D0001751

Robert Aura Smith

PHILIPPINE

FREEDOM

1946-1958

1958   New York

Columbia University Press

INTRODUCTION

The sudden death of President Magsaysay, just a little more than ten years after the Philippines had attained political independence, seemed to many persons to mark the end of an era. To most Filipinos it seemed an almost unbearable national calamity.

This tragedy focused attention on the Filipino people and their problems. It was necessary to review and to judge what had been done by them and by their American associates, in the light of all that had happened. After Magsaysay's death there was some taking of inventory, some attempt to balance the books. This wasn't "the end of the world," as some Filipinos said they felt it to be. But it was one of those stopping places, where there is a pause for breath and reflection.

What had been carried out in the Philippines by Americans and Filipinos was an unusual political and social experiment. An attempt had been made to bring together a diversity of motives in some sort of program for progress. The Filipinos had agreed, reluctantly at times, to channel their sense of nationalism into a productive and conservative course. The United States had pledged, on the other hand, that the validity of the claims of this nationalism would be respected and that its goals would ultimately be achieved.

The form of this "revolt" against "colonialism" was unique. It came to be, in the end, a joint effort of two peoples to bring about a relationship that would be fruitful to both. It was also an effort to set up in Asia a working democracy grounded in concepts that were not entirely Asian. It was an effort, often unconscious, to bring about a better synthesis of East and West. Individual Filipinos and Americans, in their relations with each other, often sensed this. Translating this sense into large political forms was a different and sometimes more difficult matter.

In the end, the political goal was reached—and not, as has too often been suggested, merely as a product of war. It was the product of an evolutionary process that would have come to its eventual fruition regardless of external disruptive forces. Philippine independence and freedom were not born on Bataan. They were born in the minds of Filipinos and Americans who had worked during long years for their ultimate consummation.

What would happen after this end was achieved was a matter of interest and concern. Could the Filipinos sustain the new responsibilities that they had so joyfully assumed? Was it possible to establish in Asia a different type of government and a different type of relationship between the rulers and the ruled? Had the periods of trial and error been really profitable? Could the great "Asian experiment" succeed?

These were the questions that the first decade of Philippine independence was required to answer. And the first decade was turbulent, unhappy, and insecure. It came to an end with the death of the one man, Magsaysay, who seemed to hold up, in his person the highest hopes of success. It was only natural that when he died it should be asked, "Can the great experiment go on?"

The pages that follow are an attempt to answer some parts of that question. Necessarily, they must trace the origins of the concept of Philippine freedom. They must show what had been tried and what had been done. They must attempt to obtain focus and perspective. The present derives from the past. One decade does not stand alone. But one decade can be a revealing period of demonstration.

If the relationship of Filipinos and Americans has been unique, it has also been singularly rewarding. Out of the welter of cross-purposes, conflicts, and misunderstandings, out of the trials and perils of charting new courses, out of the very adjustment of East to West and West to East, has come a new conception of fraternity and joint dedication. We are no longer strangers to the Filipinos, nor they to us.

What has prevailed is a great idea. It has been recognized and embraced. Men can be free, and rejoice in their freedom. They can work for, and fight for, that freedom. They may come from the nipa houses of Luzon or the cottages of Vermont, but they can be brothers. This we have learned.

It should not be unprofitable, therefore, to trace some of the elements in our learning. To that end this book is dedicated.

CONTENTS

PHILIPPINE FREEDOM, 1946–1958

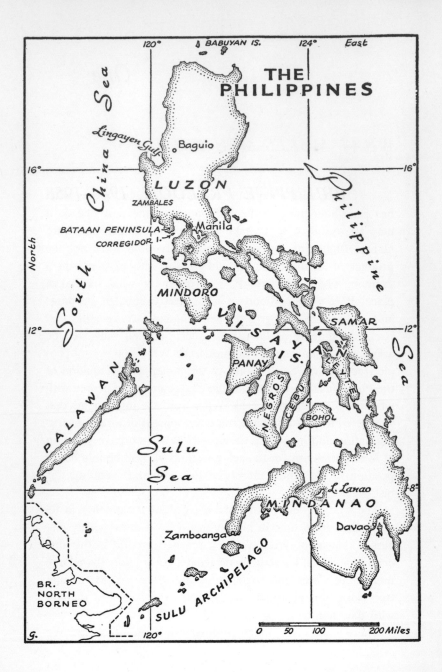

One

WHAT MAKES MEN FREE?

If we wish adequately to understand and assess what has been happening in the Philippines in the past decade it may be useful, first, to take a somewhat longer backward glance. Philippine independence and freedom were not the product of accident nor did they come into existence in a vacuum. There is a broad background for what has taken place. It is a background of ideas and events, of purposes and aspirations, of growth and change. Concerning that background there are pertinent questions that may well be asked. What makes the Filipinos free? What makes any people free? What were the aims of the American occupation of the Philippines and what was the character of the people with whom it was obliged to deal? What were the instruments that were used to make possible the development of a self-governing nation and how were they used? When we have given an at least partial answer to such questions we will be in a better position to look more closely at the dramatic events of this last decade.

The whole question of human freedom is immense in its scope and at no time in history has it been more widely discussed than now. We have even reached a point in this discussion at which we actually designate, conventionally, a large number of states and societies as the "free" world. In that free world this is usually juxtaposed in speech and thought with the "non-free," or "slave" world.

There is, however, much confusion in the use of terms. We

are confronted with two great political movements that dominate the scene. One is the rise and spread of a political system and ideology that denies certain privileges and modes of behavior that much of the Western world has come to associate with the "rights" that go with human freedom. Therefore it is often called a Communist "conspiracy" against liberty. The other is a world-wide movement toward a change in political status for many peoples from a dependent to a nondependent position. This is usually called the "rise of nationalism."

A part of the Communist conspiracy has been the effort to equate this struggle for a change in status with the urge for liberty as such and thus to permit the Communist protagonist to appear as the champion of "freedom." This has resulted in the insistent appeal to "anti-colonialism" and "anti-imperialism" as the backbone of the propaganda directed by the Communists to dependent areas and to those who have recently emerged from the dependent status. It has therefore been possible for those whose basic tenets deny what we usually think of as human freedom to appear as the spokesmen for liberty against a reactionary world.

We are prone to assume that the falsehood of the Communist position should be apparent. We are likely to become impatient with those who accept as defenders of "liberty," in the name of "anti-colonialism," the very forces that deny liberty on all other grounds. There is confusion in our minds as well as in the minds of those who are swayed by the Communist appeal. We, and they, are in need of clearer thinking.

All over the world men have been saying, "We wish to be free." The Buryats on the Manchurian border proclaimed their own little republic thirty years ago. The Indonesians rebelled against the Dutch, and subsequently some Indonesians rebelled against other Indonesians. India, Pakistan, Burma, and Ceylon changed their political relationship to the United Kingdom. Malaya and Singapore are achieving self-government. Indo-China has ceased to be French. The free state of Ghana has emerged in Africa and changes are in the making for the Rhodesias, Uganda, Tanganyika, and Kenya. Mandates in the Middle East that resulted from the First World War have been liquidated and we now deal with the independent nations of Syria, Lebanon, Israel, Jordan, and Iraq. Britain is out of Egypt and the Sudan condominium is gone. The status of Libya, Tunisia, and Morocco has been changed. In other areas, such as Nepal, a "protectorate" has given way to a changed international association in which the achievement of real self-government is the avowed aim.

Highest in this list of changes in status is the Philippines. It was the first of the dependent states in our time to become an independent republic. As such, it deserves especial attention.

It is significant that there has been, parallel to this growth, a progressive loss of freedom in the other half of the world. The Baltic states of Latvia, Estonia, and Lithuania have been swallowed up. Bulgaria, Rumania, Czechoslovakia, Hungary, and Albania have lost their power to act as independent states. Poland and Yugoslavia have been struggling for some degree of freedom of action, against heavy odds. Red China cannot be said to be truly "independent" of the Soviet Union, while northern Korea and northern Vietnam are obviously puppets.

Thus, while millions of persons have been gaining their "freedom" in the name of national independence, other millions have been losing it. Political structures alone obviously cannot answer the basic question that we have posed: What is it that makes men free?

Perhaps the most widely quoted answer to that question is the one given by Jesus, who said: "Ye shall know the truth

and the truth shall make you free." And Jesus was speaking
in an atmosphere of political as well as of religious controversy. In our day, moreover, more and more persons play the
role of Pontius Pilate and ask, "What is the truth?" The question is neither cynical nor idle. If the truth is to make us free,
we need to know what is the truth, and we need sorely to be
convinced of those things "on which we have believed." What
Jesus did, however, for his time and for ours was to take the
question of freedom out of the field of politics and into the
field of morals. This is where it ultimately belongs. To "know
the truth" is not merely a political problem. It is a moral
challenge.

This is a point at which confusion has arisen. In dealing
with the political problems of dependent areas it has been
common practice to use "freedom" and "independence"
synonymously. This, as we have now discovered, can be mistaken. There are non-independent areas that are certainly
"free" and there are "independent" states that are anything
but that. Some of the blame for the confusion of terms should
probably attach to newspapermen. They have to write head-
lines. "Independence" has eleven and a half type units; "freedom" has seven and a half. It is ofen all too convenient to use
the shorter word.

But there is a broader context. "Freedom" is one of those
"loaded" words. It has the same sort of impact as "home,"
"mother," or "honor." It carries emotional overtones in a
way that mere technical terms cannot possibly do. Thus,
Gandhi and Nehru did not describe the contest with the British as "the struggle for the evolution of constitutional self-
government in India" (which would have been entirely accurate); they spoke of "our Fight for Freedom." Similarly,
the battle cry of the Indonesians in opposition to the Dutch
was always *Merdeka* which literally means freedom.

Parenthetically, in this connection it is interesting and possibly significant that the Filipinos did not make this confusing error. They never shouted for "freedom." It was always *independencia*. There was at no time anything called a "freedom" party in the Philippines. There were simply *Nacionalistas*.

The Filipinos seemed to avoid, almost by instinct, the wrong synonymous use. Of course, they could have seen that there were or had been many politically independent states in which true human freedom was nonexistent. Nazi Germany, Imperial Japan, and the Soviet Union were conspicuous. In those cases political independence had by no means made men free. On the other hand there have been politically nonindependent areas, such as Canada prior to the Statute of Westminster of 1931, or the Philippines during the reign of the Commonwealth, in which there was human freedom in all its aspects. Indeed, it is not too much to say that in some countries that have become independent there is probably less actual freedom now than there was under a colonial status. Indonesia is a case in point.

The distinction between the two terms is revealed by the correct application of each: "independence" is a term in the field of law and politics that designates the relationship of one sovereign state to other sovereign states; "freedom" is a term in the field of philosophy and morals that designates the relationship of the individual to the society in which he lives.

On the other hand, the two terms are not necessarily contradictory. Political independence may be an important step toward freedom itself. The very pride in political independence may be used as a means of emphasizing the meaning of freedom itself. But the two should not be confused. The achievement of political independence does not solve the problems that are implicit in the struggle for human freedom, as many nations have discovered. Neither does the continuation of a dependent status, in itself, mean the denial of that freedom.

Here we must go back to some fundamental concepts. Men are free primarily as they think, believe, and feel that they are free. They are not free when they are convinced that political structures or social institutions inhibit the exercise of what they believe to be their "natural rights." It is not necessary to go into an abstruse philosophical discussion of what such rights are, or even, in fact, whether they actually exist. Men all over the world are convinced that they are endowed with such rights and that structures of government and society must ultimately come to respect them.

The rise of nationalism in our time—and especially in Asia —is, in its essence, an assertion of the conviction that these human rights may not be respected by an alien sovereign power and that their exercise and defense should lie within the indigenous society. This conviction may not always be literally true, but it is philosophically sound. It embraces a respect for so-called "customary law" in some areas, but it goes far beyond that. It is an insistence that a national or social group that can recognize its own identity and that wishes to preserve itself has the inherent right to make its own laws and to abide by them. With this there can be no just quarrel.

THE CONCEPT OF JEFFERSON

It was on those grounds that Thomas Jefferson set forth the philosophy of independence and freedom in what was to become one of the most important documents in the history of the struggle for human liberty, the American Declaration of Independence. It was obvious, from the outset, that there was no confusion in Jefferson's mind between freedom and independence since the terms are not used interchangeably in the Declaration. Moreover, its very conclusion is that the colonies were and of right ought to be free *and* independent states.

The Declaration was based, in turn, upon the conviction that a dependent status made impossible the exercise of what were held to be "natural" human rights. It cannot have been accident that priority was given to the right to make one's own laws. There were eighteen specific charges of abuse leveled against the rule of King George III. Of these, eleven had to do with the making of laws, and in each case it was charged that the right of the colonies to legislate for themselves had been denied or impeded. This making of laws was, in Jefferson's mind, held to be manifestly a "natural" right and a necessary part of freedom.

At the beginning of the Declaration, however, Jefferson laid out his case upon an even broader ground. First of all, he spoke of "one people" who were dissolving political bonds that had connected them with another. Such a people are entitled, he went on, to a "separate and equal station," by virtue of "the Laws of Nature and of Nature's God." Then came the most celebrated passage.

"We hold these truths to be self-evident, that all men are created equal. . . ." Jefferson has been many times misinterpreted on this passage: it has been said that he declared that all men were equal when it was obvious that they were not. The misinterpretation is a double one. In the first place it was not stated that these were self-evident truths, but simply that they were held to be self-evident by the signers of the Declaration and the "one people" whom they wished to represent. This is not the promulgation of a dogma, but a confession of faith. Similarly, it is not asserted that all men are equal, but that they are "created" equal. The equality here implied is one of humanity, that is, of man's status at creation, whether that creation is thought to be divine or human.

It is significant, however, that Jefferson immediately added to this statement of the equality of creation, a statement of coordinate endowment of natural rights: "that they are endowed by their Creator with certain unalienable Rights. . . ." The word unalienable is a strong one. It designates that which cannot be taken away. This is much more than to say that the rights ought not to be violated. It is a declaration of their permanence.

These rights are not restricted by the phrases that follow. "Among these," Jefferson said, "are Life, Liberty and the Pursuit of Happiness." The word "among" should be noted, but these three enumerated rights are vastly inclusive. Even if one were to try to accept the word "life" in its most restricted sense it would still be broad in all its implications. The others are almost equally so: "liberty" has been defined in dozens of ways and it is another powerful word, like its common synonym, "freedom." We have often modified the concept of abstract liberty to distinguish it from political and moral anarchy. Thus, we contrast "liberty" with "license," and speak of "liberty under law." At this point we come back to the question of states of mind. Liberty is a feeling on the part of the individual toward his society. Like freedom, it is a moral term. The "Pursuit of Happiness" is equally elastic. Obviously it, also, must be defined in terms of the relationship of the individual to the society and, also, it must refer to states of mind and feeling. Happiness itself may mean different things to different individuals. What is important in the Jeffersonian concept is that the individual's search for what he regards as happiness is a human right that cannot be taken away. But pursuit also has quite another meaning that must have been even more important to Jefferson. In this context it carries all the implications of, for example, "peaceful pursuits." Bracketed with life and liberty, it connotes a continuous state. In its simplest form this Declaration means that man has a natural right not to be miserable, and this certainly must mean that a society or a political structure that makes him miserable violates that right.

It is at this point that Jefferson moves from the philosophical to the political field, since he relates these rights directly to the function of government. "To secure these rights, Governments are instituted among men. . . ." In this, also, Jefferson has been often misinterpreted, frequently by those who have invoked his image to bless revolutionary nationalism. He is said to have declared that governments must be set up to obtain these unalienable rights for those who do not enjoy them. Jefferson did not say "obtain," he said "secure," and he was too precise a stylist to confuse the two. He was too good a logician to suggest that governments came into being to obtain for men those rights that were already inalienably theirs. Secure, in its more grammatical sense, means to make fast, safe, firm; literally, "to make secure." Under this definition, the Jeffersonian Declaration has true meaning, not otherwise. Governments are instituted, in this concept, to protect those rights and their exercise (pursuit) from invasion.

Such protection, in turn, must presume some degree of authority. Governments cannot make anything secure if they are no more than a collection of good wishes. Here Jefferson comes to the very heart of the question of freedom: "Deriving their just powers from the consent of the governed." The word "just" is important. Its use implies that some powers of government may be unjustly derived and presumably unjustly employed. Since the Declaration itself is a detailed protest against the abuse of powers by government, with repeated reference to the denial of the consent of the governed, the establishment of this criterion was imperative.

In its historical framework this was, naturally, an attack upon whatever remained of the theory of the divine right of kings, and unquestionably Jefferson meant it to be precisely that. But in making the attack he invoked a greater divine right, the right of the governed to give consent and the need to do so if powers are to be just.

This doctrine was eventually to be the real basis for the rise of revolutionary nationalism and "anti-colonialism." It was also to give birth to what was called the principle of "self-determination." It is now universally regarded as the essence of democracy.

Even those regimes that have consistently denied the enjoyment of Jefferson's "unalienable rights" have been obliged to give lip service to this principle. They have repeatedly insisted that they are installed and sustained by the people themselves, however false this may be. As a result they have confused many persons, especially in Asia, by constant references to "people's" governments and "people's" democracies. And not all of the confusion is in Asia.

There is, fortunately, a yardstick for consent of the governed that can usually be employed quickly and fairly accurately. The right to give consent must necessarily connote the right to withhold it. The Declaration itself makes this plain when it says that when a government fails to serve its proper ends, that is, the securing of these rights, it is the duty of a people to alter or abolish it. The yardstick that can be conveniently used, therefore, is simply "Look for the Opposition." When opposition is lawful, vocal, and even honored and "loyal," it is proper to assume that "just powers" are being used to secure those rights. When it is nonexistent or "liquidated," as in the Communist world, we can be sure that freedom has ceased to exist, no matter how many references are made to the "people."

This test is also useful in arriving at judgments concerning the extent of liberty in states that are emerging or have already emerged from a dependent status. They may have achieved a national independence. How far that means achievement of freedom must be determined by standards other than mere sovereign status. The degree of real government by consent is one of those standards.

In respect to opposition parties in such areas, however, a word of caution is advisable. It is sometimes more difficult to apply our yardstick than it is in the cases of longer established or even freshly conquered states. The reason is that a major function of opposition has changed and that its focus must be changed also.

In the colonial states the major drive was, and is now, for political independence. This was so overriding that it always had a tendency to bring parties together rather than to separate them, unless there were other very strong considerations. Thus, in India, the Congress party was able for years to include a wide range of political beliefs and purposes, since it was the chief standard-bearer in the march toward independence. In the early forties one American newspaperman remarked, and not at all facetiously, "The Congress party, like a tent, spreads over everything from Robert Taft to Henry Wallace, and then some!" The same thing was true, to a large extent, of the Moslem League in Pakistan in the first period after the partition. In the Philippines, prior to independence, the Nacionalista party had a virtual political monopoly for almost forty years.

What must be kept in mind, therefore, is not merely the existence of an opposition, or even its effectiveness, but rather the right to be in opposition and the right freely to exercise that role. In the cases that we have noted this was not curtailed. It is significant that opposition parties came into power in both Pakistan and the Philippines after they had become independent. Even the Congress party in India, despite Mr. Nehru's immense personal prestige, has been showing some signs of centrifugal strains now that opposition to Britain has been taken away as its major function. In contradistinction, much of the misgiving that arose, both in Indonesia and elsewhere, over President Sukarno's proposals for a "guided democracy" stemmed from the fact that he apparently planned to rid himself of any sort of annoying political opposition precisely at the time when his young government was trying, ostensibly and under difficult conditions, to achieve a real democracy.

In this connection it is worthy of note that the Communist subversive offensive has steadily worked to keep alive the cry of "anti-colonialism" in areas where it is no longer a real issue. By thus providing a false target the conspiracy can divert attention from other fields and other actions and appear as the champion of the very liberty that it denies. The effect of this maneuver upon the so-called "Asian-Arab bloc" has been clearly discernible. The championship of "anti-colonialism," even at points where colonialism has ceased to exist, has become the most popular of their causes. That this attitude serves the Communist line seems not to be important. The dead horse must still be flogged and the live bear can be left to the future.

THE DEFINITION OF RIGHTS

Now, let us go back again to the evolution of the earlier American political structures and see how they ultimately affected the Philippines. When the United States Constitution was formulated a need was felt to go beyond the mere Jeffersonian proclamation of unalienable rights. That was aimed, primarily, against a government that had been declared to be alien by the Declaration itself. But what next took shape was a definition of certain inviolable rights that was aimed at any government, domestic or alien. This definition was first formally embodied in the Bill of Rights, the first ten amendments to the Constitution, without whose inclusion the ratification by the requisite numbers of states would have been impossible. Actually, quite a bit of the Constitution itself is a bill of rights, since it limits, again and again, the powers that are vested in government and its constituted agencies. The Bill of Rights merely adds to those other limitations a group of specific provisions at points where there was sensitivity or alarm. There were enumerated certain things that no government might do in transgress of the rights of the individual. Significantly, quite a few of these strictures had to do with the processes of law and with the guarantee of the rights of the accused and tried. But the sternest prohibition of all came in the very first amendment, which deals with freedom of religion, speech, press, and assembly. "Congress shall make no law," it states, that abridges these freedoms. This phraseology is important because of its contrast to the language of some subsequent constitutions, Communist and Fascist, that purported to be democratic when they proclaimed the freedom of religion or speech "not contrary to law." The difference between that and "Congress shall make no law" should be obvious, but the distinction has not often enough been made. In the false version the defense of rights is usually garbed under terms such as "freedom of *lawful* speech." This begs the question at the very outset. It is certainly not on the model of our First Amendment, wherein the very adoption of restrictive laws is prohibited. In the case of freedom of assembly, moreover, the stricture is modified only by the word "peaceful." The term "lawful" does not appear.

The whole "Bill of Rights concept," as it is often called, is an expression of an individualistic philosophy. It was, from the outset, the negation of "statism" in any form, just as the proclamation of natural rights was the negation of divine right. The actual rights enumerated, however, in many cases arose not out of some concept of what rights were "natural," but out of some experience with their denial. For example, it is part of our constitutional law that soldiers may not be quartered upon a citizen without his consent or, in time of war, without legal authorization. This hardly seems a vital safeguard to us, nowadays, but that provision had very real meaning in the time of the Colonies. A parallel case arose when the Philippine Constitution was being drafted, almost a hundred and fifty years later. The Filipinos felt that it was essential that the Bill of Rights should include the guarantee of freedom of abode and movement. This might not have occurred to us as vital, but to the Filipinos, with memories of peonage under the hacienda system, it was a human right that needed to be reasserted and safeguarded.

Thus the details of definition may vary with time and place. What is really important is that men who have been concerned with setting up a fundamental law should have tried to define their human rights and values, and then to provide that no state, not even one set up with their consent, could violate such rights. In this way the two big concepts, government by consent and the definition of rights, became so closely intertwined in thought and feeling that they came to form the whole approach to what we call democracy.

This was, indeed, the long-standing Jeffersonian theory of

the state and the citizen. The Philippines became a modern laboratory in which it could be put to the test.

THE PHILIPPINE LABORATORY

From the very outset of the American occupation of the archipelago it was taken for granted that the islands had been liberated from Spanish domination. It was also assumed that they could and would, in due course, become independent if they so desired. There was never any intention of governing without the consent of the governed as a permanent political philosophy. Nor was there any intention of denying or inhibiting the human rights that were felt to be a part of true freedom.

The road to freedom was relatively direct and it was easily traveled. The road to political independence was more devious. It required almost half a century before that goal could be reached.

At this point it can be argued—and with justice—that one essential freedom was denied to the Filipinos over a long period. This was the freedom to be politically independent if they so chose. The argument is cogent. It was outweighed at that time by the feeling of many Americans—led conspicuously by William McKinley, Theodore Roosevelt, and Elihu Root—that the other basic freedoms might be imperiled by the too swift advent of a government that was not stable, in a society and a state that would not prove economically viable as an independent nation. Except in a very few quarters there was never any strong American sentiment that favored the permanent retention of the Philippines by the United States. Actually, ratification of the annexation passed in the Senate by a very small margin. In many quarters, however, some of them Filipino, there was a strong feeling that haste should be made slowly and that building should be permanent.

The latter view prevailed, strongly backed not only by the "manifest destiny" group in the United States, but by the first Philippine Commission. As a result, we and the Filipinos lived through a protracted "probationary" period in which the goal of ultimate independence was not denied but in which its consummation was repeatedly deferred.

This very delay added strength to the nationalist movement with its insistent demand for immediate and even unconditional independence. It served to help the creation of a more forceful political self-consciousness. At the same time, there was sufficient confidence in the goodwill and good purposes of the United States that there was no real support for the idea of "revolutionary" nationalism. It was not that the Filipinos were cowed by superior force. It was rather that there was no need for violent revolution when there was the conviction that its ends could be achieved peacefully and lawfully.

In this way Philippine nationalism became a strongly constructive and fruitful, rather than sterile, cause. Within its framework Filipinos accepted the responsibilities of self-government. They ran for office and were elected—by Filipinos. Some of their functions were limited, but they were the functions of government by consent.

Manuel Quezon, a fiery patriot, has often been quoted in his dramatic statement that he "would rather live under a government run like hell by Filipinos than under one run like heaven by Americans." That is good, and orthodox, nationalism. But what is often overlooked is that Mr. Quezon, at that point, had lived all of his adult life in a political position to which he was freely elected and in which he had assumed large responsibilities. He and his fellow Filipinos were having practice in the big field of government by consent, and this was precisely what had never been possible under the Spanish regime.

Thus the Philippines could become truly a laboratory in this search for freedom and independence. A wide latitude was enjoyed. Most of the restrictions could be self-imposed. The Filipinos were ready and eager to embrace the Jeffersonian concepts. They identified them, rightly, with the cause of their own patriots. But just how these concepts could be put into immediate practice was problematical.

Their situation may have been unique at that time although we have later seen the same forces in operation, especially in the case of the United Kingdom. Although it was not always clear to them—and to some others—they were working with a sovereign power that wished to divest itself of sovereignty. The Filipinos were under the "guidance," if one can call it that, of a people who had established and "made secure" the defense of the very rights to which they themselves aspired. In all the controversy over their status, and there was much of it, there was an undercurrent of human understanding that made some of the later political phenomena possible. Indeed, Bataan itself could happen only because of this understanding.

It is against such a background of ideas that we should turn to what has happened, and why. We are rightfully concerned with the progress of the young Philippine Republic. It is, in a sense, a part of us and of our thinking. What has happened since it became independent is a proper field for both our anxiety and our gratification. We have had the opportunity to see, in the Philippines, "what makes men free."

Two

THE GROUNDWORK
FOR INDEPENDENCE

The American assumption of sovereignty in the Philippines was, in the beginning, more the product of military accident than of political design. In 1898 the United States went to war against Spain on a group of issues that revolved chiefly around the status of Cuba. In the war fever that swept the country the name of the Philippines was not even mentioned. The idea of making some sort of political crusade into the far Pacific would have been repugnant to most Americans. On the other hand, those who were responsible for the conduct of the war were well aware of the disposition of all the Spanish forces and all the Spanish holdings. It was decided, logically enough, to strike the Spanish wherever they were vulnerable. One such place was the Philippines, where there was a small Spanish naval squadron that was precariously holding on to the remnants of Spanish sovereignty in the face of widespread revolt.

A genuinely Filipino revolution had been proclaimed in 1896 and had swept through a large part of the countryside. The most successful of its military leaders was Emilio Aguinaldo. The Spaniards made an accommodation with him and paid an indemnity to end the revolt. He went into temporary exile and later stated that he had used every centavo that he had received to further the cause of the revolution. He undertook to buy arms in Europe, but few shipments arrived. There were other Filipino patriots of intellectual stature and deep perception. When Aguinaldo eventually turned against the Americans in 1899, these patriots joined him in drafting a revolutionary constitution providing for a free and independent republic. In its time and place this Malolos Constitution was a remarkable document. It cannot be said, however, that the revolution that started in 1896 succeeded in setting up a functioning independent government. What it did was to indicate clearly that the days of Spain in the Philippines were numbered. Even without American intervention it is doubtful that Spanish authority could ever again have been fully established.

This was the situation when the American naval forces in the Pacific under the command of Commodore—later Admiral—George Dewey were concentrated in Hong Kong with orders to strike at the Spanish fleet in Manila upon the outbreak of war. The defenses at Manila Bay proved to be less formidable than had been supposed. The Spanish fleet, much out-gunned, was quickly destroyed with no loss to the Americans. What remained of Spanish military power was bottled up in Manila and it was soon obvious that surrender was inevitable.

What followed is the most sorrowful chapter in the whole story of American-Philippine relationships. The Filipinos assumed that the American forces had arrived in the role of liberators and as such they were wildly welcomed. Aguinaldo hurried back from his exile and assumed leadership of the sizable Filipino units that flocked to the Americans and gladly put themselves under their command. In the beginning, the United States did nothing to dispel this illusion and the Filipinos were certainly unprepared for what was to happen.

When the Spanish surrendered and the Americans started

their march into Manila on August 13, 1898, the Filipino "revolutionary army" was informed by the American commander that the occupation would be by Americans only and that the Filipinos must remain outside the city. He justified his action by stating that the Filipinos were insufficiently disciplined and that he was fearful of a sack. This was the beginning of a breach that was not to be healed for several useful years. Under Aguinaldo's leadership many of the Filipino revolutionary units were withdrawn to the countryside. The Malolos Constitution proclaimed an independent republic, and Aguinaldo was named its president. What came about was the bitter thing known as the "Philippine Insurrection" in the United States, and as the "Philippine-American War" by many Filipinos.

The American response was to assume both the position of being obliged to establish public order and the mission of stamping out any armed resistance. Two years of sporadic and often ugly fighting ensued. Although there was at no time a general rising of the people, there was a prompt change in the attitude of the Filipinos. The Americans were no longer liberators. They were conquerors, more benevolent perhaps than the Spaniards, but conquerors nevertheless. Aguinaldo finally surrendered and peace was restored, but fearful damage had been done.

Meanwhile, the United States consolidated its sovereign position. A fully functioning military government was set up. But much more than that, in the Treaty of Paris, which ended the Spanish-American war, the United States formally recognized a transfer of sovereignty from Spain to itself. The islands were ceded to the United States for a payment of $20,000,000.

If the Filipinos felt that they had been betrayed, there was reason. The feelings of Americans were mixed. There was some talk of "manifest destiny" and some expression of satisfaction that the United States had become an "empire" with far-flung possessions. This was not the sentiment of the majority. As has already been noted, the treaty with Spain was ratified by a very small majority in the Senate. The Democratic party quickly made Philippine independence a campaign issue. It was usually presumed that the American tenure, even if protracted, would not be permanent. Coupled with this was the feeling that the United States had assumed a responsibility for the welfare of the Filipinos that must be discharged.

Unfortunately, in this latter attitude there was something of condescension and an unconscious assumption of superiority that was irksome to Filipinos. American knowledge of the islands and their people was slight and it was too quickly taken for granted that the Filipinos were some sort of "heathens" who would, first of all, have to be "civilized." Indeed, an American battle cry during the insurrection was "Civilize them with a Krag!" This did not, of course, represent the basic aim of the Americans, either in the Philippines or in the United States, but it is illustrative of one of the attitudes that had to be overcome. It was not until the Filipinos could be convinced that the United States honestly intended to help them in their preparation for genuine self-government that it was possible to make real political progress.

A CIVIL GOVERNMENT

An imperative first step was the ending of the military administration and the establishment of a civil government. This was done by 1901 when a civil commission was set up; it was made more effective in 1903 with the installation of William Howard Taft as the first civil governor general. The broad aims of the American occupation were already beginning to appear, and its form was beginning to take shape.

First of all, the occupation was obviously benevolent. From the earliest days there were signs of this character. Surprisingly, perhaps, some of the best missionaries in this cause were the American soldiers themselves. Especially in the villages they made themselves liked and respected by their generosity and good humor. And, as is often considered typical of American soldiers, they took an interest in the children. More than one eminent Filipino was to say, laughingly, in later life, that he had learned his A B C's in English at the knee of an American corporal.

In the second place, the American occupation itself was essentially democratic. This may seem to be a paradox and so it appeared to many Filipinos. But it was quickly made plain that the rights of the "little man" were to be respected no less than the privileges of the "big man." If independence was denied at the top level by the imposition of an alien sovereignty, democracy was carefully fostered at other levels by an honest effort to give Filipinos a chance to govern themselves.

From this point of view the American occupation was also, in a sense, revolutionary. Spanish rule in the islands may not have been much worse than conventional colonial rule of the time, but it was bad enough, in all conscience. In the first place, it was fully authoritarian. Filipino opinion was never consulted at any point. There was a framework of law by decree and never by consent. That this rule was corrupt, by modern standards, goes without saying, because the whole system was corrupt. Officers were allocated, honors bestowed, and, most of all, land distributed on a basis of reward and whim. The welfare of the individual Filipino was seldom a consideration.

This Spanish rule was not usually harsh in the physical sense. Filipinos were often peons but they were not necessarily slaves. There was little discrimination on the basis of race and intermarriage was both common and respected. Many eminent Filipinos had Spanish blood and were proud of it. No stigma attached to the word mestizo. This attitude has been preserved, indeed, in one of the conventional terms for a beautiful costume of Filipino women. It is called "mestiza dress."

At this point it may be well to remember and to emphasize that the Spanish conquest of the islands was not merely political but also religious. Church and state were one in Spain, and the church had long been an instrument in pioneering. A dominant note in all the Spanish declarations of purpose respecting the Philippines was the need for propagation of the faith. This cause was remarkably successful. At the time of the American occupation about 90 percent of the Filipinos were devout Roman Catholics. The only important exceptions were the Moslem Moros in the south and the solid block of animists in northern Luzon, who were first designated as the "pagan" and later as the "non-Christian" tribes.

The effect of this religious "occupation" should not be underestimated. Some anthropologists have asserted that religious belief is so modified by local custom and usage as to become "naturalized." On this ground they are sometimes prone to discount its impact. The "naturalization" may have taken place, to a degree, in the Philippines. Later there grew up, in fact, an indigenous Catholic sect composed of the followers of Bishop Aglipay, which eventually numbered several million communicants and declared its independence of Rome. But it was a Christian and is still, in essence, a Catholic church.

CHURCH AND STATE

There were some unpleasant aspects of church control in the Philippines. The church and its various orders became the largest of all the landlords. It was not always a good landlord and sometimes a very bad one. The Filipinos, however devout, had reason to see, from time to time, that they were being exploited by a group that was not really Filipino. Revolt did not at any time take the specific form of anti-clericalism, but some of this was reflected in the writings of José Rizal, who is always called the father of Philippine independence. It was made conspicuous in the Malolos Constitution, which provided a rigid separation of church and state.

Against this should be balanced the solid contribution that the church was able to make. For almost three hundred years it was the principal, if not the sole, instrument of popular education. It fulfilled this mission better at the upper levels than at the lower and it did establish in the Philippines some distinguished institutions of higher learning. During the whole period of American sovereignty in the islands it was the proud boast that Santo Tomas was the oldest university under the American flag, antedating Harvard —as Filipinos were quick to point out. Another signal contribution was in the field of science. The Jesuit order paid special attention to the weather, and the Philippine Weather Bureau, under its guidance, was by far the best in all Asia. Its studies in vulcanology and especially in cyclonic storms— the "typhoons" of the Pacific—have been invaluable.

Some other contributions of the church were of a more

general nature. It gave a degree of homogeneity to the Filipinos. It should be remembered that in this archipelago, with a land area less than three times that of the state of New York, there are eleven major languages and almost eighty dialects. There were other divisive elements—the sea not the least of them—and there was no concept of Filipino unity as such. The church gave a common ground to all. The Filipinos became fellow-communicants and spoke the same religious language.

Even more important, as events took shape, was the fact that this religious faith laid a groundwork in ethics that made the subsequent enactment of law much easier. When there is, throughout a society, a uniformly accepted concept of what is "right" and what is "wrong" it is not hard to formulate that concept into laws that will be respected and obeyed. When it was necessary to re-codify the Spanish law under which the Philippines had been governed, to bring it completely into line with the best Anglo-Saxon practice, it was not necessary to change the ethical basis upon which it rested. "Right" and "wrong" were still the same.

Nevertheless, the American occupation was, from the beginning, strictly secular. Very few American Catholics were appointed to high office and the church, as such, was not represented in government. Indeed, one of the most devout Catholics to serve in the islands, the last Governor General, Frank Murphy, was a stern exponent of the separation of church and state. He actually earned some censure in clerical circles because of the positions that he took. For one thing, he urged upon the legislature, in a strong message, the enactment of a divorce law. He declared that divorce was as repugnant to him personally on ethical and religious grounds as it was to the majority of the Filipinos, but that there also existed in the Philippines a number of persons who did not share this view. For them, he declared, the conventional legal procedure as to divorce should be authorized.

Governor Murphy's sharpest clash with the church, however, arose from his attitude toward a celebrated criminal case. A young woman of prominent family was convicted in the lower courts of falsifying results in grading a bar examination. This was a serious offense in the Philippines. The conviction was appealed and the case was held up for several years in the Philippine Supreme Court. Her uncle was one of the justices and his proper disqualification of himself left the court evenly divided and unable to reach a verdict. Upon his death and replacement the Supreme Court promptly upheld the judgment of the lower court and the young woman was sentenced to two years in prison. Enormous pressure was then brought upon the Governor General for an executive pardon before she should begin her term. Much of it came, in organized fashion, from the priesthood on the ground that she was a devout communicant. The Governor General rejected these pleas, holding that the public must know that there was not one law for the rich and influential and another for the poor. Eventually the papal legate himself attempted to intervene with the suggestion that unless clemency were exercised he would "reluctantly" be obliged to consider the Governor General as less than a faithful son of the church. Governor Murphy replied: "And I am reluctantly obliged to remind you that I am in these islands as the representative of the President of the United States, and not of the Holy See." The young woman went to prison to make the Governor General's point about the equal application of the law, and then was pardoned, as an act of mercy, after she had served nine months.

This secular character of the American rule was further emphasized in the early days by one approach to the problem of land reform, a problem which was to be taken up in many parts of Asia. Under the leadership of Governor General Taft, the government was empowered to negotiate with the religious orders for the purchase of large estates known as the "friar lands," so that they might be broken up and sold, on easy terms, to the tenants. The program itself was not significantly successful, but it served to make plain that the Americans did not think highly of the church as an absentee landlord.

On the other hand, there was at no time any stricture upon complete freedom of worship. This right was scrupulously protected. In government offices, for example, wide latitude was given for the observation of religious holidays—and there were many of them in the Philippines. Business establishments were also lenient on this score. The Filipino had good ground for his conviction that he was completely free in the exercise of his faith and in his worship.

THE DEFENSE OF RIGHTS

This freedom was extended to the whole field of ethics and behavior. A good case in point arose when the law was re-codified and promulgated as the "uniform code of justice" for the entire archipelago. Such a code naturally came into conflict at some points with the established behavior patterns of considerable groups. The penal code, for example, provided prosecution and punishment for bigamy. That was to be expected. But there was a substantial Moslem Moro population in which polygamy, as authorized by the Koran, was not merely accepted and practiced but was actually in conformity with religious law. It was difficult to see how a Moro chieftain could be prosecuted for doing what was specifically sanctioned by his faith. Similarly, in some of the "non-

Christian" groups in northern Luzon there was a generally
accepted practice of what was, in effect, trial marriage. It
was sanctioned by long usage, fully respected, and in most
cases worked out well. Under the penal code as applied to
Christian Filipinos the young people would certainly have had
to be prosecuted for concubinage and possibly for other
statutory offenses, yet what they were doing was fully approved by the community, sanctioned by their own families,
and well established as a correct behavior pattern.

Governor General Dwight F. Davis resolved this dilemma
for the law makers by executive order. He ruled that where
established "customary law," which did not violate the accepted ethics of a special community, came into conflict with
the uniform code, the customary law should prevail within
that community.

The Dutch, in the East Indies, had long since tried out
this approach to *adat,* the immense body of customary law
in what is now Indonesia. Their experience was generally
satisfactory and they could, with justice, lay claim to non-
interference with the individual rights of their subjects on
that score.

In the Philippines, the problem was minor. Relatively few
cases arose. What was important was the enunciation of the
principle. It was part of a long process of making it plain
that the basis for independence and freedom was defense
of the rights of the individual under law.

If the defense of freedom of worship was almost automatic, the defense of freedom of the press was anything but
that. At various times the legislature enacted, or attempted
to enact, restrictive laws that purported to define libel.
Actually most of these measures were designed to protect
politicians, or their friends, from exposure of misdeeds

through the publication of the truth. The most notorious of these was the "gag law" that was put through in the early thirties. This threw away entirely the principle of "truth and good motive" as a defense in a libel action and simply provided that it was a criminal offense to publish any statements that reflected on the honor or good name of a person in public office, even if such statements were part of an official court record. This attempt to conceal the proof of wrong-doing was so outrageous that it never did survive the appeal from the first conviction, in 1932. It was subsequently repealed in 1934.

Reluctantly it must be admitted that the politicians were sometimes under considerable provocation. Newspapers sprang up and flourished throughout the American occupation, and some of them were very good. But there were some that represented anything but a "responsible" as well as a "free" press and some were definitely abusive, although the real heyday of the scurrilous press was not to come until after liberation from the Japanese. In the main, however, it was possible to keep the bad elements in the press under some degree of control by simply filing civil suits under the law (not the "gag law"), without infringing upon the true right of free publication.

On the most important political issue discussed in the press, the widest possible latitude was given. This was the question of nationalism and the campaign for independence. At no time did the American administration attempt to put a check on publications in this campaign, even when they were violently anti-American. General Wood's administration brought an action against one Filipino publisher, not on the ground that he was "nationalist" but on the ground that what he had published was manifestly false and scurril-

ous. General Wood was sustained by the United States
Supreme Court, but the punishment was eventually re-
mitted.

Statements that were obviously incorrect were repeatedly
and patiently corrected, but there was no such thing as
censorship or pre-censorship, or of closing down any publication because of its "nationalist" position.

The effect, both on the campaign for independence and on
the Filipinos as a whole, was salutary. For example, when
Manuel Roxas, in 1931, attempted to organize his Ang
Bagong Katipunan, or new brotherhood for independence,
he stumped the country urging the Filipinos to rise and throw
off their chains. He was greeted by many of his fellow-
countrymen and most of the press with a gentle "tut-tut."
It was hard to talk about chains at the same time that the
Filipinos were immensely proud of the fact that they had
what they repeatedly called the freest press in the world,
and when they could report even the most inflammatory of
the Roxas statements in full.

This guarantee of rights extended also to protection of
peaceful assembly. While the administration—Filipinos and
Americans alike—took stern measures against violent up-
risings such as those of the Tangulans or Sakdals in the early
thirties, there was no curb upon demonstrations, marches,
or public gatherings, even if they were specifically anti-
American. An interesting illustration of this policy was
afforded in 1930, when it was reported that the United
States government was to name Nicholas Roosevelt as the
next Governor General. Mr. Roosevelt, amiable and urbane,
had written a book about the Philippines in which he made
some remarks that most Filipinos regarded as derogatory.
A huge throng assembled at the Balintawak Monument on
the outskirts of Manila. They listened to an assortment of

fiery speeches denouncing all things American and they
concluded their outing by ceremoniously burning a copy of
Mr. Roosevelt's book. Some Americans resident in Manila
were angered and demanded that the demonstration should
be officially denounced and some of the offenders punished.
Governor General Davis reminded them that these people
had assembled peacefully to petition for the redress of a
grievance and that no punitive action could justly be taken.
It may have been an odd sort of petition, but the grievance
was quickly redressed. Mr. Roosevelt was assigned to another post.

Within the wide latitude that was given, and perhaps partly
because of it, there was little that could be called "revolutionary" anti-Americanism. There were many objections to
American acts and attitudes, as was only natural. In the early
days, for example, Governor Taft, with the utmost goodwill
and benignity, referred to the Filipinos as "our little brown
brothers." The remark seemed outrageously condescending
to the Filipinos and it was never forgiven. The phrase became
"fighting words" for more than a generation. Similarly, when
a group of tribesmen (and some of their comely womenfolk)
were taken to the St. Louis World's Fair in 1904 and exhibited in something less than the conventional quantity of
dress the outcry among the Filipinos was sharp and resentful.
Years later, it was still difficult to set up a good tourist service
in the Philippines because of the deep opposition to what was
called "G-string publicity."

The nearest thing to actual revolt, in the political sense,
came in the early twenties and was based, also, upon wounded
pride and sensibilities. Governor General Leonard Wood was
sent out to restore good government after the administration
of his predecessor, Francis Burton Harrison, had reduced the
treasury to bankruptcy and undermined the civil service. The

major feature of the Harrison regime had been the too rapid "Filipinization"of all the civil services, and Governor Harrison was regarded as the most "pro-Filipino" Governor General who had served. When General Wood tried to get rid of some of the Harrison appointees, to bring back or retain valuable Americans at some points, and to curtail the powers of the extra-legal Filipino "Council of State," he collided with Manuel Quezon. All the Filipinos in General Wood's cabinet walked out. This led to a period of executive rule under General Wood's so-called "Cavalry cabinet," and it led to a seven-year feud between General Wood and Mr. Quezon. These tensions contributed to the Filipino's long illness and ultimately to General Wood's death.

What had really been hurt was Filipino pride, and the hurt remained in spite of the fact that many Filipinos were quick to assert, later on, that General Wood was "the best friend the Filipinos ever had." Subsequent Governors General—notably Stimson, Davis, and Murphy—who were able to tread more softly, could accomplish much necessary "housecleaning" without rousing general antagonism.

These cases illustrate the fact that it is difficult, if not impossible, to assay the nature and aims of the American occupation without a glimpse into Filipino character. The occupation succeeded in laying the groundwork for freedom and independence in part because Americans and Filipinos were the sort of persons that they were. They discovered, ultimately, that they could get on together when they shared common goals.

"PROUD AND SENSITIVE"

It is dangerous to generalize about the character of any people who are judged as a whole. Societies are made up of individuals, and they differ each from each in the Philippines just as they do in the United States. It is fair to suggest that Filipinos run the range of good, indifferent, and bad in about the same proportions that obtain elsewhere. Some generalizations may be made, however, if only to promote a better understanding, and some things can be set down as characteristic of the Filipinos, always with the reminder that there are many exceptions.

By far the most frequently heard generalization is the one made by the Filipinos themselves, who have said it thousands of times: "We are a proud and sensitive people." There is good reason to accept this as true. But both pride and sensitivity can have good and bad aspects. Pride in achievement proved to be one of the strongest assets in the Filipino character. In its simplest form this was reflected, again and again, in the determination of the poorest peasant that his children should have better education and better opportunity in life than he had had, and in his immense pride when this could be accomplished. Without his sort of pride the whole story of the rise of public education in the archipelago would have been vastly different.

Similarly, the Filipino was quick to take pride in the exploits of his fellow-countrymen. Athletic prowess was held in high esteem. Scholarship was honored. And, most of all, political skill and advancement were lauded and rewarded. In all such cases, it should be noted, pride had a strong national overtone. The good things that were done were especially important because they were done by Filipinos.

This attitude, if occasionally somewhat narrow, was valuable for two reasons. First, it reflected and fostered a political self-consciousness. It would have been impossible to create an independent democratic state unless there were this feeling, for an honest pride in achievement is certainly a part of constructive nationalism. Second, this national pride was a factor in reducing the regional divisions that always presented a problem. It was necessary for Filipinos to learn to say, not "I am a Tagalog," "I am a Visayan," or "I am an Ilocano," but rather, "I am a Filipino." A good example of how this can work was afforded in the "Far Eastern Olympic Games" of 1932. An outstanding performer was a Moro swimmer. He was hailed as a Filipino and joyfully accepted as such. This was a better contribution to understanding between communities than a dozen punitive expeditions against Moro outlaws.

In its best aspects this pride contributed, throughout the American occupation, to the growth of individual—and eventually national—self-respect. It was transformed from a negative thing to a positive thing. Growth and progress would have been impossible without it.

There was, however, always the intrusion of a false pride at some points. There was pride of wealth, with its inevitable accompaniment of offensive ostentation. There was pride of position, with its abuse of family relationships and its contribution to a vicious type of local bossism in politics. But, most important, there was an acceptance of *amor propio,* the the false sense of honor and the wounding of it. This overlaps the element of sensitivity because it is a combination of false pride and excessive sensitiveness.

Undoubtedly two factors were at work here. There was a specific inheritance of Spanish attitudes, in the first place. This *amor propio* was a recognized part of the Spanish behavior pattern and the Spaniards cherished it. False pride and a false sense of honor have been associated with the Spanish character ever since Cervantes made them world-famous— and amusing—by the satire of Don Quixote. A deeper part of this attitude, however, may well have been the very revolt

against the subservience that had been imposed by colonial
rule. The Filipinos looked for slurs because of some considerable experience with them.

This hypersensitivity in a young nation was by no means
peculiar to the Philippines. Indeed, it has been a characteristic emotion and behavior component in almost every one
of the emergent independent states. It has been strong enough
in some cases—Indonesia for example—to affect the course
of policy and to bring down a government. In the case of
India it was partly responsible for the uproar over an American secretary of state's well-meaning but too casual remark
about the Portuguese colonial holdings, in which he appeared
to discount India's claim to Goa. Some of the basis for the
so-called neutralist attitude must certainly be found in an
excessively sensitive approach to the acts and motives of those
who had previously been in positions of authority.

In the Philippines this frame of mind sometimes worked to
the disadvantage of both the United States and the Philippines
because of the fact that some Filipinos might take offense
where none was meant. Since Americans were often too blunt,
even if well-meaning, such occasions arose frequently. As a
result it was necessary to do many things by indirection when
a more straightforward course might have been both easier
and quicker.

The basic sensitivity of the Filipino, however, goes far
deeper than any question of false pride. It has qualities of
great virtue. The Filipino is sensitive, in the best sense, because of an intensely emotional approach to life. This means
warmth of heart, generosity, quickness of response to appeal,
devotion to a family or a cause, and thus, ultimately, a flam-
ing patriotism.

It is commonplace to think of those who live in the tropics
as stolid and phlegmatic. The tempo of life, it is true, is slower

than it is in more unpleasant climates. *Mañana*—do it to-morrow—is a byword. As a result, the Filipino has sometimes been described as "lazy and incompetent." This is unjust. There is a different pattern of life in the tropics, but this does not mean that human emotion and human response have been slowed down. A Filipino may know by long experience that it does not make sense to work ten hours a day under the sun in the hot season, but this does not mean that he is apathetic. He has simply adjusted to life as he knows it. His emotions, as a person, have not been correspondingly slowed.

At one point, indeed, the Filipino is only too well, and often unhappily, known for the swiftness of his responses. He is quick to anger. This is quite apart from the sensitiveness to slurs that has been noted. It obtains throughout most of the archipelago and in most of the relationships between Filipinos, especially where women are concerned. With this hotness of temper there has been all too often a readiness to resort to violence, frequently violence with the knife. There were, during the occupation by the Americans, probably fewer crimes of violence "with malice aforethought" in the Philippines than in some other societies, our own included. But the quick, unexpected, and quite unpremeditated use of the knife was alarmingly commonplace for many years.

A widespread misconception can be corrected at this point. In the early days, and to some extent even late in the occupation, some Americans in the Philippines—and many more in the United States—regarded the Philippine bolo as essentially a weapon of violence. Young American housewives coming out to the islands shuddered when they saw a houseboy or a gardener equip himself with the heavy-bladed, short-handled instrument. They were shocked when the boy explained, simply, "But, Ma'am, I *have* to have a bolo." It was essentially not a weapon but a tool. It corresponded roughly to the machete in this hemisphere. It was put to hundreds of uses that were not provoked by anger. The amusing statement that a good Filipino could pick his teeth with his pet bolo was scarcely an exaggeration. There was perhaps some confusion in this country where Philippine tools and weapons were often put on display between the Philippine bolo and the Moro *kriss,* which was a weapon and was intended to be so used. The point is that Filipinos were not involved in crimes of violence because they had and used this tool. The knife of violence was the small one, just as it is elsewhere.

But if the Filipino was quick to strike he was also quick to forgive and forget. In northern Luzon there were, of course, long-standing tribal feuds which often erupted. And there were some antagonisms between families that were passed on through the generations. But, in the main, the Filipino was not one to cherish a personal grudge. The role of the peacemaker was usually easy. Incidentally, this has accounted for the relative ease with which some Filipinos have been able to shift from party to party or group to group in the political field, which has often been a bit bewildering to Americans.

WARMTH OF HEART

Back of these various manifestations lies another and still bigger element in this basic sensitiveness. It is the essential warmth of heart that everyone who has known Filipinos will recognize. There may be other Asians who are more carefree, in the conventional sense. Some may seem, superficially, to be more genuinely merry. But none is more basically sanguine. The establishment of friendship is often astonishingly easy. Good temper, a sense of humor, and a willingness to be accepted as just another human being have always been the best passport to any village in the Philippines. This characteristic was, naturally, of immense importance in the creation of the rapport that was required to carry out the aims of the American occupation. Filipinos were often described as "surly" in the time of the Insurrection. This was the product of the situation, as the Japanese were later to discover, and not a natural or normal part of Filipino behavior.

Depression of spirit is usually a fleeting thing, however intense it may be at the time. One American editor, long resident in the Philippines, has testified that in his whole experience he saw only two cases of genuine melancholia. One was based on a deep domestic maladjustment. The other was induced by the Japanese occupation and became psychopathic.

The Filipinos have always been ready to sing and dance on the slightest provocation. They are deeply fun-loving. Every village celebrates fiesta after fiesta and the national carnival has become an institution of significance and importance, carried on as a public enterprise with governmental sanction and participation.

Another phase of this sensitiveness and warmth of heart that was and is conspicuous is the renowned Filipino generosity and hospitality. Nothing was too good for the guest. Entertainment was regarded as one of the best things in life, and nothing was spared.

This, however, had its drawbacks. Time and again individuals and families impoverished themselves to play the role of good host. One Filipino secretary of finance once told the legislature: "Do not forget; the usurious moneylender makes his living on marriages, births, and fiestas." The future was all too often mortgaged for the present. This was a fixed behavior pattern and some of the impoverishment of the country was deliberate self-impoverishment. Frugality is not really a general trait, nor, indeed, a highly regarded one. This may help to explain, also, the very widespread, and often criticized, addiction to gambling which has sometimes been called the curse of the Philippines. That these various attitudes should eventually be reflected in political life is not at all unnatural.

We are concerned here, however, with the impact of these elements in the Filipino character upon the American occupation and its aims. Obviously they made some phases of the American administration much easier. This was particularly true at the village level where the American official or teacher was again and again received as an honored guest. If he was willing to accept Filipinos as they were and to be accepted, in turn, for what he was, he was able to exert tremendous influence. And he did.

The understandings that were reached brought out another trait in the Filipinos that was to be of great significance. This was the capacity for an intense loyalty, both to a person and to a cause. This received its world-wide testimonial on the battlefields of Bataan, but it had been an integral part of the growth of government and society in the Philippines for many years. There was, for example, a pervasive loyalty of subordinates to their superiors in the whole business of administration. Sometimes, it is true, this was miguided or based upon improper consideration of family or other attachment. On the other hand, it would have been quite impossible to carry out the work, say, of the Bureau of Science unless there were devoted men who respected their jobs and their mentors. Teachers were dedicated to their profession even when they were badly paid and not always well treated. The Philippine Constabulary would never have been able to reach the high degree of morale that was shown for many years without the *esprit de corps* that came from a conception of loyalty to group and to cause. The same spirit made the Philippine Scouts a well-disciplined and effective fighting body, as we later discovered.

Beyond this is the intricate pattern of personal loyalties that marked every phase of Filipino-American relationships. When the Americans were interned in Santo Tomas literally hundreds of them were kept alive by the gifts, attention, and services of their former employees. The case of the former houseboy who walked more than a hundred miles and went through the Japanese lines to bring fruit to Santo Tomas merely on the off chance that his former employers might be there was not unique. Some important American business structures, with warehouses concealed and books in order, were surreptitiously kept intact by Filipino employees throughout the Japanese occupation. But long before these events dramatized this relationship there had been a working pattern of good faith and loyal service. It was possible, for example, to publish an American newspaper in Manila for years with an almost entirely Filipino staff, most of whom were as hotly loyal to their paper as the most wide-eyed American reporters in the United States.

It may seem paradoxical that the Filipinos, intent upon their independence, should give this official and personal loyalty to the power and the persons that appeared to stand in the way of the achievement of their aims. The case, however, is not unique. The British could testify to similar experiences of loyalty in India throughout the great Indian Civil Service and in the lives of individual Britons. The real difference in India was that the massive civil disobedience movement was meant to be an expression of basic disloyalty to the ruling power. There was no corresponding development in the Philippines. There, nationalism, even when most flamboyant, remained a constructive force designed to reach its goal through lawful processes of agreement. And loyalty to the law and to those who enforced it—Filipinos and Americans—was part of the process.

This, then, was the human material with which the Americans set out to work in the occupation. That is was good material goes without saying. The Filipinos were quick to learn and quick to appreciate good motive. They remained "proud and sensitive," but they were able, eventually, to use these traits for their own good cause in cooperation with an alien administration that tried to respect them.

Naturally, there were periods of stress and strain and there were mistakes on both sides. Many of these arose from the very fact that there were two "sides" and that what was happening was too often viewed as a contest rather than as a period of experiment and growth. The experiment succeeded, but the growth within it was sometimes too slow to suit Filipino aspirations.

There was not, however, even in the days of General Wood, any fundamental departure from the essential aims of the American occupation. The first of these was to make secure and to preserve for the Filipinos those rights whose exercise is the essence of human freedom. The second, which developed more slowly, was to help to prepare the Philippines for full and successful self-government and for complete independence. This involved, as we shall see, an economic and social revolution, and the creation, by Filipinos and Americans, of a new political and social state unlike any that had previously appeared in Asia.

Three

THE INSTRUMENTS OF

INDEPENDENCE AND FREEDOM

The foundation for the eventual independence of the Philippines and for the freedom of its people had been laid, as has been noted, in several firm and basic elements. There was a common idealism, nationalistic in the Philippines, benevolent in the United States. There was a Filipino character, volatile in some instances, but capable of no small degree of stability when the occasion required. There was a people capable of growth and eager for it. The American occupation brought with it certain aims that were lofty, and that could be accommodated to this people. There were conflicts and confusions but they could be resolved. An ultimate goal had been recognized. It was human freedom.

On that foundation, however, there had to be careful, and sometimes slow, building. A new group of institutions, political and social, had to be evolved. This process often seemed painful. There was always that shining ideal to be held up. In spite of the pain, nevertheless, the building was good.

It was necessary, from the beginning, to devise or perfect certain instruments that could be used in the achievement of independence and freedom. There was need for an enlightened electorate, for a better mode of civil and public service, for a better code of justice, for an all-out war upon disease and hunger. The Philippines could become independent and the Filipinos could be free, but only if skill and imagination were brought to bear to work out the use of these instruments of growth and development. The process was eventually to succeed, and for that reason the means may be examined with profit.

PUBLIC EDUCATION

First of these instruments was the establishment of a system of free public education. Americans will note, with interest, that this is in the Jeffersonian tradition. Jefferson's own contribution to education was no less than his contribution to statecraft; his thesis was that a true democracy could rest only upon an enlightened electorate. The extension of this concept to the Philippines, when the basic aim was to set up a self-governing democracy, was only natural.

It was, however, also purposeful. This was made clear by President McKinley in his instructions to the Philippine Commission that was setting up civil government in the islands. These instructions set forth the purposes of American occupation and administration and were, in a sense, the chart of the American course. Addressing the Second Philippine Commission, President McKinley said that it should "regard as of first importance the extension of a system of primary education which shall be free to all, and which shall tend to fit the people for the duties of citizenship and for the ordinary avocations of a civilized community." The use of the word "civilized" was again unfortunate in this context, but the emphasis upon the duties of citizenship is significant. At the very outset the function of the school was tied to the growth of the state.

It is a mistake to say or suggest, however, that the United States "imposed" a system of free education upon the Philippines. This was far from the case. What the United States did was to meet a demand that had been made in the Philippines for several generations. Each one of the revolutionary constitutions or proclamations had given high place to the need for free public—and secular—education. Spain had bowed to this insistent demand about thirty years before the final revolt and had set up a system of public education of sorts to supplement the parochial schools. It eventually enrolled about two hundred thousand pupils. But the Filipinos wanted much more and much better than had been suggested or provided.

The American moves to establish a functioning, nationwide system of free primary education were therefore hailed with a great enthusiasm which never waned. Eventually this ardor was to take form in the Philippine Constitution itself, in which it was ordained that the provision of a system of public education, not merely primary but also adult, and education in citizenship itself, were proper functions and duties of the government.

The best evidence that the system of education was not imposed, however, lies in the simple fact that there was not a compulsory attendance law until the last years of the Commonwealth. No one had to go to school. But in spite of this, and in spite of the fact that the Insular—i.e., central—government spent about a third of its total appropriations for education, the facilities that could be provided were never large enough to meet the demand. We have noted that possibly two hundred thousand children were in public schools in the last days of the Spanish regime. By the time of the Commonwealth this number had grown to two million. It is now more than four million in a population of twenty-one million and represents 85 percent of the children of school age. There was no need for compulsion, or imposition. What was needed was only to supply an answer to an insistent demand. For this reason it was not an "American" school system. It was Philippine.

What the United States did impose, however, was the use of English as the language of instruction. This was to have far-reaching consequences in the formation and growth of the state. English was designated in the first Public Education Law of 1901, and its use was mandatory thereafter. The Tydings-McDuffie Act, the charter of independence, carried the provision that English should remain the language of instruction throughout the period of the Commonwealth. In his instructions President McKinley had originally suggested the use of the vernacular languages in the public schools. His administrators in the islands, however, overruled the suggestion and stood fast for the use of English. There were practical as well as ideological reasons for their decision.

In the first place, there was the question of textbooks. There were none in the vernaculars and the few in Spanish were not suited to the needs of the Filipino children, who were to move into a new world. In the beginning, therefore, American textbooks had to be imported. This has sometimes been called unrealistic, because those textbooks were written by Americans for American children, whose background was totally different from that which obtained in the Philippines. References to snowflakes, for example, were completely meaningless. The Filipino child, in short, was being taught to live in an American world of which he knew nothing and in which he would probably never have occasion to live. Gradually, over a period of some years, this defect was remedied. First, Americans began to write textbooks specifically for Filipinos, using the Philippine frame of reference. Later, Filipinos themselves took up the writing of their own texts for their own people, although the books were actually

printed in the United States. Competition in this field was
keen and helped to sustain a high quality in the material that
was turned out.

The use of American texts for primary instruction had,
however, an important effect in the field of nationalism. Children learned about George Washington, Abraham Lincoln,
and Patrick Henry. This was something that supplemented
what they had heard of Filipino heroes such as José Rizal
and Andres Bonifacio. That they should translate what they
learned of American nationalism into the terms of their own
country was inevitable. One story of this translation has become a classic in the Philippines. The Filipino boy was asked
to write a composition on "The Cow" (he had of course never
seen one in the land of the carabao), and his eloquent conclusion was: "The cow gives milk, but as for me give me
liberty or give me death."

It is significant that the American teachers, from the beginning, encouraged just such reactions. Pride in country and
love of country were approved and there was no suggestion
that the material in the textbooks ought to be foreign to the
Philippine scene. Eventually the schoolrooms were adorned
with busts and pictures of Filipino heroes, such as Rizal and
Mabini, in the same way that our schools display the like-
nesses of the founding fathers. The singing of the Philippine
national anthem was part of the daily exercises. And over the
schoolhouses, eventually, the American and Philippine flags
flew side by side. Some of this should be traced to the effect
of those early textbooks in English.

A second factor in the choice of English was the teacher
problem itself. About one thousand teachers who were Spanish left the islands after the occupation. The number of
trained Filipinos was entirely inadequate. Americans had to
be imported. The first contingent, composed of several hun-

dred American volunteer teachers, was brought out on the United States Army transport "Thomas." They became known as the Thomasites and took pride in the name. The first teachers were obliged to teach in English because it would have taken too long for them to become sufficiently proficient in any one of the vernaculars to do their job. Meanwhile, they had to carry on while Filipinos were being trained.

It was never intended to staff the Philippine schools permanently with American teachers, and normal schools were established for Filipinos from the beginning. But as late as 1915, in the elementary schools, more than 10 percent of the teachers were still Americans. In the intermediate and secondary schools the percentage was much higher and the division superintendents, the backbone of the administrative system, were all Americans. Gradually this, too, changed, and by the time of the Commonwealth, in 1935, American teachers in the elementary schools were less than one tenth of one percent, while those at the higher and administrative level numbered less than forty.

If the use of English dictated the use of American teachers, it served to bring into Philippine life, at the village level, a profound influence from the outside world. The teacher was the very center of village life. He, or she, was regarded as the model of deportment, the repository of all learning, and the court of last resort. The Americans, with very few exceptions, discharged this heavy responsibility with good grace and great success. There are many Filipinos in public life today who testify gladly and eloquently to the influence and example of American teachers in their childhood.

The third reason for the imposition of English in the Philippines was even more political in its implications. This was the need to provide a lingua franca if the scattered islands were ever to become truly a nation. Language complexities in the

Philippines have sometimes been exaggerated, as, for example, in the frequently quoted statement that there are "about eighty languages" in the archipelago. This is not true, since a total of eighty would necessarily be comprised by some dialectal variations that are so slight as to form no barrier to understanding. But H. Otley Beyer, the most outstanding linguistic anthropologist in respect to the Philippines, has stated that one must recognize at least eleven distinct languages in the islands, not including English and Spanish. It would have been quite impossible to set up an effective central government on such a polylingual basis. Spanish had been the official language and it was retained in that capacity to some extent, but it was the American design to make English the language of government and the common medium of exchange in communication. To do this it was necessary to make it the language of the schools.

Thus English became an instrument in national unification and to that extent an important instrument of nationalism itself. And it was in English that the important state papers of the emerging nation were framed. The Constitution, the messages of President Quezon and of Mr. Osmeña, the declarations of various Governors General, the writings of persons such as General Carlos P. Romulo, will remain as part of the political heritage of the nation.

This factor is sometimes obscured by the natural drive for a national language in a newly independent state. In the Philippines it is now the law that the national language is to be a "modified" Tagalog, and Filipino scholars have been working for almost a generation on the required modifications. In time, when this modified Tagalog becomes the language of instruction in all the public schools it may be adopted. But that time is still in the future. Tagalog is a mother tongue to less than one quarter of the Filipinos. There is, and will continue to be, resistance to it in many areas.

English continues to be the principal language of government and the principal language of business. Between four and five million Filipinos, a quarter of the population, are literate in English and it forms the most useful tool for general intelligibility in a multilingual society. It is also, still, by far the most important language of publication. In Manila, for example, the circulation of newspapers in English considerably exceeds that of newspapers in all other languages combined.

How long this will continue to be the case is problematical. English does not have a stigma attached to it as does, for example, the use of Dutch in Indonesia. The patriotic urge for an indigenous national language is not anti-English and in no sense anti-American. But it must be understood that English never did become, in spite of the school system, the natural language of the villages. And even among those who are highly literate in English it is not often the natural language of the home. Among a relatively few and usually upperclass families Spanish is still a home language. But for the vast majority the mother tongue is one or another of the vernaculars.

Meanwhile, however, English has served the cause of nationhood to excellent purpose. It has been valuable in the formation of the structure of the law. It has been useful in government and in business. It has been a big window on the outside world. It has helped to give Philippine nationalism an international character. These things are obvious; how far the use of English as the medium of public instruction has been a factor in creating a more genuine national unity cannot be quite so readily estimated.

It should be remembered that the use of English was only one aspect of a general uniformity in the Philippine educational pattern. From the very beginning the school system was centrally administered. It was an Insular function of government. Its revenues were derived from the Insular government. Methods of instruction were the same throughout, as were standards for teachers. This excessive centralization has often been criticized because it gave rise to a certain inflexibility— and the criticism is just. At the same time, a uniform pattern of public instruction has undoubtedly been a factor in creating a national consciousness that is above regional interest.

The next point at which the growth of a great public school system had its effect on the growth of a free government was that of literacy. Filipinos and Americans alike felt from the beginning that this was perhaps the most important tool on the workbench of democracy. Perhaps the wisest of them knew that there is no demonstrable organic connection between literacy and basic intelligence. At the same time it is much easier to carry out the day-to-day workings of government, and especially self-government, if a majority of the people can read and write. Experiences in India have demonstrated that it is humanly possible to carry out a free and democratic election even in a countryside that is largely illiterate. But they have also shown how difficult and complex is this task. It is obviously easier to hold an election if the voter can read a ballot and sign his name to a registration roll. It is easier to set issues before the public if the spoken word can be supplemented with the written one.

Literacy in the Philippines at the time of the American occupation was certainly less than 20 percent. Within two generations it rose to more than 40 percent. It is now well over 60 percent. If these figures seem low, they should be compared with those in other Asian countries: only Japan has had a higher literacy rate than the Philippines in the past half century. An interesting development is that the rise in literacy is not merely literacy in English, for there is a corresponding rise in other languages (except Spanish). It is thus the impact of an educational system as a whole, and not merely in its English aspects, that has helped to bring about this growth.

One reason why the rise in literacy has not been even more rapid is the relatively high mortality rate in school attendance. By far the largest part of the huge numbers of Filipino children who flocked to the schools did not reach even the fourth grade. It was obvious that no really substantial fluency in a totally foreign language could be reached in that time. This was a good argument for teaching in the vernaculars since the imposition of a double burden on the pupil could thus be avoided, and presumably the attendance survival rate could be raised. Yet the experience of the Dutch in Indonesia did not bear this out. Primary instruction was in the vernaculars but the literacy rate remained at about one tenth that of the Philippines.

The Filipinos have been well aware of the loss through this excessive dropping out at the primary levels. From the beginning of the Commonwealth, President Quezon insisted that the Philippines must have compulsory education at least through the first four grades, but that was not economically feasible. And even now, with far from the whole school-age population actually in school, both the physical plant and its budget have been strained almost to the breaking point.

Nevertheless, the influence of a school system that reached a majority of its pupils for even less than four years was enormous. In that time the Filipino child learned new modes of thought and behavior. He learned something about uncontaminated drinking water and the proper disposal of waste.

He learned about the toothbrush. And most of all he learned that there was a world other than that into which he was born. There was a chance for rapid advancement for the gifted and ambitious. And for all there was an equality of opportunity. These were lessons that could be readily learned even if the English was difficult, and they played a vital role in the forming of a nation.

It is not too much to say that the basic function of this whole system was social and political rather than intellectual. It was not designed to develop scholars. This does not mean that scholarship was not valued nor that the Philippines was deficient in encouraging its growth. The Filipinos produced more than an expectable quota of really first-class jurists, scientists, linguists, and technicians. The scientists made outstanding contributions, in the laboratories that grew up, to pure research and to its practical application. But this was not essentially the contribution of the public school system, which served in quite another way.

Reduced to its essence, the American occupation was actually an experiment in a gigantic social revolution. It proposed to change the actual mores of a whole people. Rightly or wrongly, it was believed that in no other way could they become truly free and enjoy their freedom. Such a revolution would have been quite impossible without the enthusiastic cooperation of the Filipinos themselves. They were not only willing but eager to change modes of behavior and they embraced the public school system as the natural instrument for making the changes. They were not "imitative" in the derogatory sense that the term has often been applied to the Japanese. But they were ready to accept American patterns of thought and behavior and to emulate them. For one thing, the Americans had learned how to live in freedom, and that was their own goal.

In this way the function of education was to start the individual into a new pattern of living and to give him a chance to adapt to a changed environment. At this point, also, the system was often attacked as unrealistic because the world for which the Filipino was being prepared was not necessarily the Filipino world. The degree to which education should be "vocational" was a much-argued point from the start. "Vocational" really meant the teaching of skills and techniques that had an immediate and practical application in the business of earning a living. And so even primary education had some vocational aspects. There was instruction in basket-weaving, in furniture-making, and in rudimentary home economics. Machine-shop instruction was out of the question in the earlier stages because there were no machine shops. Later on, there was resistance to this type of vocational training because of the Filipino preference for the "white-collar" job and the tendency to look down upon mere vocational training as opposed to the academic. The whole question of vocational education in the Philippines was brought into sharp but not unsympathetic review in 1930 by the findings of the study commission headed by Dr. Charles E. Prosser. It was then held that the opportunities for sound vocational training had been woefully deficient, but that the biggest obstacle to them was the attitude of the Filipinos themselves.

Twenty-five years after Dr. Prosser, the situation had not materially changed. There were far better opportunities for technical training but there was still a "white-collar" surplus and "white-collar" unemployment. The law, for example, was the pathway to political advancement and the Philippines has been cursed with a surfeit of lawyers for more than two generations.

Behind this attitude lies the fact, of course, that simple work with one's hands was associated in the Filipino mind with a previous state of political servitude. "Freedom" often meant freedom from the necessity of doing manual labor. The Americans tried, by precept and example, to change this attitude but they were not significantly successful. It is only in the most recent years, and particularly with the rise of Ramon Magsaysay, that it is possible to see any great change at this point.

To the extent, therefore, that the system of public instruction did not make a sufficient contribution toward the better adaptation of the Filipino to his immediate environment it must be said to have been less than successful. Against this must be weighed its contribution to adaptation to a larger and a changing environment in the world of ideas. This was the very essence of nationalism and of social revolution. As such it was embraced by the Filipinos as the very heart of their cause. It was a true cornerstone in the national building. It was an instrument of freedom.

PUBLIC HEALTH

The school system also played a vital role as a transmission belt in the establishment of a public health service. The school was the first point of instruction in hygiene and sanitation. It was, in the beginning, the place at which smallpox vaccination was introduced. The teachers were not usually medically trained but they had an outlook on health problems different from that which had obtained, and their pupils, in turn, became little medical missionaries in every family. The schools, moreover, were able to cooperate fully with the public health agencies that were set up and many school buildings were actually used, in part, as clinics and dispensaries. There was also close coordination at the top. The Bureau of Health and the Department of Education were combined by law in 1916 as a single department under the direction, ex officio, of the Vice Governor. It was not until 1941 that a separate Department of Health and Public Welfare was created.

It was apparent from the first day of the American occupation that there had to be sweeping changes and vast improvement in the health field if the Philippines was ever to enjoy freedom and indeed even to survive as a nation. If it is true, as Dr. Howard Rusk has said, that no people can be truly free unless they are relatively healthy, there was little chance for freedom among the Filipinos. Certainly there was little chance for political and economic viability as a state. It is usual to think of Asia's teeming millions; these islands, on the contrary, were underpopulated as a whole, despite some local congestions. In a land area about the size of New York, Pennsylvania, and Ohio there were not more than six million persons. Malnutrition was high, production was low, and the outlook bleak. It was certainly not the physical material out of which to create, overnight, an independent nation in which there could be the pursuit of happiness.

In another time and another place it is hard for us even to imagine the appalling health—or lack of health—conditions that prevailed in the Philippines at the time of the American occupation. The annual death rate throughout the islands was estimated by the First Philippine Commission to be more than fifty per thousand, although vital statistics were meager. The first medical census in 1903–4 showed it to be more than 40 per thousand in the city of Manila itself. Life expectancy was in the low thirties. In spite of high fecundity and a high birth rate, the survival rate was so low that the population had not increased in more than a quarter of a century. A contributing factor was an infant mortality rate so high as to seem almost incredible. In the city of Manila at the time of the occupation

infant mortality (within the first year) was one out of every
two living births and in some districts four out of five. There
was no pursuit of happiness for little Mrs. Juan de la Cruz,
but only the annual pilgrimage to Cementerio del Norte.

Tuberculosis, malaria, and the dysenteries were endemic.
Malnutritional diseases, especially beriberi, were prevalent.
The parasitic-disease incidence was beyond estimate. Early
health officers acted on the assumption that it was 100 percent. Hansen's disease (leprosy) was common and widespread. The lesions of yaws could be seen in every village.
On top of this was the constant scourge of epidemic. There
were 40,000 deaths from smallpox every year. And in any
year when there were less than 50,000 deaths from Asiatic
cholera, masses were celebrated in the churches in thanks-
giving for the deliverance of the islands. Bubonic plague frequently paralyzed the ports. There was relatively little typhus,
but typhoid often wiped out whole villages and came merely
under the classification of "fever." It was regarded as something of a cross between malaria or dengue, and dysentery.
Its relationship to transmission sources was unknown.

In the light of what we know about these killers now it
seems almost surprising that the Filipinos survived at all.
They were fighting a deadly handicap and they were not on
terms that were better than even, until there was a change
in regime and in outlook. Winning the battle for health had
to be part of winning the battle for freedom, and the Filipinos
threw themselves into it with vigor and enthusiasm. They had
good, and often inspired, leadership in the American doctors
who went to and served in the islands. Their story has been
well and often told, as it deserves to be. But there was also
the growth of a distinctly Philippine health tradition. After
all, José Rizal himself had been a physician. The medical

schools which were set up or greatly expanded under the American regime were quickly overcrowded. There were always more candidates for study abroad than could be accommodated. When public health nursing was thrown open to Filipino women there were Filipinas ready to take up the task.

Even more important, there was a general recognition in most of the archipelago that a public health program was an essential component of a properly functioning state. There was, for example, surprisingly little resistance to the scheme of general vaccination against smallpox that was initiated in the first decade of the American occupation. This was later extended to immunization against cholera. Filipinos and Americans working together—with the aid of laboratories throughout the world—developed a practicable serum for this use. The Filipinos may have been afraid of it in the first place, but they were won over. Here, again, the schools played an important part.

It is significant that in the very fields where public cooperation was essential the results were spectacular. By the time of the Commonwealth smallpox had ceased to be a consequential health problem. In place of those masses in praise of deliverance because cholera casualties were only in the tens of thousands, the situation changed, until if there were a hundred deaths from cholera in any year someone in the Health Department was likely to lose his job. Bubonic plague was brought under control by the establishment of a rigid port quarantine service set up and operated under the United States Public Health Service from 1901 on. Ship masters were held rigidly to task—and punished—if the adequate ratguards were not provided and in place. As a result the Filipinos were able, later on, to read the weekly reports of the epidemiological service of the League of Nations as it applied to various Asian ports, and to see, time after time, the simple note: "Plague—Manila—Clean."

By far the largest health job was, and still is, that of public sanitation. The provision of uncontaminated drinking water was a problem for every village. It was possible for engineers to set up a public water supply for a city such as Manila, put it to rigid and continuing tests, and then make the justified boast that Manila was one city in Asia where anyone could "drink water out of the tap." In the village, however, the source of water supply was usually the community well or the adjacent stream. The wells were seldom adequately safe-guarded against pollution and the streams served for bathing, laundering, and for sewage disposal. The latter was also often left to the pigs, living under the little bamboo houses on their stilts, that were the principal scavengers. It was into such a situation that the department of public health and the school system had to step with a massive program of education.

It is not that the Filipinos were not personally clean. Far from it. In all of Asia probably only the Balinese were more completely addicted to bathing. But this was a community, not a personal, problem. Once the villagers could be taught that there could be such a thing as group uncleanliness, in the medical sense, even among those who scrubbed them-selves assiduously, a long forward step could be taken.

Once again, the provision of the required services became a "national" project and it, also, contributed to the growing political self-consciousness. The organization of the Bureau of Health was based upon administration by provinces but the control was centralized. An adjunct of major importance was the central Bureau of Science, set up in 1905, which was to do not only the major laboratory work in the development of vaccines and serums, but was also to provide the best training ground for scientists and technicians to reinforce the strictly medical personnel. An Insular Bureau of Animal Husbandry was set up, primarily to grapple with the problem of epizootics. It met some local resistance when it ordered provincial quarantines and even required animal slaughter. But the control of rinderpest was too important to be left to uninformed communities. The carabao was the economic backbone of rice farming and the loss of work animals could mean near starvation to a whole area. The Bureau developed successful means of inoculation and compelled their general use. As a result it was possible to report triumphantly in 1930 that there was not a single new case of rinderpest in the archipelago. The Bureau was then able to devote further efforts to developing better animal strains and introducing new types, to teaching means of better care and feeding, and to promoting public understanding of a better animal economy.

Another example of the coordinated attack upon a great scourge was in the work done against Hansen's disease. Prior to the American regime there had been a few sporadic isolation points, notably the San Lazaro Hospital in Manila, but the work was ineffective and in most cases the disease itself bore the ancient stigma and patients were held as "prisoners of God's will" until slow death released them. In 1905 there was set up in the Philippines a tremendous colony on the island of Culion where persons who suffered from the disease could be isolated and at the same time treated as human beings. This was not the first such experiment (good work had been done in Hawaii) but it was one of the best. Culion was later to become, also, one of the finest laboratories for the study of the disease. At this time, it should be remembered, the use of chaulmoogra oil was the only known specific treatment and not nearly enough was known about it. It was not until the discovery of the possibility of using the sulfone compounds in therapy—two generations later—that great changes in treatment were possible.

The work did not stop with Culion. Eleven provincial segregated hospital colonies were eventually established and some of them were almost as important in the society as Culion itself. At the time of the death of General Wood, a group of Americans and Filipinos determined that the enduring monument to the man who had done so much for public health in the Philippines should be a Leonard Wood Memorial fund, devoted to the care and treatment of leprous patients in the Philippines. It was through this fund that the splendid Eversley Childs Memorial Hospital and Clinic was set up in Cebu. It was here that Dr. Rodriguez, a Filipino, was able to develop and prove the first definitive test for the incidence of the disease in children.

Unfortunately the whole system of the treatment of the leprous patients was to become, in the early days of the Commonwealth, something of a political football. Segregation was held, in some quarters, to be much too severe, and the whole insular program was attacked. The ostensible issue was the right of suffrage of those who were hospitalized but this was merely the means of gaining political capital from the situation. The subsequent Japanese occupation, on the other hand, and the tremendous advances in therapy, on the other, eventually made much of this discussion academic.

This was not the first stormy chapter in the story of the Philippine health service. The greatest gains were made in the period 1901–14, when the whole pattern of human survival was changed. The period 1914–20, characterized by generally slackened controls, was one of loss in which some good things were undone. Then followed the administration of General Wood, when a major purpose was to "revitalize" the

health service. This was successful and by 1926 its full worth
was restored. Early in the thirties, with independence in sight,
there was again a tremendous forward surge under the inspiration of Governor General Frank Murphy, with the invaluable help of his extraordinary adviser in the field of public
health, Lieutenant Colonel George E. Dunham. Commonwealth President Quezon threw the whole weight of his government behind a new health and welfare program and it
became, once more, a great patriotic cause. It was again a
part of the crusade for independence and freedom.

It was this factor that made the achievements in the Philippines most significant. Otherwise, gains in the health field
were not unique. The first part of this century was a period
of immense advances in many parts of the world. But in the
Philippines it was possible to see, within a precise area, what
could be done when the change in the whole health pattern of
a people became a deliberate national cause. What actually
happened was almost incredible.

The whole survival pattern was changed. Birth rates remained constant but the death rate in Manila, for example,
dropped from 40 per thousand in 1903 to 23 per thousand
in 1914. By the time of the Commonwealth, in 1935, it had
dropped to 12. It is now, 1957, 9.6. Infant mortality in the
same district where the rate at the time of the American occupation was 80 per hundred, dropped to 54 per thousand in
1933, less than two generations later. Instead of expecting that
four out of five of her children would die in infancy, Mrs. Juan
de la Cruz could confidently expect that fourteen out of fifteen
would survive. The whole population was tripled in less than
two generations. Life insurance ceased to be put on a tropical
rate basis and its sale became an important factor in economic growth. The outlook on life itself was changed.

This was the product of a nationally directed effort. At

the advent of the Commonwealth 49 public hospitals had
been set up. A thousand dispensaries were functioning. There
were more than four thousand maternity and puericulture
centers. In the first year of the Commonwealth public health
nurses performed more than half a million immunizations.
These were functions of the state, state-supported and a part
of it. If a people should be healthy to be truly free, the Filipinos had come a long way on the right road. Public health
and its promotion were an instrument of freedom.

A VIABLE ECONOMY

Public services such as those noted here cost money. It
readily became apparent that if there was to be real progress
in the Philippines there must be a sounder basis for it than
existed at the time that the Americans moved in. Potential
productive wealth was there but had not been used. Public
revenues were small and standards of living were pitifully
low. Something had to be done.

After several experiments and after recurring appropriations for administration in the islands, the United States took
its major step in 1913 with the adoption of the Underwood
Tariff Act, which provided that products and exports of the
Philippines should be admitted to the United States duty-
free. From that point on the immediate problem of solvency
in the islands could be met, but larger, far-reaching questions
were raised through the establishment of a peculiar economic
relationship that made the ultimate achievement of independence more complicated. Actual survival in the Philippines became dependent upon the free American market.
Political independence could be welcomed. Real economic
independence had been made impossible. Initially, however,
the problem of economic viability had been solved. The Phil-

ippines prospered beyond even the most sanguine expectations. The money that was needed for those programs of health and education was available.

National defense was, and continued to be, the responsibility of the United States. It was paid for by American appropriations. The Coast and Geodetic Survey, which had important work to do, was taken up as a joint Philippine-American enterprise, and its cost was shared. Otherwise, government in the Philippines was self-sustaining and it paid its way. It will be observed that the continuing assumption of the defense burden by the United States made it possible for the government in the Philippines to channel larger amounts into such fields as health and education than would otherwise have been the case. In the thirty years that followed, these fields could and did use more than 30 percent of the Insular revenues. This was an unusual situation and a valuable one.

The first effect of the American legislation was to channel export production into relatively few goods and to send these directly into the American market. This had both good and bad aspects in the long run. Money was being earned by the Philippines that could be used in local growth and development—and it was. But those earnings created an increased dependence upon a free American market, whose fluctuations would affect the whole economy of the islands and whose ultimate withdrawal, when independence came, could imperil the entire economic structure. It was a case of choosing the short-term gain as against the long-term danger, and the decision was made in favor of the short term.

Production was concentrated upon four major export products. They were sugar, coconuts, abacá (Manila hemp), and tobacco. These were supplemented with smaller exports such as pearl buttons, embroidery, hardwoods, and, later on, minerals. Together, these products constituted the backbone of an export economy and for more than twenty years they accounted for more than 75 percent of the Philippine exports. Most important, they were going directly into a free and protected market. Up to the time of the Japanese invasion the United States absorbed, regularly, about 85 percent of the total Philippine exports, and supplied about 70 percent of the total Philippine imports. This, moreover, was the characteristic trade pattern, with the archipelago enjoying an expectable annual balance of trade of about 15 percent. Prosperity was the order of the day.

Even the great depression of the thirties in the United States did not materially affect this prosperity. The shipments of sugar, coconuts, and abacá remained relatively constant, and the price drop was not large enough to affect the basic pattern. Moreover, it was just at this time that the Philippines was caught up in a tremendous mining boom that more than offset any depressive effects of the American slump. Gold was the leader; the Philippines quickly passed Alaska and shot into a position second only to California as a producer of gold under the American flag. There was also an enormous expansion in the base metals field. Iron, manganese, and copper went to Japan; chromite and zinc went to the United States. Three stock exchanges were operating in Manila at one time.

This was actually the situation when the Commonwealth took over. The country was rich and prosperous. There was a free market for its exports. Standards of living were rising. There was a truly viable economy for the state and if the Filipinos were optimistic it was with cause.

There is another side to this bright picture—a considerably less bright one. The objective in the economic pattern that was set up was to obtain money for a growing and developing state. It did that, successfully. It did not, on the other hand, set up a sound, diversified, independent economy. Ultimately it created as many problems as it solved.

In the first place, this money-crops-for-export program was not sufficiently related to the basic question of subsistence. Rice was and is the chief food, and the expansion of its cultivation barely kept pace with the population increase. In the twenty years before the Japanese invasion the situation was always so precarious that every factor in a given year had to be favorable if rice production was to be adequate for local needs. Naturally this favorable conjunction rarely took place, and the Philippines, a major rice producer and consumer, was repeatedly forced to go into the foreign market to buy rice.

Moreover, the position of the majority of the rice farmers was and continued to be lamentable. Irrigation was inadequate to provide for uniform double cropping and secondary crops were insufficient to make up the difference. The typical rice farmer was virtually idle for several months in every year and he paid the penalty. The middleman, the warehousing agent, or the landlord had him in an economic vise. Every crop was mortaged in advance and the interest rates were scandalously usurious. Governor Murphy once solemnly estimated that more than 80 percent of the rice farmers in the Philippines were hopelessly in debt from birth to death. It was no accident, therefore, that the Communist-led Hukbalahap explosion ultimately centered in the rice lands of central Luzon.

Similarly, the type of economy that was developed made no contribution to solving the problem of tenancy and land ownership. In many cases, indeed, the effect was to increase the tenant relationship rather than to promote freeholding. Americans will be shocked to realize that during their ad-

ministration in the Philippines the percentage of tenant farmers actually went up instead of down and that at the advent
of the Commonwealth almost half the farm population was
tenant. In some cases, such as the model Calamba Sugar
Estate south of Manila, the landlord-tenant relationship was
highly paternalistic and benevolent and many farmers actually
preferred to work for the estate as tenants rather than to
accept the responsibilities of independent cultivation. In
other cases, and many of them, there was a high degree of
absentee landlordism and the tenant condition was pitiful.
This was to become politically explosive.

From the political point of view, however, the crux of
the problem was that the United States, wittingly or unconsciously, had set up a genuinely colonial economy. The protected American market was an irresistible magnet for Philippine goods. With a tariff of two dollars a hundred pounds
on sugar the Filipinos competed successfully with Cuba, even
with the latter enjoying a 20 percent differential in the United
States. They could not have done so in a free market. They
could sell cordage in the United States and build up a rope-
making industry, where in the world market they could
merely supply the raw material. Japan took advantage of this
and through a variety of subterfuges eventually got control
of more than half of the abacá output by 1934. But it was
baled hemp, not rope, that went to Japan. With the American
tariff protection on vegetable oils it was profitable to mill
coconut oil in the Philippines and not to be dependent merely
upon the shipments of copra into a free market where the
competition was overwhelming. Subsequently, the United
States government put a processing tax on oils milled in the
United States. The proceeds on Philippine raw material were
returned to the Philippine government and constituted the

"windfall" of the early thirties that made further progress in the islands easier. Philippine exports of cigars and leaf tobacco to the United States made possible the imports of American cigarettes which found a big market in the islands.

What all this added up to was a critical dependence of the Philippines on that free American market. It meant, in short, that while the United States had taken important steps to prepare the Philippines for political independence it had followed a course that made economic independence precarious if not impossible. When the first outline of independence laws began to be discussed with the visit of Senator Vandenberg to the Philippines in 1931, prominent Filipinos put their case clearly to the Senator. "We are obliged to realize," they said, "that such a thing as our school system, for example, is directly dependent upon that three-quarters of a million tons of sugar that we ship to the United States." This was literally true. The public services were Insular functions, not local, and dependent upon Insular revenues. Those revenues, in turn, were directly dependent upon exports to the free and protected American market. The question was thus not some abstraction in economics. It was a question of the standard of living for every Filipino.

At this point it must be confessed that not all the support in the United States for Philippine independence was entirely idealistic and altruistic. American and Cuban sugar interests, the American cordage industry, and American dairy farmers had a stake in the grant of Philippine independence if it put Philippine competitors outside the protection of the American tariff wall. The Filipinos found themselves with an assorted group of strange friends and allies in their campaign for independence. In a depression-ridden United States these were men and interests who were less concerned with independence of the Philippines from the United States than with the independence of the United States from the Philippines.

The result was that a major part of the achievement of a plan for the Philippine independence had to be centered upon some sort of program that would permit economic survival for the new nation. It was Senator Vandenberg who first formally proposed the establishment of United States import quotas on major Philippine products and the gradual imposition, over a period of years, of American tariffs. This principle has been an integral part of all subsequent legislation dealing with Philippine independence and with Philippine-American relations. The problems that it raises have not yet been solved.

From time to time some Filipino leaders have asserted that they were willing to take the chance on economic survival and would prefer to cut the economic ties to the United States, once and for all. This is good nationalism but it is not humanitarianism. It might have been possible, very early, gradually to lay the foundation for a truly independent Philippine economy. Another course was chosen and it could not later abruptly be abandoned. What was done has contributed to the growth and well-being of the Philippines. It has helped to make secure some of those precious rights. It has been an instrument of freedom and with wise understanding and adjustment both there and here it can continue to be that.

CIVIL SERVICE

In the growth of self-government and the preparation for independence a vital role was played by the development of an adequate civil service. When the time came for the transi-

tion to the Commonwealth and then for the proclamation of
the Republic there were Filipinos properly trained for every
major administrative post. Many of them had long experience. Most of them had repeatedly justified the confidence
that had been placed in them.

The Philippines thus escaped the administrative breakdown that took place in some other colonial areas when independence was granted but where an adequate corps of indigenous civil servants had not been sufficiently built up.
Over the years there had been established, in the Philippines,
a familiar pattern of expectable behavior and a large body
of public servants was prepared to carry it out. The path
trod by the civil service was occasionally rocky but it was a
path of progress and it led, ultimately, to the desired goal.

This civil service was set up in 1900 on a strictly merit
basis. In this respect the Philippines was some years in advance of the United States where the "spoils system" had
by no means disappeared. The merit system had special
significance in the Philippines because it came in conflict
with, and was obliged to replace, one of the fixed behavior
patterns. The Filipinos embraced and followed what was
called the *pariente* system. *Pariente* means a relative, and
in the society it meant that those members of a family who
were more fortunate accepted the responsibility to provide
for those who were less so. Thus nepotism could be a virtue
rather than the contrary. The merit system made the application of this family pattern more difficult and contributed
to the quality of the service. There were infractions and
evasions, of course, as there would be anywhere, but in the
main the system worked. By far the larger part of the *parientes*
got into positions or minor jobs that did not come under the
civil service.

In the first fifteen years of the American occupation the

administrative framework of the civil service was almost entirely American. Good men were attracted to the service. Some of them proved to be brilliant and gave their entire careers to public service in the Philippines and for the Filipinos. We have already seen what was done in health and education. Beyond that there was substantial service in forestry and fisheries, in finance, in land survey, and in public works. Some of the men who went into these fields were expert to begin with. Others acquired their *expertise* under the pressure of crying need. And all the time they were helping to train the Filipinos who could eventually assume their responsibilities.

By 1914 there were more than twenty-five hundred Americans, properly qualified, who were working in this civil service. At that time, under the administration of Governor General Harrison, an attempt was made to Filipinize all the services. As a result, in about six years, the number of American civil servants in the Philippines dropped from 2,623 to 614. Simultaneously, the merit qualifications were relaxed and the value of the service was imperiled. Under the existing conditions the Filipinos were not yet ready for the sweeping changes that were made, in spite of the good motives that prompted them.

It was into this situation that Governor General Wood was obliged to step. He put a stop to the wholesale departure of Americans from administrative posts and tried to restore merit standards for the Filipinos. Naturally, he was regarded by many Filipinos, and especially by some political leaders, as being anti-Filipino, and a period of tension ensued. After General Wood's departure, and ultimate death, a new period set in. Henry L. Stimson, following the Wood administration in 1929, took up the role of "conciliator" and succeeded. And even more important, a Filipino statesman, Sergio

Osmeña, worked out and presented the plans under which Americans could leave the Philippine service with dignity and pension and under which Governors General could have the help of technical advisers in special fields who were neither in cabinets nor under civil service. The plans worked and the cooperative character of the civil service was fully restored.

By the time of the Commonwealth the Americans actually in the public service had been reduced to a handful, most of them in administrative positions in the field of education. The Filipinos continued to function. The transition was completely orderly. The training had been good and the civil service had proved its worth. It, also, was an instrument of freedom.

REPRESENTATIVE GOVERNMENT

The most easily understood, and in some ways the most spectacular, development in Philippine progress was the growth of the legislative instruments of self-government. Here was actual practice in government by consent and in government by Filipinos. The Philippine legislative bodies became the continuing center of nationalism, of political growth, and of the considered expression of Filipino aims. They became, also, a yardstick of progress and a means by which that progress could be made.

Law in the Philippines was, in the beginning, a matter of American fiat. The first legal instrument was the instruction to the Second Philippine Commission by President McKinley in 1901. This set up the framework of government, but it was not government by consent. This was followed, in 1902, by Congressional action, the Philippine Organic Act, that solidified this framework but that also paved the way for

Filipino participation in government, for eventual free elections and the evolution of a Filipino legislature.

The idea of election was no novelty. Even under early American military rule it had been applied at the village level. When an American officer went into a town he asked for the "headman." If he was told that there was no such person he usually retorted, "Well, get together and choose one." Self-government began at the rice roots. But it was several years before it could take form at the highest level, although municipal and provincial elections were carried out by 1903.

From 1900 to 1907 the legislative and executive powers in the Philippines were concentrated and vested in a Philippine Commission, appointed by the President of the United States. After the first year Filipinos were regularly included in the appointed members of the Commission. They could not, however, be said to have been chosen representatives of the Filipino people, although they were often eloquent spokesmen.

By 1907 a census had been taken, electoral rolls made out, and the groundwork laid for a genuinely popular ballot. The lower house of a Philippine legislature was to be chosen. There was adult male suffrage, with a literacy or property qualification. A person who paid enough taxes could vote even if illiterate. All literates could vote. The upper house of the new legislature was to remain the Philippine Commission, but it was augmented, and by 1913 the Filipinos, chosen by popular election, were in a majority on it. Some appointed posts were reserved in the lower house, also, to represent the tribal groups, but the principle of a Filipino-elected legislative body, for Filipinos, was firmly fixed and was never compromised. Domestic legislation, including appropriation, originated in the lower house. The upper house could over-rule, but this was infrequent.

Most chroniclers of the 1907 election give especial at-tention to the fact that it brought into the forefront of the Philippine political scene the two men who were to be the leaders of Philippine nationalism and Philippine political thought for almost forty years. They were Manuel Quezon and Sergio Osmeña. Both were sent into that first legislature and they continued in office until the death of Mr. Quezon in 1944 and the retirement of Mr. Osmeña after the advent of independence. They made an interesting contrast and a steadily successful political team. Mr. Quezon was small and fiery. He was a magnificent orator, a shrewd politician and often a ruthless one, a tough fighter and sometimes an unscrupulous one, a "leader" in the Philippine sense of the word. Mr. Osmeña, with some mixture of Chinese blood, was more reserved. He early won a deserved reputation for high integrity and for balanced judgment. He accepted the post of second to Quezon with good grace and rarely chal-lenged the leadership of his colleague. On the few occasions when they split, such as in 1933, their differences were composed quickly and they could again present a united political front. They were joined later by a younger man, Manuel Roxas, who became the speaker of the lower house with Mr. Quezon's blessing. Mr. Roxas was also a gifted orator, but he was above all else a parliamentarian. In this role he was an invaluable third member of the triumvirate that dominated the legislative and political scene for a quarter of a century.

From the strictly governmental point of view a serious weakness in this situation was the lack of an effective opposi-tion. Quezon, Osmeña, and later Roxas, were "nacionalistas," that is, proponents of national independence at the earliest possible date. Subsequently, that became the party name. There could be no successful challenge to such a central party plank. Prior to and during the first national election, in 1907, there was a short-lived Federalista party that centered in a relatively few conservative intellectuals. It held that the interests of the Philippines could be best served by some sort of permanent attachment to the United States, possibly culminating in statehood. This party was said to have had the blessing of Governor Taft, probably because he was personally friendly toward some of its members. He denied, specifically, that he had ever given any such blessing, and the Federalistas faded out after the first election. Subsequently some other opposition parties were formed, the strongest of which was the Democratas. But these parties, while they could win an occasional local election and perhaps even send a few representatives to the legislature, were not effective instruments at the national level. It was, in the main, one-party government.

This put the burden of serving as a functioning opposition all too frequently upon the American-appointed executive branch. The result was frequent friction, much of which might have been avoided had there been a Filipino opposition strong enough to act as a check on the majority party. Up until 1916 the upper house was still the appointed Philippine Commission and disagreement between the two houses was often inevitable. But from the beginning the American opposition could be expressed in the veto of the Governor General, which continued to be in effect until the advent of the Commonwealth, although it ceased to be absolute (that is, vetoes could be appealed) after 1916.

The occasional Filipino nationalist charge that the veto power was arbitrarily misused—leveled especially against

General Wood—will not withstand examination. The vetoes were in the interest of good and better government, almost uniformly. What can be sustained is the charge that the basis for veto was not always explained with sufficient clarity and emphasis. This defect was subsequently corrected and, beginning with Stimson, Governors General made it a practice to send precise and detailed veto messages to the legislature. The results were good. Governor General Davis, for example, actually vetoed more measures than did General Wood without creating any atmosphere of tension or hostility. One reason was that in many cases the Governor General could honestly say that he had returned a measure because of imperfect drafting. He could state that he was in sympathy with the aims of the legislation that had been put before him, but was convinced that the measure as it stood would not achieve those aims and he was therefore returning it to have "its imperfections remedied." With such a procedure there could be no legitimate quarrel.

In this connection a word should be said about "government by indirection." Stimson, Davis, and Murphy were masters of this technique. When they wanted a particular thing done they made it a practice to call in a responsible Filipino leader and suggest that he espouse such a particular cause. The Governor General stayed out of the picture. Filipinos did the work and Filipinos got the credit for it. When Governor General Davis, for example, felt that there was need for a considerable clean-up in government he did not order investigations. He suggested that a young member of the lower house introduce a resolution asking for a special report on the operations of some departments, giving attention to what he hoped were mistaken charges of corruption. The result was the celebrated "Ruiz investigations" (not the Davis) that shook up several government departments. Another result was that when Governor Davis was ready to leave the islands, two thousand Filipinos gathered at the Manila Hotel Pavilion and sang with gusto and obvious enjoyment a little song for the occasion:

> D. L. Davis, D. L. Davis,
> De los tennistas, primador;
> D. L. Davis, D. L. Davis,
> Por los grafters, matador.

Similarly, when Governor Murphy determined to put through a new program of health and welfare he called in Manuel Quezon and laid it out in detail. It became the Quezon program of "social justice" that was not only immediately successful and effective but was later to be reflected in the very text of the Constitution.

Obviously the Filipinos were not unwilling to work in this fashion. On the contrary, they respected a mode of administration that could give them responsibility and credit. It was not a subterfuge. It was cooperative government by consent.

In the growth of government structures a great forward step was taken in 1916. The American Congress adopted the Philippine Organic Act of 1916, commonly called the Jones Law, that was to be a basic charter for Philippine freedom and independence. It made the subsequent legislation possible and established a basis upon which a working Filipino government could be set up.

So much attention was immediately focused upon its sometimes controversial preamble that some of the significance of the legislation itself was lost. The preamble stated that it was the intention of the United States to accord independence to the Philippines as soon as a stable government should be set up. Naturally, this immediately raised the problem of defining a stable government. The Filipinos insisted that they already had one and were certainly capable of sustaining it. Unfortunately, at that very time, the government was not especially stable. The maladministration of the Harrison regime had undermined the civil service and departmental operation. The subsequent report of the Wood-Forbes mission, which detailed this precise instability, was not a recommendation for immediate independence. But the preamble was continuously held up as the great American pledge, which it most certainly was. It was a declaration of intent and purpose, with that one condition. It would have been an obvious breach of faith had the United States not exerted its efforts to create that stable government that was set up as the prerequisite for independence.

Actually, the Jones Law set up the instrumentality through which that very thing could be accomplished. It was precise and detailed. Fortunately, it was not as long as the massive India Act of 1935, but it served a corresponding purpose, twenty years earlier. It set forth, in detail, the scope and functions of a working government. It made that government representative and responsible. (Responsible is not used here in the parliamentary, but in the moral, sense.) It placed an immense burden upon the Filipinos but gave them the means by which to carry it.

Perhaps the most important single provision was the creation of an all-Filipino legislature. The Philippine Commission ceased to exist. Henceforth the upper house was to be a Senate, elected by Filipinos. The few appointive seats for the tribal peoples were reserved in both houses, but they were soon filled by Filipinos, not Americans. This Senate became the concentric point for constructive Philippine nationalism. The President of the Senate became the position of highest leadership among the Filipinos, a position which was elective. Naturally, Mr. Quezon filled it.

To suggest that this Philippine bicameral legislature was always inhibited by the veto power is to be short-sighted from the point of view of the evolution of a government by consent. It was an instrument in political growth that was to be of continuing significance. It was a place in which self-government could actually be practiced. It was a place in which petitions could be formulated for address to the sovereign power. It was a greenhouse—one could almost say a forcing house—for constructive Philippine nationalism.

Another immediate outcome of the Jones Law adopted in 1916, was the drafting and adoption, within one year, of an Administrative Code for the Philippines. This was the work of Filipinos. They were acting under American authority, it is true, but they were setting up the framework of a government. They set forth how that government should operate. If the American-enacted Jones Law laid a foundation for building self-government, the Filipino-enacted Administrative Code made possible the splendid building upon that foundation.

It is not too much to say that the great Philippine Constitution had its first step toward enactment in the formulation and adoption of the Administrative Code.

THE CONSTITUTION

In the late summer of 1934 an extraordinary assembly came to order in Manila. It was the constitutional convention, authorized in the Tydings-McDuffie Act that had been approved in March of that year by the American Congress and President. This was the immediate instrument through which subsequent independence could be achieved and freedom made secure.

Independence legislation had had something of a stormy

course up to this point. The first independence act to be adopted in Congress, the Hare-Hawes-Cutting Bill of 1932, had been vetoed by President Hoover and then enacted over his veto in 1933. When it was submitted to the Filipino electorate they rejected it. They were led, in this case, by Senate President Quezon, in opposition to Osmeña and Roxas, who had worked for the bill. Mr. Quezon's ground for objection was that the economic provisions were too onerous and the provision for the retention of American bases in the Philippines so vague as to compromise eventual Philippine sovereignty. Quezon easily won a test in the legislature—which was interpreted as a rejection of the measure—went to Washington himself, and returned with the new legislation, the Tydings-McDuffie Act, that was not materially different from its predecessor in substance but that made occasional changes in phraseology, some of them more advantageous to the Philippines.

Quezon promptly took the bill to the country as the paramount issue in a further contest against Osmeña and Roxas. He won a smashing victory, and it was correctly interpreted as approval of the American legislation. This may not have been a "plebiscite" in the strict legal definition of the term, but it was certainly an expression of popular will, freely given. It was another instance of genuine government by consent. No further election or "plebiscite" was required to demonstrate that the Filipinos were solidly behind the course that was outlined.

A first step in this course was the election of a popular assembly to draft a constitution for the Philippines. This election was held in the early summer. It was somewhat different from anything that had happened previously in the Philippines. It was nonpartisan. Delegates were chosen from local districts, presumably without any intervention whatever of party machinery. Mr. Quezon and Mr. Osmeña, who had already composed their political difference, did not even present themselves as candidates. This was to be a body that represented the people as a whole, not one party or another.

Naturally, however, men with political experience were predominant among the candidates. There were members of the legislature, provincial governors, justices and former justices, former cabinet members, and even Filipino Resident Commissioners who had served in the United States. Significantly, there were almost no candidates from any branch of the civil service. But in addition to the professional *politicos,* doctors, lawyers, merchants, and farmers were chosen. When those 202 men assembled they could honestly believe that they were a good cross-section of Philippine public life. They were fitted to draft an organic law by Filipinos and for Filipinos. This was a truly Philippine body.

This aspect of its character was quickly dramatized. Governor General Murphy was invited to preside at the opening session. He promptly declined. Then he was invited to attend as the "guest of honor." Again, and gracefully, he refused with the explanation that he wished no suggestion that this convention was anything but Philippine in its entire character. Some of the Manila newspapers cried "Snub," but the attitude of the more thoughtful was sharply set forth in an editorial in the influential and highly respected *Manila Daily Bulletin.* It said:

Governor General Murphy acted with wisdom and tact in declining to be present at the first session of the constitutional convention. The delicacy of his behavior was greatly appreciated by those who have the utmost confidence in him and would have welcomed his presence. Murphy's conduct is a symbol of the fact that the administration wants the constitution to be a truly great Philippine and Filipino achievement, and does not wish to bring pressure to bear at any point. To the convention a free hand has been given.

This attitude continued. The United States Attorney General refused to make any ruling, in advance, on the validity of certain items in the first draft that were submitted to him by cable from Mr. Quezon. The Attorney General explained that under the law it was merely the entire document that required the eventual approval of the President of the United States, and that any sort of prior rulings would not be in order nor in accord with the spirit of the law. Similarly, no American official took any part, at any time, in the deliberations of the convention, although they were always welcome in the visitors' gallery, as was the public.

This does not mean that American influence was not felt. The very fact that presidential approval was to be required was in itself the strongest deterrent to the adoption of any course that could have been held repugnant to the American concept of constitutional government. More than that, while the Governor General would not be present officially his legal staff—and it was a good one—was always at hand to help, privately, on questions of drafting. American lawyers, businessmen, and newspapermen were often consulted in a friendly way, especially on questions of phraseology. Furthermore, the United States Constitution itself, and the American-legislated Organic Acts were to serve as models in many cases.

But the American requirements laid upon this convention were surprisingly few and simple. Actually, there were only two specific stipulations. The Philippine Constitution must provide for a government that was republican in form and it must contain a bill of rights. In this, emphasis had to be placed upon a required guarantee of freedom of worship. Within those limits the Filipinos could make their own state.

The so-called "mandatory provisions," stipulated under the Tydings-McDuffie Act, but not necessarily a part of the Constitution, came in an entirely different category. These related to the status of Americans in the islands, the status

of American holdings, and, above all, the terms upon which
Philippine-American trade was to go forward. There was
also the provision that English should continue as the
language of public instruction throughout the ten-year Commonwealth period, that the Philippine peso should continue
to be pegged to the American dollar at two to one, and that
the President of the United States might intervene to void
any legislation that undermined the fiscal stability of the
Commonwealth. But the Tydings-McDuffie Act also provided
that these "mandatory provisions" could be incorporated
either in the Constitution or in an ordinance merely appended
to it.

This provision changed the whole character of the constitutional convention. The "mandatory provisions" were incorporated, in full, and virtually without debate, in an "Ordinance Appended to the Constitution." They were to be
operative for the period of the Commonwealth. After that
they could simply be dropped, as a body, from the basic law
of the land. Thus the convention set about to draft a constitution, not for an interim Commonwealth, but for an independent Republic of the Philippines. This fact gave the
members a greater dignity and a greater sense of responsibility.
They were building for a hundred years, not ten, and their
building was good.

At the outset Governor General Murphy's refusal to preside at the opening session created a minor political crisis.
Senate President Manuel Quezon was the next obvious person
in line to open the sessions, but he had just been through
some stormy political campaigns and his opponents charged
that his appearance would give a political tinge to the whole
proceedings. But the choice of Mr. Quezon was logical and
inevitable. The whole responsibility for electing a constituent
assembly and convening it had been laid, in the American

law, upon the Philippine legislature. Mr. Quezon was the senior officer in that body. He could convene the assembly in the name of the legislature itself, and he did. He stayed on the rostrum just long enough for the delegates to elect a chairman pro tem and then retired. The convention then elected its permanent president, a distinguished jurist, Claro M. Recto.

With the help of Manuel Roxas who was, as we have noted, a gifted parliamentarian, the machinery for operations was readily established. The ground to be covered in the final document was divided and subdivided and committees were appointed to study each designated field. These committees, in turn, reported their findings to a central drafting committee. The drafting committee attempted to put the provisions upon which committee agreement had been reached into acceptable form, assisted by a committee on "style." These provisions were then submitted, in turn, to plenary sessions of the entire convention. Thus the constitution was tacitly and provisionally approved, part by part, before it was finally submitted to the assembly as a whole.

This method was actually not as cumbersome as it sounds. From a practical point of view it was imperative. It must be remembered that this constituent assembly was multilingual and that the language barriers were often difficult to surmount. Actually six different languages and many more dialects were heard on the convention floor. The ultimate text had to be English, and the Constitution had to be submitted, in that language, to the President of the United States. The drafting committee had a huge task, therefore, not only in substance, but in form.

There were constant cries in the press that the convention was "dragging its feet" and frequent accusations that too much time was being consumed in petty disputation. Considering the necessary mode of operation, this criticism was unfounded. The convention was able to complete its work in about five months, which by our legislative standards could hardly be called dilatory. More than that, it produced a document that not only obtained prompt presidential approval but that won the justified admiration of much of the world.

Meeting the basic requirements of the Tydings-McDuffie Act was no problem. The Filipinos were in entire agreement that they should have a republican state and that the Constitution should embody a Bill of Rights. Just what constituted a "republican" state could have been the subject of debate, but there was little on that issue. The convention assumed, correctly, that this meant that there should be an elected government, headed by an elected president, sustained by an elected legislature. There was to be a Republic of the Philippines, and there is. The convention, however, left no doubt on this score. Article II of the Constitution is a "Declaration of Principles," and the first sentence in it reads: "The Philippines is a republican state."

But at that point the delegates went directly from a question of form to the very heart of self-government, and of freedom itself. The sentence that followed was the most dramatic proclamation of principle that had appeared in Asia up to that time. It says, simply: "Sovereignty resides in the people and all government authority emanates from them."

A quarter of a century and a world war later we might take that for granted. Indeed we have seen the abuse of the word "peoples" in connection with spurious "democracies" until we are sick of it. But in 1935, in Southeast Asia, that was revolutionary doctrine of the first order. It should be remembered that residual sovereignty, in the technical sense, was still vested in the United States and would continue to be so vested for the period of the Commonwealth. Yet the delegates were writing, not for the interim, but for the future. This was to be a "republican" state and much more. It was to be a state of the people themselves. The reading of the Gettysburg Address in those little village schools had borne a triumphant fruit. When all government authority emanates from the people they may, truly, be said to be free.

The Declaration of Principles went on to include some other interesting components. The next paragraph declared that the defense of the state was a prime duty of government and that, in fulfilling it, the state was empowered to require by law that all citizens "render personal military *or civil* service." (Author's italics.) This was highly controversial and it was hotly debated. Compulsory civil service could be interpreted to mean forced labor. The dispute was not resolved until it was made plain in the Bill of Rights that this provision could not be so interpreted. Paragraph 13 of the Bill explicitly states: "No involuntary servitude *in any form* shall exist except as a punishment for a crime whereof the person shall have been duly convicted." (Author's italics.)

The next item in this declaration had also a novel addition. It stated that the Philippines renounced war as an instrument of national policy, paraphrasing the language of the Kellogg-Briand Pact, but then the paragraph went on to say that the Philippines adopted "the generally accepted principles of international law as a part of the law of the Nation." There was a sharp attack upon the vagueness of this statement. "Generally accepted" is difficult to define, and to adopt that as part of the organic law was certainly a sweeping commitment. Presumably, of course, the Philippines could reserve to itself the right to determine what was or was not "generally accepted," but even so the implications were broad. In defense of this phrase—and its proponents carried the day—was the argument that the new nation wished to make plain, from the very beginning, that it proposed to be an orderly, law-abiding member of the community of nations. Such an objective was above reproach and the argument was accepted as cogent. The Philippines has, since its independence, scrupulously respected the "generally accepted" principles of international law, but in how far those principles are part of the "law of the Nation" is still subject to discussion and further interpretation.

The remaining items in this declaration of principles are admonitory rather than definitely operative and indicate, in each case, what the state should do, rather than what it must do. They are unusual and interesting and reflect the trend of Filipino thinking at the time of the drafting. Section 4 provides that the government should give "aid and support" to the "natural right and duty of parents in the rearing of the youth for civic efficiency." Again the terms are vague and the language is permissive, but the intent is clear. Filipinos are to be brought up, by their parents, as good citizens in this young state. The emphasis upon the family is natural but significant. Elsewhere the Constitution enjoins upon the state the duty to provide adult education in citizenship, but in this section it recognizes that this is also a problem for parents. Equally interesting is the suggestion that the preparation of youth for "civic efficiency" is a "natural right," as well as a parental duty.

In still a further declaration of principle the Constitution states that it "should be the concern" of the state to promote "social justice to insure the well-being and economic security of all the people." This is another way of phrasing the "general welfare" clause of our own constitution, but it makes the specific addition of "economic security." This was a reflection, in part, of the experiences of the United

States in trying to cope with the depression of the early thirties and the growing American conviction that the state had an obligation in the field of economic safety for the individual. But the declaration, as a whole, was the expression of a conviction on the part of Mr. Quezon and others that the Philippines could and should establish its own version of a "welfare state." The term "social justice" had come from Governor General Murphy and embraced a wide range of projects for human betterment. It was taken into the Constitution with this background and the Filipinos had a firm feeling as to what it meant. There was some criticism of this section on the ground that it opened the way for "socialism," but that was not in the mind of the convention. What it actually meant, certainly, was that the Filipinos wished to preserve a somewhat paternalistic conception of the state in which government should be held responsible for aid to "civic efficiency," and for social amelioration and a degree of economic security.

It should be remembered that the delegates and their leaders were influenced by currents of political thinking in other parts of the world. They had seen the rise of the Labour party in Great Britain. They had studied the constitution of republican Spain and of the German Weimar Republic. They had seen the beginnings of the New Deal in the United States. They were discussing the functions and obligations of government at a time when there was a growing feeling that governments should be stronger, not weaker, and that the scope of their activities should be enlarged rather than curtailed. The idea that the state which governs least governs best had definitely been discarded. As a result the Philippine Constitution provided for a central government with broad powers in various fields. It had control over lands and public utilities, over the national composition of stock com-

panies that could deal with natural resources. Indeed, it was
held that the development of natural resources was essentially
the duty and prerogative of the state itself. It was not suggested that there should be outright state ownership of the
means of production and distribution, but there were vested
in the government more than the usual strong powers of
regulation and control.

Many of these powers were vested in the executive branch
as such. The office of the president was made quite powerful.
Many Filipinos felt that it was too powerful and urged a
modified form of "responsible" cabinet government in which
the legislative branch would have wider authority. This view
did not prevail and the structure, as it evolved, provided
for a full separation of powers, similar to that in the United
States. The legislature enjoyed a wide field in which law-
making was permissive. The President, however, was to be
strong in his own right and not merely the mouthpiece of a
legislature or a party.

When such a government was contemplated it was only
natural that additional emphasis should be given to the question of a Bill of Rights. This became, in time, the center of
the best discussion and debate in the convention and eventually the declaration of human rights became the very heart
of the Constitution. The American law had stipulated merely
that the Constitution should contain "a" Bill of Rights. The
Filipinos went to work to see to it that this requirement was
more than fulfilled. This was not lip service to an American
law. It was a vital expression of the determination to be free.
If sovereignty was to reside in the people, it was determined
that the people should be fully protected in their natural
rights as individuals against even a strong government and
that those rights should be spelled out in detail.

This, of course, was not a novelty. The first instrument

of law in the Philippines under the American occupation, the McKinley instructions to the Second Philippine Commission, had contained an elaborate enumeration of what government for the Filipinos should provide. In those instructions, almost every one of the enumerated rights in the first ten amendments to the United States Constitution was spelled out in detail. In the subsequent Jones Act of 1916 an even more elaborate bill of rights was incorporated, with all the provisions that were operative in the United States. The Filipinos had lived under a real bill of rights long before they set out to compose one of their own.

The additions and modifications that were made, however, are extremely interesting and enlightening. They reflect the character of the Filipinos and the society in which they had lived. They reflect, best of all, the devotion to the principles of individual human liberty, of "unalienable" rights that no government or society can take away. It was no accident that the Bill of Rights appeared almost at the beginning of the Constitution. It constitutes Article III and follows directly upon the Declaration of Principles. It contains only one section, but that section is made up of twenty-one specific paragraphs, each one sharp in its phraseology.

The first three paragraphs deal with due process of law and equal protection, with the right of the individual to be secure in his person and property, his "life and liberty." The protection against "unwarrantable search and seizure" is even more explicit than that in our own Constitution and stipulates "persons, houses, papers and effects" and provides that warrants must particularly describe the things to be seized.

Paragraph 4 makes an interesting addition, and provides a freedom not guaranteed in so many words in our own Constitution. It states: "The liberty of abode and of changing the same within the limits prescribed by law shall not be impaired." We might take that for granted, but there were delegates in that convention who could remember the hacienda system and its peonage in which the right to change one's abode had repeatedly been denied or impaired. It was to be written in the basic law of the land that this could not happen again—and Filipinos understood why.

Another interesting addition was made. Paragraph 8, providing freedom of speech and press, also carried, in identical words, the American declaration of the right to assemble peaceably to petition for redress of grievances. But before that, the Bill of Rights directly stated in Paragraph 6 that there should be no abridgment of "the right to form associations or societies for purposes not contrary to law." This, also, came out of a long memory of the time when such association and societies had been arbitrarily outlawed and suppressed.

In the guarantee of these rights and liberties the Filipinos usually followed the American pattern of "no law shall be passed." A good example of this is in the paragraph dealing with freedom of religion. It will be remembered that the inclusion of such a guarantee was a stipulation of the Tydings-McDuffie Act. This was sensitive ground because of the power and preponderance of the Catholic Church in the Philippines. The delegates met this stipulation and this problem with a clear and unequivocal declaration. It went far beyond what would have been required, technically, to meet the stipulation. It added one more great document to the literature of religious freedom, and it could serve as a model anywhere in the world. Paragraph 7 says:

No law shall be made respecting an establishment of religion, or prohibiting the free exercise thereof, and the free exercise and enjoyment of religious profession and worship, without discrimination or preference, shall forever be allowed. No religious test shall be required for the exercise of civil or political rights.

This paragraph was no small achievement. It was adopted by a convention in which there was virtual unanimity of religious faith in a society in which the church was strong and had been so for centuries. But the freedom that was guaranteed went far beyond that of worship within one religious community. The phrase "without discrimination or preference" had strong meaning. And the ban upon an established church made plain that the Philippines was to be a truly secular state.

The paragraphs that deal with rights in the courts follow closely the American pattern. There is the guarantee of habeas corpus, of a speedy trial, the confrontation of witnesses, and the assumption of innocence until the contrary is proved. There is a ban upon self-incrimination and double jeopardy, and upon excessive bail and cruel and unusual punishment. The right of trial by jury is, however, conspicuously omitted. At the time of the drafting a Philippine judicial system was working well without it. The right of appeal was well established and the Philippine Supreme Court had, time and again, served admirably to protect and preserve the rights and interests of individuals. Jury trial was not felt to be essential to the preservation of those rights and its introduction, constitutionally, would have presented a variety of problems with which the young nation did not need to cope.

Three other provisions, however, which were different from those in the United States Constitution, were added, and these also came out of the experiences of the long past. It was stated, first, that no law might be passed impairing the obligation of contracts. This was meant to make plain that even the strong must make good their commitments to the

weaker. Following almost immediately was the stipulation
that no person might be imprisoned for debt or for nonpayment of a poll tax. This was the final blow against the cedula
system. Finally, the last paragraph of the Bill of Rights in-
troduces a new note. The equal protection of the law had
already been affirmed, but that was not enough for the Filipinos. Paragraph 21 says: "Free access to the courts shall
not be denied to any person by reason of poverty." This
was an innovation in constitutional law at the time and reflected the general atmosphere of social consciousness in
which the Philippine Constitution was drafted.

This, then, was the Philippine Bill of Rights. To most
Filipinos it was the very heart of the Constitution, the permanent affirmation of human liberties. Other provisions were
secondary. They could be amended, and some of them were.
For example, the Constitution originally provided for a six-
year term for the president, without reelection, and for a
unicameral legislature. Both of these provisions were changed
within four years and the presidential incumbency was put
on a four-year basis with one permissive reelection. The
Philippine Senate was reestablished, to consist of twenty-
four members elected at large. Universal adult male suffrage,
with a literacy but no property qualification, had been established, but there was an additional proviso that the ballot
should be extended to women if 300,000 qualified women
voted in favor of it in a national plebiscite. They promptly
did.

The Filipinos rightly felt that these were largely matters
of form. What was really important was that an organic law
had been drafted by and for Filipinos. It delineated those
rights that were to be made secure. No other document quite
like it had ever appeared in Asia. It made the transition to
fuller self-government and to eventual independence relatively

easy. It was the greatest single instrument in the achievement of real freedom.

The Constitution was unanimously approved by the convention on February 8, 1935. It was promptly submitted to the electorate in a national plebiscite and was overwhelmingly adopted. A great experiment in the search for human liberty had borne fruit.

Four

THE TRANSITION

On November 15, 1935, the largest crowd in the history of the Philippines assembled in front of the Legislative Building and in the park facing it. It was estimated at not less than a quarter of a million. These Filipinos had come to see and to celebrate the inauguration of the Commonwealth and of Manuel Quezon and Sergio Osmeña as its President and Vice President.

The temper of the crowd was good, its mood festive. One Filipino reporter called it "the happiest day in our history" and declared that it would remain so until that greater day, ten years later, when the Philippines would become fully independent. The police had a little trouble keeping the enthusiastic crowd behind the barriers until the big parade had passed, but there was no disorder. An anti-Quezon demonstration, planned and threatened by Aguinaldo, did not materialize. Governor General Murphy had talked him out of it. Filipinos and Americans rubbed elbows in the crowd and smiled pleasantly at each other. They were entitled to a sense of joint achievement.

In the inauguration ceremony the United States was represented by Vice President Garner, Secretary of War Dern, the Speaker of the House and several other members of Congress, and by the last Governor General, Frank Murphy, whose status changed that day from Governor to High Commissioner. The Philippines was represented by the full membership of the legislature, the full body of the Supreme Court, all the department heads, and by its elected representatives for the highest offices. An air of solemnity was apparent and it permeated the crowd as they heard a message of felicitation from the President of the United States, heard the Philippine and American national anthems sung, and saw the Philippine flag run up alongside the Stars and Stripes. The throng was hushed as Quezon and Osmeña took their oaths of office.

The speeches were short, and for the most part grave. Tribute was paid to the goodwill and generosity of the United States, but it was not fulsome. On the other hand, emphasis was laid upon the duties and responsibilities that had been undertaken. It was soberly pledged that they would be discharged. A new step had been taken and the Filipino leaders were conscious of its import.

Quezon and Osmeña had been chosen on September 17, previously, in a free and popular election. It had been a curious three-cornered affair. Once the two leaders had composed their differences and agreed to head a ticket together, there was never any doubt of the outcome. But General Aguinaldo, relying on the support of his *veteranos,* had also presented himself as a candidate. He felt that he was on strong historic ground, since he had been the first president of a Philippine "Republic" under the Malolos Constitution. The third entry was Bishop Gregorio Aglipay, head of the Independent Church. He offered himself as the representative of his communicants (he claimed three million, which was a gross exaggeration) and also as a spokesman for the Ilocano group, as opposed to the Tagalog (Quezon) and the Visayan (Osmeña), since it was in that group that he had the strongest following.

When the ballots were counted, Quezon and Osmeña had

polled more than two thirds of the total, more than twice as many as Aguinaldo and Aglipay combined. The voters were not confused, either by Aguinaldo's justifiable, if by then somewhat unrealistic, reminiscence or by Aglipay's sectarianism and sectionalism. They knew their leaders and trusted them. Aguinaldo was quick to cry fraud, to demand an investigation, and to threaten to "demonstrate." But as the Manila *Daily Bulletin* pointed out, if every one of the ballots that he challenged as fraudulent had been thrown out, or even given to him, the outcome would not have been changed in the least. It was true that Quezon and Osmeña had a powerful and dominant political machine. But it was also true that the electorate had a chance to express its will and did so. In the Commonwealth, also, there was government by consent.

Eloquent testimony to this fact was given by the vote cast for Vice President Osmeña. He ran more than 120,000 votes ahead of Quezon, more than 15 percent of the total cast. His margin, moreover, was not merely composed of votes from his home province; he received them from almost every part of the islands. What this meant was both that many Filipinos wished to pay tribute to a distinguished "elder statesman," and also that the Filipinos were able and willing to split a ticket if they so desired. It was the best possible answer to the charge of a "manipulated" election. Quezon certainly could not and would not have "manipulated" this impressive preponderance of votes for his running mate.

The use of election machinery was not new in the Philippines. It had been part of the pattern of growth. But the plebiscite on the Constitution and the election of the first Commonwealth officials dramatized the fact that a political goal had been reached. The Filipinos had ratified the form of government under which they wished to live and had chosen, freely, the men who were to carry out their aims. This was another milestone.

COMMONWEALTH PROBLEMS

The physical transition to the Commonwealth took place with barely a perceptible ripple. High Commissioner Murphy moved into a suite at the Manila Hotel until a suitable residence could be found or built, and Mr. Quezon moved into Malacañang Palace. On November 16, government business went on as usual. The same men did the same jobs in much the same way, except for the air of fiesta that lasted for several days. This, also, soon evaporated, for the Commonwealth had some big problems to meet and their solution was neither obvious nor easy.

These were problems of life and death. First was economic survival; second was national defense. The projected closing of the American market precipitated the first; the militant expansion of the Japanese Empire made the second a grim reality.

It was hard for the Filipinos to realize the extent of the threat to their economy that they had so enthusiastically accepted. Their orators had always said: "If there are dangers and difficulties to be faced, we will face them." But few of those orators had ever thought to spell out, in detail, just what those dangers and difficulties were. "Quotas" were already a reality, but they were generous. "Progressively increasing export taxes" was a vague term that had never been translated in the popular mind into a matter of pesos and centavos. Besides, the taxes would not even begin for another five years, and when they did the revenue collected would be returned to the Philippine government. *Mañana* would take care of itself.

On the other hand, the existing prosperity was real and obvious. The law provided that 850,000 long tons of sugar annually could go into the duty-free market in the United States, that 200,000 long tons of coconut oil could be freely marketed in the United States each year, and that 3,000,000 pounds of cordage would enjoy yearly, for another five years, that protected outlet. These quotas could be respected, and they were, without hardship. Exports continued to rise.

Even the collapse of the mining boom did not make a dent in the economy as a whole. Early in 1937 Mr. Quezon had suggested that he was prepared to order a sweeping investigation of all mining stock transactions and had even intimated that he was ready, if necessary, to nationalize the mining industry under the natural resources clause of the Constitution. What collapsed as a result was the mining stock market, not the industry. Paper profits were lost by the million. One exchange went out of business. Scores of dubious "mines" were taken off the other boards and what had been called "the promotion of cow pastures and golf courses as gold mines" was stopped. But the sound properties were sounder than ever. Production in both gold and base metals continued to rise. The speculative profits on the exchange had never been an honest part of the gross national product. The production of gold, chromite, iron, manganese, and copper was a part of that product—a real, not a speculative one—and it continued.

If most of the Filipinos were inclined to sustain their mood of optimism, the United States certainly did nothing to dispel it. On the contrary, American policy contributed to an artificial prosperity that was divorced from anything that the Filipinos could ever hope to continue indefinitely. The terms of American agricultural legislation were applied to the Philippines and Filipinos were paid to keep land out of cultivation. Agents of the United States Department of Agriculture toured the Philippine provinces handing out checks to sugar planters who had reduced their acreage, in spite of the fact that the quota limitation on sugar was itself designed to keep Philippine production within the proper bounds. Even more importantly, the United States had adopted a processing tax of two cents a pound on vegetable oils. As a matter of conscience it was determined that the proceeds of the tax, when applied to coconut oil from the Philippines, should be returned to the Philippine government. This procedure itself was not a novelty. The United States had, for many years, levied the customary Federal excise tax on Philippine cigars in the American market and then returned the proceeds to the Philippines. But the processing tax on oils was on a larger scale in total income.

No challenge could be made to the thesis that the United States action was honorable and high-minded. Its net result, however, was to channel back into the Philippine economy a sum roughly equivalent to the expectable government revenue from all other sources in any given year. This was the "windfall" to which reference has been made. It enabled the Philippine government to embark on ambitious programs of public works, to build needed roads, schools, and hospitals, and to give the legislature a "pork-barrel" holiday with specific sums allocated for each district. It contributed to the sense of economic well-being. In so far as the additional revenue was directly translated into a change for the better in the lives of the poorer Filipinos it served a good purpose. In so far as it created an artificial sense of a prosperity that could not be sustained it was deceptive. As one American writer put it: "The United States was preparing the Filipinos for a beer income by sending them on a champagne spending spree."

Among the more thoughtful of the Filipino economists and political leaders, on the other hand, there was a ready realization that this condition could not last indefinitely. There was also the realization that the imposition of the terms of the legislation, beginning with the progressively increasing export taxes to be levied in 1941, would bring immediate hardship. Within a year after the Commonwealth was inaugurated, therefore, a new slogan came into being. There was a demand for a "realistic re-examination" of the terms of the Tydings-McDuffie Act. Some Americans misinterpreted this as a demand for a re-examination of the whole question of Philippine independence. This was not accurate. The Filipinos still wanted their independence, but some of them were beginning to be concerned with economic survival.

Their case was subsequently presented to Washington and it fell on sympathetic ears. Economic depression pressures in the United States had lessened somewhat by 1938 and attention was being fixed upon other dangers. The Tydings-McDuffie Act was re-examined and amended. It was provided that the quotas should continue but that the more onerous provisions should not come into effect until 1961. The basic economic problem was not solved. The evil day was merely put off. There was business as usual—and it was good business.

The next matter of concern was national defense. Again, the Filipinos were optimistic. They had had strong reassurance from General Douglas MacArthur on two counts. In 1936 he had given his judgment that the Philippines could be adequately defended, within the limits of its resources, by a citizen army of 400,000 men, a navy made up primarily of torpedo boats (the mosquito fleet), and a modest air force. In 1939 he declared that neither Japan nor any other power "coveted" the Philippines and that, in any case, the cost of invasion to Japan would be so great that the astute Japanese would not be foolish enough to attempt it. Subsequent events proved him wrong in both these judgments, but the judgments were popular with the Filipinos at the time they were made.

It is impossible to appraise what happened without some knowledge of the unique position and prestige of General MacArthur. More than any other then living American soldier he had a close attachment to the Philippines. His father had served in the islands. The distinguished son had a command post there from 1922 to 1925 as commander of the District of Manila and of the Philippine Division, United States Army—the highly respected Philippine Scouts. General MacArthur returned to the Philippines in 1928 to become the commander of the entire Philippine Department. In 1930 he was called to Washington to take the highest position in the United States Army, Chief of Staff. President Roosevelt continued him in that position beyond the normal tour of duty because he regarded his services as "indispensable." He was not relieved until 1935.

Meanwhile the question of the defense of the Philippines had been debated in Congress and concomitantly with the adoption of the Tydings-McDuffie Act, legislation was introduced to provide for an American military mission to the Philippines that would assist in planning that defense. Upon his retirement as Chief of Staff, General MacArthur was named to head that mission. He returned to the islands with the inauguration.

President Quezon was delighted. He had discussed Philippine defense planning with General MacArthur in Washington and had found the General sympathetic toward Philippine political aspirations and confident that a defense program could be carried out. The Filipinos were rightfully impressed by the fact that the United States had sent its first soldier to assist them. The rank of Field Marshal of the Philippine Army was created, and it was bestowed upon General MacArthur.

Much more than that, President Quezon made national defense the first order of business of the Commonwealth. The first measure to be enacted by the new legislature was the National Defense Act. It reaffirmed the declaration in the Constitution that national defense was the first responsibility of the state and of its citizens and undertook to set up the machinery through which it could be provided. It became the Quezon-MacArthur defense plan.

In fairness to the Filipinos and to General MacArthur it must be remembered that there was a rigid limitation on this plan. That limitation was economic. It was assumed that once the Philippines became independent it would be obliged to take over the full burden of national defense, previously carried by the United States. Means had to be devised, therefore, that were within the fiscal possibilities of the Commonwealth and the forthcoming republic. A further assumption, and this one was mistaken, was that the program would have a full ten years in which to come into operation. The costs, accordingly, were made as light as possible and the time schedule was generous.

The Defense Act provided for an annual draft of 40,000 men. They were to receive five and a half months' training, after which they would go into a "citizen reserve," and be recalled at the end of five years for a refresher course. In this way, by the end of the ten-year period there would be a trained citizen army of about 400,000.

It was obvious that the Philippines could not build and maintain a first-class navy. Accordingly it was decided to rely upon a fleet of fast motor torpedo boats, numbering between thirty and forty. Thinking along this line was obviously influenced by the story of the Italian "mosquito fleet" in the Mediterranean and it was assumed that such torpedo boats could be an effective deterrent to invasion. Also, they were within the financial possibilities of the new Commonwealth. The first ones were put on order in Great Britain. Two had actually been delivered when the Japanese struck.

This "navy" was to be backed up by a fleet of medium bomber planes that could presumably intercept any invader well offshore. It must be remembered that this was in 1935 and 1936 when it is stated that this bombing fleet was expected eventually to reach as many as sixty planes and that the defense plan called for the training of up to one hundred Filipino pilots by 1946. At that time General MacArthur— and a great many others—had an inadequate conception of how large a part the air arm was to play in future warfare. General MacArthur had stated that in his view the air arm was a logical extension of the cavalry and that its major function was reconnaissance. Manila was to learn that the Japanese air arm was an extension of the artillery and that its function was bombardment.

But that was in the future. Meanwhile, the Philippine draft went into operation. It functioned reasonably well, but it did not reach the set goals at any point. At the end of six years, roughly 130,000 men had actually received training. There were several reasons for this. Physical facilities were inadequate. Materials were costly and some experiments with providing various items of equipment from local manufacture were unsuccessful. There was also a critical shortage of trained officers and noncommissioned officers to carry the load of the training of recruits. As many officers as possible were brought from the Constabulary and the Philippine

Scouts, but there were not enough. A "West Point of the Philippines" was established, and it was good, but it took time.

Money was also a factor. The Commonwealth was trying to live within a budget and the legislators kept a sharp rein on expenditures for defense. They even went so far as to suggest an investigation of General MacArthur's emoluments and his dual status as an officer of both the United States Army and the Philippine Army. General MacArthur retired from the United States Army at the end of 1937 and continued in the service of the Philippine Army, only, until he was recalled to United States Army duty on July 6, 1941.

These facts are brought up here, not in a sense of criticism or recrimination, but simply because they had an important bearing upon some Filipino attitudes that were to become critical and controversial later on. It cannot be denied that defense planning for the Philippines was woefully inadequate. The fiscal limitation was one factor. The presumptive time element was another. It is reasonable to assume that if the ten-year program could have been carried out it would have reached its goals or have approximated them. A civilian defense force would have been provided. The naval and air strength, if it could be called that, would have come into being. And it would have been done within the financial framework of the Commonwealth.

But the plain, and sorry, fact was that the Japanese menace was not taken seriously. When the Japanese launched their full-scale attack upon China in 1937 it was confidently asserted that they would "bog down in the vast morass" of China. Even when they took Hainan Island in the South China Sea, directly facing the Philippines, it was blandly assumed that their target was the French position in Indo-China, not the whole of Southeast Asia. A few voices, such as the courageous one of Dr. J. Ralston Hayden, former Vice Governor of the Philippines, were raised in warning. But the suggestion that the Philippines was gravely endangered was likely to be dismissed as "war-mongering" and as unfriendly to the idea of Philippine independence.

It was not until midsummer of 1941 that really stronger defense measures were taken. General MacArthur was recalled to active duty in the United States Army with the grade of Lieutenant General, and later raised to General. He was placed in command of American armed forces in the Far East, and the Philippine Army began mobilization. The Scouts, some Constabulary elements, and the Filipino reserves were called to the colors, along with volunteers, both Filipino and American. The naval force was slightly augmented and the United States consigned some fighter planes to the Philippines. Most of these, however, did not begin to arrive until November.

This was the situation when Japan struck. The army in the Philippines was relatively small, conglomerate, and only partly trained. The "mosquito fleet" was virtually nonexistent. The air force was totally inadequate and a large number of the new planes that had been sent out were still in crates on the docks. Except for raw courage the islands were almost defenseless.

American intelligence, military and civilian, had made the worst of strategic errors. The striking power of the enemy and his readiness to strike had been gravely underestimated.

JAPANESE OCCUPATION

The heroism shown in the defense of Bataan and Corregidor made history. It may also have influenced it. From the time that the American-Philippine force was swept back from the central Luzon coastal plain and retreated to the mountains of the Bataan Peninsula, in January, 1942, after Manila had been declared an open city, it was apparent that the archipelago could not be held unless massive reinforcement was immediately dispatched from the United States. No such reinforcement was possible and the American-Philippine force was doomed to fight merely a holding and delaying action, facing inevitable defeat and ultimate surrender. There has been no disagreement among military historians on the point that the stubbornness of the defense completely upset the Japanese timetable for the southward swing and may therefore have been the first real step in the ultimate turning of the tide against Japan. From December to May, Japan was obliged to commit large forces to the Bataan-Corregidor conquest, and in that time it was possible to mobilize better defense further south. The Australians, for example, have always been lavish in their praise of the defense of Bataan, feeling that it was a factor in "saving" Australia.

A valuable lesson can be learned from Bataan, also, and how far it will affect future planning and action in the Philippines remains to be seen. This was the fact that the defenders had to fight not only the Japanese but malaria as well. In the end, the latter was an even more formidable enemy. Bataan was known to be one of the most heavily mosquito-infested areas in the islands. Several plans had been put forward to clean it up but none had been carried out. A battle ground had been chosen, in advance, and the retirement to it was a masterpiece of military operation. It had been rehearsed, but the battleground itself had not been prepared as it should have been, and it was insidious and deadly. The Japanese, with vastly superior numbers (and possibly a little more immunity) could cope with the malaria.

The defenders could not, and it was part of the price that was paid for shortsightedness in defense planning.

In the long run, however, the greatest thing that came out of Bataan was not military, but political and social. Filipinos and Americans fought side by side in a common cause. The Americans who survived have testified, again and again, that the Filipinos were magnificent. The Filipinos have testified that they were fighting, not just for the United States, to which their loyalty was pledged, and not just for the Philippines, which had been invaded, but for liberty itself.

Bataan thus became a symbol to the Philippines of the value and the triumph of an idea. The Filipinos showed that they were not beguiled by the Japanese talk of "Asia for the Asians" or the "Co-prosperity Sphere." They had had a taste of human freedom and saw it threatened, not by Americans, but by the Japanese who sought to pose as "liberators." It was for this ideal of freedom that Bataan was stubbornly fought. That the Filipinos proved their loyalty to the United States was only part of the significance of the situation, however gratifying it may have been to the Americans. They were proving also that their loyalty to the concept of freedom was unshaken. They were ready to pay for it in their blood.

Bataan also brought a basic change in the relationship between Filipinos and Americans. They were no longer our wards; they were our allies. Our sons had died together. It was right to believe that we could live together, in fraternity.

That the Japanese ever understood this is doubtful. They had assumed that they could play upon a deep resentment of a colonial people against the colonizers, of a pigmented people against the "whites," of Asians against the non-Asians. Their liberator pose could therefore be heroic, and they expected appreciation of it. The Japanese were shocked, chagrined, and then violently angered by the depth of Filipino resistance to them. They soon realized that the Filipinos, in the main, hated and despised them and all they stood for. There was more than mere guerrilla activity. There was quiet, stubborn, passive resistance. The Japanese saw "sullen" Filipinos.

This lack of understanding and the consequent chagrin may account, in part, for the almost incredible stupidity of the Japanese occupation policies. If these had been genuinely benevolent and if the Japanese had really made some concession to the Filipino desire for freedom they might possibly have won some support for their cause. They would probably have been able to blunt some of the fierce edge of resistance. They might even have had some real "collaboration" on a far wider scale. The American reconquest of the archipelago would have been more difficult.

Instead of benevolence and understanding, however, the Japanese brought an outrageous arrogance and a calculated cruelty that made more and more enemies for them. Some of their bad behavior can, no doubt, be attributed to the mere ignorance of junior officers and enlisted men who had never before been outside Japan and who, after having themselves been repressed, found an outlet in a conquered country. At the higher levels there seems to have been such an unshakable prepossession with Japan's inherent superiority, divine mission, and glorious destiny that the very idea of resistance was intolerable heresy. The Filipinos soon observed, moreover, that Japanese behavior reflected, in part, the Japanese fortunes of war. When things were going well for Japan the conquerors were often inclined to be lenient. When Japan suffered reverses the Filipinos were made to suffer. In the later stages of the war most Filipinos knew well enough, by the increase in Japanese cruelty and the progressive tightening of all restrictive measures, that Japan was being defeated.

It is true that the Japanese had rather ostentatiously proclaimed the "independence" of the Philippines. They set up a puppet republic with the help of some Filipinos who were willing to cooperate with them. These Filipinos seem to have been governed by a variety of motives, which will be discussed later. What is important is the fact that this puppet regime did not command any popular support or arouse any enthusiasm. The Filipinos knew, through their own elaborate grapevine, that at the elbow of every Filipino official was a Japanese ready and willing to tell him just what he could and could not do. Some of these Filipinos tried to circumvent their Japanese "advisers" and paid for it with their lives. The Filipinos knew that, too. They knew that this was not government by consent.

This is not to suggest that the Japanese entirely neglected any attempts to win over the Filipino mind. They organized youth societies, but destroyed their value by dictating everything that could be said or done in them. They took control of newspapers and radio, and made it plain that they would determine precisely what the Filipinos were to print or hear. This was a far cry from freedom of speech as the Filipinos had known it, and the clandestine audience for broadcasts from the Americans grew steadily. In the light of later events it is hard to believe that the Japanese made even a dent in Filipino thinking.

Any Japanese propaganda was handicapped, of course, by the extent of atrocious Japanese behavior. Hundreds of Filipinos suspected of anti-Japanese feelings or activities were tortured and killed. Hundreds disappeared behind the grim walls of Fort Santiago, never to be heard of again. Villages suspected of harboring guerrillas were razed. Work animals were slaughtered. The whole population was put on a starvation basis. And personal indignities never ceased. Robbery was not merely condoned, it was authorized. Rape was a commonplace. And everywhere the Filipinos were required to bow respectfully before every Japanese. This, in the name of "liberation." It is small wonder that so many Filipinos took to the hills. The Japanese could have expected it.

The story of the Philippine guerrillas is a fascinating one and has been told several times. Almost every province had its local hero. In Cebu, for example, Tomas Confessor defiantly sent word to the Japanese that if they wanted him they could come and get him. They never did. In the southern islands Ruperto Kangleon was the acknowledged resistance leader. He could not be taken. A functioning provincial government was set up in the mountains of Negros. There was an American-directed intelligence center and a functioning administration in Mindanao.

Actual physical damage done by the guerrillas to the Japanese occupying force was not large, although considerable casualties were inflicted. But the guerrillas served a great purpose. In the first place, they kept alive the idea of continued Filipino resistance. The people were unconquered as long as those units operated "in the hills." There was always a final refuge for those who had come under suspicion or who had found the Japanese "liberators" intolerable. There was still that standard of freedom to which men could repair.

Of hardly less importance was the fact that the guerrillas were able to serve as a large intelligence network. American submarines operated in Philippine waters from the beginning of the war and they kept up steady contact with resistance units. Their operations against the Japanese, moreover, were frequently dependent upon what had been learned from the guerrillas. One unit of the resistance, for example, was credited in an official American citation with having supplied the information that led to the sinking of some fifty Japanese ships in Philippine waters. General MacArthur is reported to have said that "We had history's most effective fifth column working for us in the Philippines." One of his staff officers put it more graphically, when he said: "Before we landed on Leyte we were in a spot where if a Japanese buck sergeant, anywhere in the Philippines, even went to the latrine we knew about it in half an hour." This is a perhaps pardonable exaggeration, but it is true that when the Americans went into Lingayan Gulf they had advance knowledge of the location of every Japanese gun emplacement and were able to take advantage of that knowledge.

THE LIBERATION

American forces made their dramatic landing on Leyte Island on October 20, 1944. General MacArthur had returned. But something else had returned as well. This was free civil government. At the time, the spectacle of the great naval engagements in Surigao Strait and in and around Leyte Gulf may have temporarily obscured what was taking place in the political field. But there could be no doubt of American purposes. One of General MacArthur's first announcements after the Leyte landing was that the United States Army had no intention of setting up a military government in the Philippines.

At the time of the Japanese invasion the United States had taken Commonwealth President Quezon and Vice President Osmeña out of the islands. They remained in the United States as the recognized heads of the Philippine Commonwealth. President Quezon died in the United States on August 1, 1944, and Mr. Osmeña succeeded him in the presidency of the Commonwealth and was recognized in this office. When General MacArthur landed in Leyte, President Osmeña went ashore with him.

Within three days, in a formal ceremony at Tacloban, the Leyte capital, General MacArthur turned over civil government to President Osmeña with the declaration that he was restoring "government by constitutional process under the regularly constituted Commonwealth government as rapidly as the several occupied areas are liberated and the military conditions will permit." Filipino Civil Affairs units had gone ashore with the troops from the beginning and they began to function. Schools were reopened, civil hospitals set up, and relief supplies distributed.

Liberation in Luzon, which followed early in 1945, was centered in most American minds upon the freeing of the several thousand Americans who had been interned by the Japanese in three major concentration camps. In Santo Tomas, in Baguio, and in Los Baños, the Americans were set free even while the last stubborn battle for the Walled City in Manila was still being fought. Some Americans died in those last days and some Filipinos were executed by the Japanese in a final defiant gesture.

There was still smoke over the Walled City on February 27, 1945. But on that day, in a simple ceremony at Malacañang Palace, not more than a mile away, General MacArthur turned over to President Osmeña full civil authority in all the Philippines. A free government had been reestablished. President Osmeña called the legislature into session. Courts were reopened. The civil service began to function. The Constabulary went to work. Radio Manila began to broadcast and a free press sprang back into life.

That the Americans were made welcome should go without saying. Indeed, it would be an immense understatement.

Some of the Filipino attitude was expressed in a letter that a fifteen-year-old girl wrote to an American broadcaster. He had been a friend of her father and mother who had been killed by the Japanese. She heard that he had made a broadcast to the Philippines paying a tribute to her parents, and she wrote to him:

I'm sorry I couldn't hear your broadcast, but we don't have any electricity yet. One of my friends told me about it. We haven't heard a thing about Mummy and Daddy but we still hope they will come back to us. We are living out here in Singalong with Auntie. Buddy and I can't go back to school yet because all the bridges across the river are blown up. But we are getting along all right. Buddy and I can bring water from the Singalong market [that was a mile and a half away] and we are getting more rice. The streets are pretty much torn up. But *nothing matters,* now that the Americans have come back.

This was the faith of the Filipinos. It was imperative that the Americans justify it.

As a war measure, the United States Congress in June, 1944, had authorized the President to advance the date of the grant of Philippine independence if it were deemed advisable. Its resolution reaffirmed the intention of the United States to "restore as quickly as possible the orderly free processes of government to the Filipino people, and thereupon establish the complete independence of the Philippine Islands as a separate and self-governing nation." The Filipinos did not feel that it was necessary to change the timetable. The Tydings-McDuffie Act had provided that the Republic should come into being on July 4, 1946, and there was no doubt that this pledge would be kept.

Meanwhile there was much to be done, including the election, early in 1946, of the man who would serve as first president of the independent Philippine Republic. Manuel Roxas presented himself as a candidate. He had served in several capacities under the Japanese and he had been called a "collaborator." But immediately after the landing in Luzon General MacArthur had attached Mr. Roxas to his staff with a statement that he had been in continuous touch with Mr. Roxas, who had been loyal and faithful to the United States. The implication that Mr. Roxas had served in some counter-intelligence capacity was obvious, and his exoneration was accepted as complete.

Mr. Osmeña, who would have seemed to be the logical choice for the office since he was already the Commonwealth President, refused to make an election contest. He said, simply, that his services to the Filipino people were well known. If they wished him to continue he would do so but he would not make a popular appeal for votes. He retired to his home province and sat out the campaign. Mr. Roxas was elected.

On the following July 4, 1946, the independent Republic of the Philippines was formally inaugurated and Mr. Roxas was sworn in as its first President. Manila was still a shambles of shattered buildings, shacks, and quonset huts. War damage had hardly begun to be repaired. The beautiful harbor was littered with wreckage. Too many Filipinos had not enough to eat that day. The price of rice was fantastic. The American troops were riddled by a Communist-encouraged "we want to go home" campaign.

But there was faith and hope in the Philippines. The dangers and the difficulties were all too present. Nevertheless there was confidence that they could be overcome. There was also confidence that the United States would not prove faithless to its obligations. The first of these had been met. The Philippines had become independent. They could hope to be free.

Five

TRIBULATIONS OF A NEW STATE

That the Filipinos could have been joyful and optimistic on that July 4, 1946, is a tribute to three things. First was the essentially sanguine character of the people that has been noted. Second was their satisfaction over the attainment of the goal of national independence. This had been set forth for years by the political orators as the immediate solution to all problems and there was no inclination among the mass of the people to disbelieve this. Third was their unshaken confidence that the United States would not fail to discharge its responsibilities and that if help were needed it could and would be had from a rich and powerful protector.

To these factors should be added the feverish excitement of change, the hum of rebuilding, the sense of release from captivity. There was a curious sort of "gold rush" to the cities. Manila was quickly crowded far beyond its capacity.

But Manila, like many other points in the archipelago, was still a shambles. The destruction had been appalling. General Eisenhower said that of all the wartime capitals only Warsaw suffered more damage than did Manila. The old Walled City, last center of Japanese resistance, had been totally destroyed and a few hundred miserable persons were living in caves that had been clawed out of its rubble. Beautiful residential areas had been burned over and abandoned. There was wild cogon grass growing within a hundred feet of the famous Luneta. Dewey Boulevard, running along the bay, was a series of gutted shells of what had been fine residences and hotels, and beside it was a harbor that was choked with the wrecks of sunken ships. The estimate that Manila had been 50 percent destroyed was conservative. General Romulo put the figure at 80 percent.

This was Manila only. The damage extended to almost every part of the country. Road transportation was virtually paralyzed since more than five thousand bridges had been destroyed. Food production was almost at a standstill in many areas because of the loss of work animals. Rice cultivation had been dependent upon the carabao and the Japanese had recklessly slaughtered these essential animals for food. They had taken a heavy toll also of the pigs and chickens that had played an important part in giving a diet balance. Three years after the Japanese had been driven out, the total animal population of the archipelago was still not half what it had been before the invasion.

There was a wide range in the monetary assessment of actual damage. An early figure was set by the United States War Damage Commission at three quarters of a billion dollars. This was in 1945. In the next year the Philippine Census Bureau put the figure at a billion and a quarter, and when the Filipinos began to talk about reparations from Japan they set a base figure of eight billion. This was unrealistic, but it reflected the Filipinos' own idea of the extent to which they had suffered.

Physical damage was only a part of the problem. President Roxas, in his inaugural address in 1946, declared that the health and education services had been set back a quarter of a century. This was an understatement. They had been all but destroyed. Epidemic disease had come back in full force. A whole generation of children was growing up that had never seen the inside of a schoolroom. Worse still, those young people—and some of their elders—had come to take it for granted that the normal mode of behavior was to deceive, to rob, and to kill, since that had been forced upon them by the Japanese.

ECONOMIC CHAOS

The broad economic situation was chaotic. Long before production for export could be restored there was a wildly clamorous market for imports. The Filipinos had been deprived of necessities, amenities, and luxuries for four years, and they were "hungry" in more senses than one. When United States assistance began to put some degree of purchasing power into Filipino hands, imports ran wild. In that first year of independence they reached almost $300,000,-000. A year later the imports were still double the value of total exports.

Some of these imports were sound enough from the economic point of view. There was a critical shortage of textiles, and the Filipinos had to be clothed. There was a food shortage, and they had to be fed. There was a shortage of building materials, and they had to be housed. But there was also a demand for items that were nonessential, in the strict view, but that were part of the psychological hunger of a newly liberated people. The trade in lipsticks and nylons zoomed. Quite a few Filipinos bought Cadillacs instead of tractors. Almost anything that could be sold had its buyer because of this intense will to buy. And American assistance provided purchasing power.

Some of the immediate help came from UNRRA. In the first two years after the liberation this agency authorized and provided about $8,000,000 worth of goods in direct relief. Other and larger help was to come. A Rehabilitation Act, adopted by Congress in 1946, shortly before Mr. Roxas was

inaugurated, provided for war damage payments up to $400,-
000,000. A War Damage Commission was set up and in five
years, from 1947–1952, it considered a million and a quarter
claims and paid out $390,000,000. A transfer to the Philip-
pines of $220,000,000 worth of Army surplus property was
authorized, of which more will be said later. The Reconstruction Finance Corporation provided a loan of $100,-
000,000. Veterans' pensions and payments to guerrillas who
had been enrolled against the Japanese began to be made.
Eventually much of the assistance was pulled together under
the Mutual Security Program in the early fifties, and later
under the Economic Cooperation Administration. The total
amount of American help in the first eight years of the independent Philippine Republic is usually placed at about
$2,000,000,000.

It has often been stated that this was generous and that it
should have been adequate to give the young nation a sound
chance for economic recovery. Several factors were at work,
however, that were to make the effect of this help less significant than it might have been. The "hungry" market has already been noted. It was simply impossible, from the human
point of view, to channel the required assistance into fields
where it would do the most good in restoring productive
capacity. Copra and abacá production came back fairly well.
Sugar was slower. Gold and base metal production lagged.
The total of new investment from private sources was dis-
appointing.

Under those conditions some form of inflation was inevitable. It hit the Philippines hard, and where it hurt worst,
in the price of rice and other simple living costs. In the first
year of independence, 1946–47, the index of living cost was
approximately six to one over the last prewar years, 1939,
1940, and 1941. This was forced down to four to one, by

1949 and finally to about three to one, where it stands now, but the inflationary pattern remained. The peso, it should be remembered, was arbitrarily pegged to the dollar at two to one, so there was never a "runaway" currency inflation. But there was this steady high cost of living that hurt every Filipino and that hurt the little man worst of all.

Meanwhile some persons were getting rich—and not always by ethical means. Private profiteering could have been expected; before long it began to reach official circles and eventually to bring about the charges of wholesale corruption that blackened the name of the young republic in the press of the world.

THE SURPLUS SCANDALS

Some of the worst offenses and abuses stemmed directly from what could and should have been a gigantic aid program. This was the disposal of surplus American military property. The Philippines had been set up as the staging area for the eventual assault on Japan and the sudden end of the war found an enormous concentration of materials there that would not be used and whose return to the United States was deemed to be impractical and uneconomical. The rough estimate of the replacement value of this material was about $600,000,000. The Rehabilitation Act of 1946 put a procurement value of what could be declared surplus at $220,000,-000, and authorized its transfer to the Philippines.

A double process was set up. Some items, such as vehicles and heavy machinery, were turned over directly to government agencies. The remainder—by far the largest part—was put up for sale at auction, with the proceeds to accrue to the government.

What happened was appalling. In the first place, the mate-

rial was not properly warehoused and guarded, and theft was
widespread. The charge that the American guards, as well as
Filipinos, connived at this was published in the Manila newspapers. Several years later one of the Huk leaders declared
that his organization had used, from the beginning, military
supplies that had been filched from the "surplus." He stated
that the reason his men were unwilling to turn in American-
made arms was that they had abundant American-made ammunition for them.

But theft, even widespread as it was, did not reach the
proportions of losses that came from the scandalous sales.
The American inventories were totally inadequate and often
false. Many of the Americans expressed themselves as being
interested only in "getting rid of the stuff" and in "getting
out of here." This was the time, it will be remembered, of the
Communist-inspired "get the troops home" movement in the
Philippines, that was strongly felt among the United States
forces. Surplus property disposal was one last unpleasant
chore for men eager to get home, and their inclination was
to get it over as quickly as possible.

Items were auctioned off by case lots and by number.
There was an obvious profit to be made by foreknowledge of
what a number represented and there was a brisk traffic in
this information. In many instances designations of case lots
were careless and misleading. Subsequent testimony in the
Philippine courts revealed that some airplane engines and
even surgical instruments had been sold under the label
"scrap metal." One lucky Filipino bought, for a few pesos,
a case of microscopes that was labeled "socks."

A substantial part of the surplus found its way into a black
market and thus eventually satisfied some consumer needs.
But it was sold at fantastic profits and contributed to the
general inflationary trend. The largest scandals were in the

field of building materials, especially galvanized iron, since this was so largely in demand. Several persons of high position in public life were ultimately involved in these deals. One senator was forced to resign and go abroad and one well-known personage was ultimately cleared by the Philippine Supreme Court only after four years of appeal.

The loss to Philippine morale and reputation was obvious. The monetary loss was also substantial. The government eventually realized less than one fifth of the value of the materials whose transfer had been authorized. The final total was only $40,000,000. And in the meantime a pattern of private and public corruption had been established and accepted which persisted for several years.

THE COLLABORATION ISSUE

It was against this background of economic chaos and to some extent of moral breakdown that the Filipinos and Americans tried to come to grips with one of the most complex and troublesome of problems in the society, that of previous collaboration with the Japanese. Under even the best conditions its solution would have been virtually impossible. Under the conditions that prevailed, it merely added one more component to an atmosphere of unrest and unhappiness.

That some Filipinos had actively assisted the Japanese was obvious. It was also painfully true that some Filipinos had informed against others to curry favor or obtain material reward. Several cases were settled swiftly and privately by assassination. How many such cases of summary judgment and execution took place will never be known.

But above and beyond that was a whole body of officials that the Japanese had set up. Men who had held positions of high honor in the Philippines before the war were installed as officers of a presumably independent Philippine government, under Japanese supervision. A former senator and justice of the Supreme Court, Jose P. Laurel, was named "president." Members of the Japanese-ruled "cabinet" included Judge Claro M. Recto, who, only a few years before, had presided over the Philippine constitutional convention. Such men were no common criminals but under the procedure that was set up they had to be brought to trial before an American-established military tribunal for having aided the enemy. Filipinos were associated with the proceedings.

Immediately after the liberation, a counterintelligence service which was put into motion examined complaints of collaboration that ran into thousands. Some of these were false and obviously merely spiteful. There was more than one attempt to settle a private grudge by making a complaint. But there were also cases in which a long and friendly association with the Japanese, well before Pearl Harbor, could be clearly established. Filipino lawyers had represented Japanese commercial companies in Manila for years. There had been a friendly Japanese-Philippine Society. Some educators had established a "Japan Institute," primarily to teach the Japanese language. There had been travel back and forth, and even Quezon himself had at one time received banzais in Tokyo. How far such associations were innocent and normal and how far they had actually and deliberately served the cause of Japan to the detriment of the Filipinos was no easy question to answer.

At the higher levels there was a spirited defense against the charges. As the former puppet-president, Mr. Laurel was the most important of those arraigned, and he made a strong case for his actions. He testified that before Commonwealth President Quezon had been taken out of the Philippines by the Americans, Mr. Quezon had issued specific instructions. These, given to Mr. Laurel and presumably to some others, were to the effect that the leaders who remained were to make the best accommodation that they could with the Japanese in the interest of the Filipino people. Mr. Laurel testified that he had obeyed this order of his chief of state to the best of his ability. Moreover, he was convinced that what he had done accomplished precisely what Mr. Quezon had had in mind. He felt that his actions had spared the Filipinos from an even worse fate during the Japanese occupation and that he had been able to ameliorate their lot in many cases. His words carried weight and his subsequent rehabilitation in political life, which was complete, demonstrated that most of the Filipinos were confident that he had spoken the truth.

A further argument, advanced by some others—among them Mr. Recto—had considerable cogency from the legal point of view even if it had less popular appeal. This was that at the time of the Japanese invasion the United States was still the sovereign power in the Philippines. As such, it had the primary obligation of defending the archipelago. This duty had obviously not been discharged, and the sovereign power had been driven out. It was therefore illogical, it was urged, to hold the Filipinos responsible for any defection from what was, at the time, a lost cause, and from what was also an alien sovereignty. If the United States could not hold its position, it was argued, the Filipinos could not justifiably be accused and tried for not having held it for the Americans and for having come to the best possible terms with the power that had driven the Americans out.

This argument, and it is a good one, may have had some bearing upon the later attitudes and statements of Mr. Recto, which were often described as "anti-American." It certainly had, and should continue to have, a large bearing upon American defense commitments to the Philippines. The "sovereign" obligation no longer exists, and the original failure to discharge it may be said to have been wiped out by the subsequent liberation. But the Filipinos have a moral right to insist upon adequate guarantees that they will not again be "let down" if they make reciprocal commitments to the United States.

Whatever legalistic merit this position may have had, it was not widely accepted among the Filipinos for an obvious reason. The Filipinos had made common cause with the Americans, fully convinced that this cause was their own freedom. The men who fought on Bataan were not unwilling mercenaries in the service of a foreign power. They were patriots fighting for their own homeland. The massive resistance to the Japanese occupation was certainly based upon no desire to vindicate the sovereignty of the United States. Collaboration with the Japanese was not generally regarded as a disloyalty to the United States but rather as a form of disloyalty to the Philippines and to its ideals.

Moreover, the prompt actions of the United States at the time of the liberation made it plain that the confidence in the achievement of independence, once the Japanese had been driven out, had not been misplaced. The American Congress had, in fact, authorized the President to proclaim Philippine independence at an earlier date than the one already stipulated, if that were desired. This may have been merely a propaganda move, designed to offset the spurious Japanese declaration that an "independent" republic had been set up, but no Filipino has said so. Later events showed that it could be taken, rather, as a further earnest of American good faith. With the liberation, there was no appreciable demand to speed up the advent of the free republic. The original timetable was accepted as valid and logical. The whole idea of "collaboration" was thus discredited and the men who had declared that they were fighting for freedom were proved to be right.

By far the best defense of those accused of collaboration, however, was that they had acted under great duress and extreme coercion. In some cases, unfortunately, as we have noted, this was not true. Some Filipinos had freely given aid and comfort to the enemy for their own advantage, but it was clear to every Filipino that coercion was the very heart of Japanese rule. It was known that this coercion went far beyond the physical abuse, or torture, that was commonplace. Men who would have died under frontal attack rather than give way could sometimes be reached more subtly.

For example, one well-known Manila newspaperman was asked by the Japanese to take over a job of editing and broadcasting on their behalf. He refused. Later in the day, two Japanese officers walked into his office and said: "Look, friend, we have your two little boys downstairs in the car. We should *hate* to have anything happen to them." The Filipino did the job required of him, but the story of why he did spread so rapidly that it is doubtful that his work was of any value to the Japanese. This technique of using hostages as a means of compulsion was so common that it was usually believed that Mr. Laurel himself was forced because his son was taken to Japan and held there. Mr. Laurel did not make this plea, but many felt that he could well have done so. Long before the psychological theory of "every man's breaking point" had been widely expounded, the Filipinos had seen its various ramifications at close range.

What was hardest to determine was when and how the breaking point was reached in any individual case. After the liberation, a young Filipino lawyer, who had been active in the underground resistance, was questioned closely about his own attitude toward those who had collaborated and was asked for his own analysis of the moral issues involved. Without the slightest trace of bitterness, he made a penetrating reply:

When you come right down to it, I suppose it's something like this. There are roughly two kinds of persons in this world. Some men are born brave. Some are born not brave. Now, when the man who was born brave does the brave thing he does no more than we have a right to expect. If he does that which is not brave, he is a coward and deserves our contempt. Then there is this little fellow who was born not brave. If he does the thing that is not brave, that also is only natural. If he does the thing that is brave, he is a hero and deserves our highest honor. But the whole trouble is that only God knows which way we were born. So I think, in the long run, that we'll have to leave the judgments to Him.

This was the conclusion that was eventually reached in the Philippines. It was morally as well as physically impossible to try all the cases that had been brought. Many of them would have required the wisdom of Solomon, and more than that, it was conservatively estimated that to carry out the trials would have kept the Philippine courts clogged for at least thirty years. President Roxas did the sensible as well as the humane thing. He proclaimed a general amnesty. The judgment was left to God. The problem of collaboration was thus solved.

ECONOMIC RELATION TO THE UNITED STATES

The political provisions of the original independence legislation were carried out in full and on schedule. It was quickly realized, however, that the economic provisions would have to be modified. The imposition of export taxes or American tariffs, right at the beginning of the life of the republic, would have made it difficult if not impossible for the major producers to restore production. Accordingly, even before the Republic was inaugurated new economic legislation was presented in Congress which was designed to give a breathing space to the Philippine economy. Three months before Mr. Roxas was inaugurated this legislation was enacted so that there could be a firmer basis for rebuilding the economic relationship of the Philippines to the United States and so that the new government could have a better chance of survival.

There has been a confusion of names in this connection that should be clarified. The basic economic legislation of 1946 was introduced in the House by Congressman C. Jasper Bell of Missouri, and naturally it came to be called the "Bell Bill." Four years later, another Mr. Bell, Daniel W. Bell, a banker, headed an economic mission to the Philippines and presented the "Bell Report," which was the basis for further economic planning. The two men were not related or connected, but the identity of name has made some writing about the Philippines confusing. For purposes of clarity, therefore, it will be wiser to designate the original Bell Bill by its eventually accepted title, the Philippine Trade Act of 1946. This was, and remains—with some subsequent amendment—the definitive instrument in Philippine-American economic relations.

In general, this legislation followed the previously accepted pattern. There were to be quotas on certain products, a period of free or preferential exports to the United States, and then gradual imposition of the normal American tariffs. The schedule, however, was changed. The preferential period was to be twenty-eight years. During the first eight years there was to be free entry of Philippine products, subject always to quota limitations, and thereafter the American tariffs were to be imposed gradually, with a progressive increase of 5 percent annually for twenty years. This was more generous than the provisions of the Tydings-McDuffie Act and promised some hope of recovery. It also set forth a plan for eventual economic independence.

The quotas that were established did not differ too greatly from those that had previously been authorized, but some categories were added. In addition, a change was made: after the free-trade period some products—cigars, tobacco, coconut oil, and buttons—would be subjected, not to increasing American tariffs, but to a progressive reduction of the admissable duty-free quota. This was to become an issue in the revision discussions of 1954. The act of 1946, however, set up these quotas: sugar, 850,000 long tons; coconut oil, 200,000 long tons; cordage, 6,000,000 pounds; tobacco, 6,500,000 pounds; cigars, 200,000,000; buttons (shell or pearl), 850,000 gross; and rice, 1,040,000 pounds.

These provisions were not onerous. It is true that they provided a check against expansion in any field—sugar for example—but they gave an opportunity for the restoration of export trade to satisfactory levels. Beyond that, they were designed to channel Philippine production into more diversified fields. This was not entirely realistic since copra, the raw material of coconut oil, and abacá, the raw material of cordage, remained on the free list. Likewise, the quota on sugar provided that not more than 50,000 long tons of refined sugar could be included. The "colonial economy" had not been disestablished, but a step had been taken in that direction.

In spite of vigorous debates on whether long tons or short tons should be the standard of measurement, the quotas were not the really controversial part of the legislation. The big argument centered on the so-called parity clause. This provided that during the preferential period Americans in the Philippines should enjoy the same rights and privileges in the exploitation of natural resources and the operation of public services as did the Filipinos. It was parity in the Philippines, but the Filipinos were quick to point out that it was not a true parity since there was no corresponding extension of rights and privileges to Filipinos in the United States.

The objective in the parity clause was sound. It was felt that the Philippines needed a prompt influx of foreign investment, especially American, to assist recovery. One of the most attractive fields would be "natural resources," which meant mining. But the Philippine Constitution specifically declared that in the exploitation of natural resources preference must be reserved to Filipinos, and that no stock company could operate in this field unless a majority of its shares was held by Filipinos. For parity this would have to be revised to say "Filipinos or Americans."

Thus, at the outset, the Philippine Trade Act of 1946 meant that the Philippine Constitution would have to be amended before the law could become operative. This was asking quite a bit of a new nation that was sensitive on the score of its nationalism.

There was a further adverse factor. The Rehabilitation Act of 1946, which provided substantial funds for assistance, was adopted virtually simultaneously with the Trade Act. They were not necessarily interdependent, but the Filipinos were quick to assume that they were. The Manila press cried out immediately that the Filipinos were being blackmailed and bludgeoned into taking a "package deal." This was not true in so far as the Rehabilitation Act was concerned. It was true in respect to the Trade Act. If the Filipinos wanted the eight years of free trade and the gradual imposition of tariffs, they

would be obliged to amend their Constitution and accept
"parity" as well. It was a blow to national pride.

President Roxas accepted the challenge squarely. He felt
that the Trade Act was imperative. Under his direction the
proposed amendment was adopted in the legislature and
then the president went to the country to campaign for its
ratification in a plebiscite. He was tireless and he was successful. The amendment was approved in a popular election
and came into force in March, 1947.

Even with favorable legislation and with the continuation
of American disbursement in the Philippines, recovery was
slow. The population had increased, and although some
major products began to approach prewar output, the per
capita production was still far from its previous level. Trade
with Japan began to come back slowly, but it was impeded
by the failure to reach any sort of agreement on the question
of Japanese reparations.

The peso was pegged to the dollar at two to one, but the
financial structure was shaky. The Joint Philippine-American
Finance Commission was established in 1947 to make a comprehensive study of the problem. Its major finding was that
the entire tax organization was unbalanced. Income taxes
were disproportionately low and because most imports were
coming from the United States, duty-free, there was no de-
pendable volume of revenue from tariffs. Tax on the land
could not be raised without even more hardship and so ex-
cises, luxury, and usage taxes had to compensate. Even more
serious was the fact that the tax collection machinery was
not functioning. This was nothing new in the Philippines,
where tax evasion had always been a problem. But it was
especially serious when the country was in dire financial
straits.

Reserves were being depleted since even American help

could not bring about a budgetary balance. In 1948 and 1949 there was an actual trade decline and the imports exceeded exports by almost two to one. The "hungry" market was still importing beyond the nation's capacity to pay.

Remedial measures were taken. A Philippine Central Bank, with wide powers, was set up in 1948 in an effort to bring the fiscal situation under better control. A year later more drastic steps were taken when the Government undertook outright limitation of imports. Controls were set up, first on luxuries, and later on general imports as well. In December of 1949, exchange controls, under the authority of the Central Bank, were established.

In 1950 the situation had begun to improve somewhat, but it was still precarious. It was obvious that further American assistance would be necessary. In the United States it was decided that a closer study of needs was required to supply the basis for that assistance and the result was the dispatch to the Philippines in July, 1950, of the Bell Mission. This was a distinguished group, headed by Daniel W. Bell, made up of five members and a staff of twenty. It went vigorously to work and in October was able to submit a comprehensive report and detailed recommendations.

It was proposed that the United States should supply $250,000,000 over a five-year period and that its use should be under American supervision. Moreover, it was recommended that any such help should be contingent upon certain basic reforms in the Philippines. What was required, it was stated, was an overhaul of the tax structure, enactment and enforcement of a minimum-wage law for agricultural as well as for industrial labor, social and land reform, and sound planning for economic development.

Many Filipinos felt that the language of the report was harsh and that its tenor was unsympathetic. The facts, however, could not be denied. Once more the cry arose that the Philippines was being coerced in its courses of action by the threat of withholding American aid. To some extent this was true, since the Bell recommendation was that further assistance should be contingent upon what was done in the Philippines. It was also felt, in many quarters, that some degree of coercion was needed, since the Philippine administration had already fallen into some disrepute.

President Elpidio Quirino, who had succeeded to office upon the death of Mr. Roxas in 1948, and had been elected in 1949, ably faced the situation. He had already weathered the storm of the imposition of the unpopular import controls and charges of a fraudulent election, and he took the Bell Report in stride. In November 1950 he met with William C. Foster, the American Economic Cooperation Administrator, and they evolved what came to be known as the Quirino-Foster Agreement. President Quirino pledged that the legislation necessary to implement the assistance would be adopted. Mr. Foster pledged that the aid would be forthcoming.

Early in the spring of 1951 some of the legislation was adopted in the Philippines. The measures were not as sweeping as those recommended by the Bell Mission, but they were enough to warrant the carrying out of the agreement. American aid began to come in, and the budget was brought closer to a point of balance than it had been at any time since the war. The export-import position, however, continued to show an adverse balance of trade, and the continuation of the import and exchange controls was imperative.

In the ensuing years the fiscal and trade position fluctuated. There were good times and bad. Wages remained too low and living costs too high. But there was continued rebuilding, and there was a five-year development program of sorts. Under a more vigorous and competent administration there could have been even more rapid recovery. But the first crisis had been passed. There was to be no real economic collapse; the Philippines was back in business. The field of gravest danger now shifted to the political, and democracy itself was to be threatened.

THE AMERICAN BASES

A further problem in the postwar adjustment of relations with the United States required solution. This was the question of the United States military establishment that was to be maintained in the Philippines. The liberating army was to be withdrawn, of course, as speedily as possible, and this was done. But the independence legislation had authorized the United States to retain naval and fueling stations in the Philippines, on a leasehold basis and by agreement.

Accordingly, in March, 1947, the Bases Agreement was reached. Under its terms, the United States was to retain certain positions on a ninety-nine year leasehold basis. There were actually five centers authorized, one army and four navy. These were to be supplemented by ten auxiliary or service positions of a less permanent status. It was also agreed that these centers should be well removed from any major concentrations of population. This was a wise stipulation. It was also agreed that the jurisdiction on the bases should rest with the United States except when both parties to any case were Filipinos.

Under the terms of this agreement the United States closed out its establishments in and near Manila. The air base at Clark Field, well north of Manila, was retained; the naval base at Olongapo, across the peninsula from Manila, was enlarged; and a new naval air station at Cubi Point, also remote, was built.

There was Filipino dissatisfaction with the agreement almost from the outset, and this discontent became increasingly vocal. The establishment of any American jurisdiction on Philippine soil was held to be an infringement of sovereignty. There was the question of which flags should fly. A serious incident arose when Filipinos were prevented from working a small mining claim that ran into a part of the Clark Field Base. And eventually there arose the question of "status of forces" and the demand that American personnel, off the bases and off duty, should be tried in Philippine courts for any offense committed.

The clamor for a revision, and above all for a clarification of the provisions, eventually became so insistent that it could not be ignored. It became something of a football in local Philippine politics. Some persons urged that the time limit be put at twenty-five instead of ninety-nine years. Some urged that the bases be withdrawn altogether. All insisted that Philippine sovereignty must not be compromised.

The United States, therefore, began a series of discussions with the Philippines, at different levels and in different forms, as to how the agreement could properly be modified. No easy agreement could be reached. A special negotiating mission was not successful. Talks in the United States were initiated, suspended, and then initiated and suspended again.

At the time of this writing, late in 1957, the whole question was still hanging fire. The right basis for a genuine meeting of minds had not been found. Meanwhile, however, the entire defense picture in the Far East had changed through the establishment of the Southeast Asia Treaty Organization, in which the Philippines was a primary member. There began to be more hope that the impasse could be broken through a completely different approach. The implications of this development and the Philippine-American Mutual Defense Pact will be discussed later.

Our concern here has been to set forth some of the vexing problems with which the young republic was confronted. Except for the question of collaboration they were and are continuing problems. The economic relationship, as we shall see, has again been modified. Like the military one, this relationship continues to be fluid. Meanwhile, however, some initial problems were gradually being solved. But it was during this very period of problem-solving that a critical challenge to the political integrity and, indeed, to the very physical life of the republic began to take shape. Once more, sheer survival became the issue.

Six

DEMOCRACY IN DISREPUTE

SUBVERSION ON THE MOVE

President Manuel Roxas died suddenly in April, 1948, after less than two years in office. Many Filipinos felt that this was the most severe blow that the young nation could have suffered. Mr. Roxas was dynamic and forceful. He was a "leader" in the accepted Philippine sense. He dominated his party and his government, and was indefatigable in his efforts to speed postwar rebuilding. A strong administration was obviously needed, and Mr. Roxas gave it.

His vice-president, Eipidio Quirino, succeeded to the first office. He was a different person from his predecessor. He had been a successful, respected, and conservative politician. He was sensitive and intelligent and widely experienced. But he was not a dominating figure in the way that Mr. Roxas had been. He was, at best, one of a group, and the group soon took the reins out of his hands.

In the hundreds of charges of corruption that were subsequently hurled at the Quirino administration no one suggested any lack of personal honesty on the part of the president. His own specific integrity was not challenged, but this could not be said of the men with whom he was surrounded, for he was virtually walled in by those who were far from scrupulous. It could be said, in a kind way, that Mr. Quirino was merely weak. But this weakness invited the depredations of men who were not weak in the same sense.

CREEPING CORRUPTION

This creeping corruption began at the very lowest levels of government and extended all the way to the top, except for the president himself. It soon became generally accepted that a suppliant could not enter a government office without being prepared to pay some sort of bribe. There were little deals at the bottom, big deals at the top.

The newspapers and magazines began to have a field day. Many of their charges were not proved, but they were widely aired. The clamor became so intense that President Quirino was obliged to call a caucus of his chief supporters and tell them that there must be a "clean-up" campaign. Much of the value of this move was lost when one of the newspapers put a reporter under an open window of the room at the presidential Palace in which the caucus was held. His paper came out the next morning with a partial transcript on the meeting in which one of the persons closest to the President was quoted as having said: "But what's the use of being the majority party if we can't have a little honest graft?"

It was the cynicism of the remark that stung, and it was equaled by the cynicism with which the Filipinos were beginning to regard all the functions of government. Democracy was rapidly coming into disrepute. The Philippines was getting an increasingly bad press in the United States and there was a loss of confidence in this country in the ability of the government to weather the storm.

The possibility of obtaining further American help was definitely jeopardized because of the growing belief that it would be ill-used. It was impossible to forget what had happened to the surplus military property, and although the blame for that fiasco could not attach directly to the Quirino administration there was skepticism, both here and there, as to any future efforts.

One of the worst effects of the Quirino maladministration was the breakdown of the tax structure. After two years of his incumbency it was charged that not more than 25 percent of the taxes due were actually being collected. Tax evasion had been taken for granted, but not on such a scale. National bankruptcy was inevitable if this were to be accepted as the normal functioning of government.

Politically, a crisis came in the election of 1949. Mr. Quirino was the candidate of his Liberal party. He was opposed by Jose P. Laurel of the Nacionalistas who obviously wished to establish, once and for all, that the charge of collaboration that had been brought against him was unfounded. This, however, was only a minor issue in the campaign, for the real battle was waged over corruption in government. The attacks on the administration were savage.

What eventually happened bore out some of the charges. This election quickly became known in Philippine annals as the "dirty" election. It was all of that. The Liberals took advantage of their majority party position to "fix" the naming of election inspectors and the counting of ballots. Much more, they turned out "goon squads" to intimidate the voters or to keep them away from the polls. There were scores of clashes and several hundred persons lost their lives.

In the end, of course, Quirino and his Liberals won. He was returned to the office of president while his party took 68 out of the 100 seats in the House and captured the 8 Senate seats to be filled in that election. It is quite possible that had the election been entirely free and fair Mr. Quirino would have won in any case. Naturally Mr. Laurel and the Nacionalistas thought otherwise and added the word "stolen" to the word "dirty." What could not be denied was that this was far from an orderly and democratic expression of the popular will.

The realization of this fact was to have far-reaching repercussions. There were many Filipinos who believed in real democracy and were prepared to work for it. A National Movement for Free Elections was organized. Mr. Quirino had been returned to office but he was not returned to real public confidence. His administration became less rather than more effective after his election "victory." Its days were numbered.

THE HUKBALAHAP REVOLT

It has often been suggested that it was the breakdown of good government in the Philippines that brought on and fed the flames of the Communist-led Hukbalahap revolt. It may have been a factor but it was not the sole cause. In the beginning it was also often said that the revolt was a natural agrarian uprising of an oppressed peasantry and that its Communist connections were only incidental. This, also, is an oversimplification.

In retrospect it is possible to see that what happened followed a definite plan in which the Communists had been carefully schooled. They were instructed to take advantage of nationalist movements wherever they could and to capture them if possible. They were trained to capitalize on discontent and to foment it. The conditions in the Philippines after the war were ideally suited to these purposes. Thus the Hukbalahap movement was not completely spontaneous. The organizational ground for it had been carefully laid in Communist party machinery, and trained leaders were ready.

The Communist party in the Philippines was organized as early as 1930. That date is usually chosen because it was in that year, or late in 1929, that Tan Malaka, the Indonesian Communist leader, paid a quiet visit to Manila. But he found at hand several Filipinos who had already been to Moscow and had had their basic training in Marxism-Leninism. The two most important were Guillermo Cappadocia and Mateo de Castillo. They became the real founders of the party. Cappadocia continued in positions of importance for almost twenty years.

Leadership in Manila was soon taken over, however, by a rising young labor leader, Crisanto Evangelista. He made the mistake of trying to get direct action too soon. In addition to preaching the Communist doctrine, he stirred up a series of strikes that could not be ignored. In 1932 he was arrested and charged with sedition. He was convicted and his Communist party was outlawed. In 1934 he was pardoned and the legal status of the party was gradually restored. Evangelista promptly went to Moscow and the party went largely underground, until it emerged, in 1938, in a "United Front" with the Socialists.

Just how much the Communists had to do with the bloody Sakdal uprising of 1936 has never been established. This was, truly, a peasant uprising. The name Sakdal means protest and it was a protest against absentee landlordism, provincial maladministration, and what seemed to be government indifference. Not far south of Manila the rebels attacked a Constabulary post, armed themselves, and planned a march on the capital. They were quickly put down, but not without serious losses of life and not without considerable alarm in Manila. Subsequently they took on a degree of political respectability and actually elected two members to the legislature. They were a protest party.

It is now usually assumed by Filipinos who look back on these events that the Communists were involved behind the scenes. Their hand was not shown. It may have been merely a practice maneuver, but it did establish the fact that there were grievances out of which capital could be made. This was not lost sight of and became vital later on.

The hard core of the Hukbalahap movement took shape in the later days of the Japanese occupation. Its name is a contraction of a Tagalog phrase that has been translated in various ways, but that means "People's Anti-Japanese Army." The members were guerrillas and they fought the Japanese. More than that, they accumulated a sizable store of weapons and ammunition. Still further, they came under the leadership, by 1945, of a dedicated Communist, Luis Taruc.

It became clear immediately after the war that the Huks were not just another guerrilla group. They had maintained their own unique organization and had not cooperated with other resistance units. They had set up indoctrination schools and eventually their own politburo. The large center of their postwar activity was in central Luzon, north of Manila, but there were branch operations in two provinces south of the capital and several in the central, or Visayan, islands.

At the time of the liberation the Huks refused to join with other guerrillas in presenting their case to the Americans as veterans. And, most important, they refused to surrender their arms. In 1946 they openly declared their Communist orientation, took the field as an antigovernment Hukbalahap party, and actually elected seven men to the legislature. The legislature refused to seat them and Taruc, who was one of those elected, went back to the countryside and raised the standard of armed revolt against the government.

By the combination of promises and terrorism he obtained a fairly large following in central Luzon. The condition of the rice farmers was pitiful and the promise of land was persuasive. The Huks made the most of every type of discontent—and discontent was all too abundant. But the movement was also lawless, and village after village was terrorized into submission. The Huks could strike swiftly, usually at night, and the villagers had no means of coping with them.

At this stage it was natural to raise the question of just how far the Huks were acting under direct orders from the Soviet Union. There was no satisfactory answer. There were repeated rumors that the Huks were obtaining arms and supplies from Russian submarines. Taruc had often boasted that the "mighty power" of the great Soviet Union was behind his revolt. A little later he added the name of the Chinese Communists, after they came into power on the mainland. The submarine story seems improbable. It may have arisen from the well-known fact that American submarines had been active in supplying resistance units during the Japanese occupation. The Huks may well have promoted the story themselves to create an impression of greater strength, just as they promised that there would be a gigantic Soviet aerial intervention to support their eventual capture of Manila.

The facts do not bear out the boasts or rumors. Actually there was no need to supply the Huks with small arms and ammunition, such as could be sent in by submarine. Their arms, a mixture of what they had received as guerrillas, what they had taken from the Japanese, and what they had obtained through theft and the black market in surplus were ample for their needs. Other supplies could be—and were— obtained from the countryside.

There is also reasonable doubt that the Huks ever operated under any sort of direct orders from Moscow. There may have been some sort of transmission belt, but that it was concerned with day-to-day or even month-to-month operations is highly unlikely. One point of connection was clearly established with the discovery that Communist agents in the United States Army in the Philippines were in contact with the Huks. One of them, a Sergeant Pomeroy, went over to the Huks, married a Filipina girl, and eventually became the chief theoretician and schoolmaster for Taruc. He actually set up a little "Stalin University" in the mountains.

Physical direction from without, however, was unnecessary. The Huk leaders had been well trained. Some of them had been to Moscow and they had learned their lessons. The various manifestoes that were issued were couched in the familiar Marxist jargon, although there was heavy emphasis upon "landlordism," just as there was in China. And the government was always pictured as the "tool of American imperialism."

In Moscow itself there were occasional expressions of bland sympathy for the "righteous cause" of the Huks, and some publications in the United States had quite a bit to say about the terrible conditions in the Philippines that had made the revolt inevitable. The Huks were defended in some quarters as merely "peasant reformers" at heart, and the need for reform could be proved. But by the end of the decade this was much more than a "reform" movement. It was even more than subversion. It was open revolt against law and government. And it was, by its own declaration, Communist.

How large the Huk force actually was could not be firmly established. At one time Taruc boasted that he had 30,000 trained and equipped "regulars" under arms and at least a million peasant supporters in the countryside. This may have been an exaggeration, but it was plain that at least five provinces were partly under the control of the Huk bands. The area north of Manila stretching almost to the Benguet mountains came to be known, with a false jocosity, as "Huklandia." Even in Manila itself an informal curfew came into being. It was not safe to wander abroad at night. There were cases of murder and arson almost within the city limits. The damage was, however, more than physical. The very tension of terror that prevailed was paralyzing, and with it was the increasing feeling that the government was unable to cope with its enemies. This was part of a political as well as a psychological breakdown.

At this stage the maintenance of public order was, theoretically, the responsibility of the Constabulary. But the Constabulary was a far cry from the strong, disciplined, and competent force that it had been before Pearl Harbor. The best of its officers and men had gone into the armed forces at the outbreak of the war. Many of them had died on Bataan. Some survived the Death March and the prison camps. Many did not. During the occupation the Japanese had reinstituted a Constabulary of sorts, under their own direction, and it had no savory reputation. It was a common saying that the Japanese had emptied the jails to fill up the Constabulary. After the war there had not been time carefully to rebuild.

When the Huks began their systematic attacks Constabulary units were sent out to "protect" the villages. It was not long before the charge was made that the depredations of the Constabulary were as bad as those of the Huks. Constabulary units were accused of making off with everything that they happened to want and of "living off the country." Some of these charges were exaggerated, but they were good grist for the Communist propaganda mill. In many cases the Huks actually offered their services to "protect" the villagers against the Constabulary!

Shortly after he took office in 1948, President Quirino tried a new tactic. He arranged a conference with Luis Taruc, in Manila, to discuss the terms of a general amnesty. Taruc came in, and it was agreed that the Huk-elected members of the legislature would be seated. There would be no prosecutions and the Constabulary could be called off. The Huks had merely to come in and surrender their arms.

It was on this last point that the amnesty plan foundered. Taruc insisted, later, that the agreement was merely that the Huks should "register," not surrender, their arms. In any case, the question became academic. Less than a hundred of the Huks actually complied with the amnesty terms and surrendered themselves and their weapons. The possession of these weapons was the very heart of the Huk tactic. The Huks were not nearly strong enough to gain control by peaceful and political means. They had put up a front of legality in electing members to the legislature, and they had trumpeted a vast program of reform. But they knew that if they were once disarmed they had no chance. Amnesty based on real disarmament was, therefore, out of the question. Taruc went back to the hills.

After the collapse of the amnesty plan the Huks were again outlawed and the Philippine Army was called upon to wipe them out. The Army had no more success than the Constabulary. There were fewer charges of looting villages, it is true, but the Army was ineffective. It was an "arm-chair" army. Its leadership was not inspiring and its campaigns were not well directed. A barracks position would be set up and from time to time a unit would go out to "attack and disperse" a Huk concentration. The soldiers would thereupon take the field, fire a few volleys into the air, and return to their post with the report, "mission accomplished."

The truth is that they had no stomach for such a fight. They had no conception of a national cause. The only thing of importance was to get it over as quickly and as painlessly as possible and to get back behind the barbed-wire road blocks. Meanwhile, their superiors back in Manila could report to President Quirino that the campaign was progressing satisfactorily, that hundreds and even thousands of Huks were being killed or "dispersed," and that ultimate victory was in sight.

A climax came in April, 1949, when Mrs. Aurora Quezon, widow of the Commonwealth President, was ambushed and murdered by the Huks. Mrs. Quezon was traveling with an official entourage to the province of Tayabas, in eastern Luzon, which had been renamed Quezon in honor of her husband, to dedicate a monument to him. The automobile in which she was riding was riddled with machine-gun bullets at a narrow point in the road and she, her daughter and son-in-law, and several high officials were killed.

It was a senseless crime. It is probable that the Huks thought they were shooting at President Quirino. They certainly had nothing to gain by killing Mrs. Quezon who, by this time, was no power in politics but who was a national symbol of the revered memory of her husband. With that act, the Huks put themselves beyond the pale, both in the Philippines and abroad. They were no longer "agrarian reformers"; they were cold-blooded killers. The demand for sterner measures against them began to swell.

The Army was ordered to step up its campaign and it tried to do so. But the Army was crippled by the fact that the Huk network of intelligence was, at this stage, far superior to that of the Army itself. If an Army unit went out, the Huks, well-informed in advance, simply dispersed in the Candaba swamp or in the jungle area around Mount Arayat, and the soldiers were powerless.

All this time the Huks were creeping closer and closer to Manila itself. It became known that the politburo was actually living in and working from the capital. Finally, a target date was set. Manila was to be taken on Christmas eve, 1950. That was the situation when Ramon Magsaysay appeared on the scene.

Seven

THE TRIUMPH OF DEMOCRACY

The life of Magsaysay has occasionally been over-dramatized. It is such perfect Horatio Alger material that the temptation to embellish has sometimes proved irresistible. Actually, the embellishment is unnecessary. The facts speak for themselves. Often in history a critical situation has seemed to call forth an exceptional individual who was able to cope with emergencies, to provide a new leadership, and to win out in what appeared to be, at the beginning, a lost cause. We commonly speak of the "man of the hour." Sometimes we speak also of a "man of destiny," but with more reservation. Both phrases have been applied to Magsaysay in recognition of the fact that he filled a unique place in meeting a critical situation and that he did so, in part, by virtue of his own personal characteristics. Trying times may call forth great men, but it is good to realize that the greatness is there to be evoked.

It is not true to state that Magsaysay came from a "poor, illiterate peasant family." Only the word poor is accurate—and that even in a relative sense. Magsaysay's father was not a peasant. He was a village schoolteacher and a part-time carpenter and blacksmith. The atmosphere in which Magsaysay, second in a family of eight children, grew up was that of emphasis upon the value of learning and of devotion to it. The father was also a man of great rectitude and high principles. The family believed in making its way and paying its debts. Advancement was taken for granted.

There may have been some effect exerted upon the young Magsaysay by his physical surroundings. Certainly they were to play an important part in his later career. He was born on August 31, 1907, in the province of Zambales. This is on the west side of the Island of Luzon, north of the Bataan Peninsula and facing the South China Sea. It is not part of the central Luzon coastal plain. It is largely mountainous country. It is not overcrowded, as are the rice-growing provinces to the east. It is good land, but it is rugged. This may have imparted something to the character of the people. No one has ever called the Zambaleno "easy-going."

Certainly there was no listlessness in the Magsaysay household. The children walked to school. The boys helped in the blacksmith shop and in the farm-gardening. The older children, as always, helped to take care of the younger. There was enough to eat, but there were no luxuries. They were not expected. It was a good family, comparable in some ways to that of a rural teacher or preacher in the United States two or three generations ago. There was plenty of hard work. But there were also loyalty, righteousness, generosity, ambition, and, if one judges by the Magsaysay of later days, much good humor.

The blacksmith shop must have had something important to do with the molding of the life of the young Ramon. He showed an early passion for making and fixing things. When he was still in high school he managed to acquire an old Ford automobile, and he put in many hours keeping it running. He learned the ways of motor cars and also the roads of Zambales, such as they were. This, also, was a part of "destiny."

After his graduation from the local high school young Magsaysay went off to Manila to further his education. He was not a distinguished student in the academic sense. But he was vigorous and was regarded, even then, as something of a leader among his classmates. In Manila he enrolled in the University of the Philippines but did not find the atmosphere congenial and transferred to a smaller institution, Jose Rizal College, where he was graduated with a degree of Bachelor of Science in Commerce.

Meanwhile, he had been obliged to make his living. He did so by following his bent for motor mechanics and began his work in a garage and transportation company. His skills were recognized and he won promotion. Eventually, after two years' courtship, he married the charming daughter of the owner of the company, and then went back to Zambales to take over the supervision of its bus lines in that province.

The situation was made for him, and for history. He was no idle superintendent. He went out on every line to every village. He got to know every curve in the roads, and more important, got to know men and women at every bus stop. He liked them, and they loved him. The company prospered, as could be expected.

Then came the war. After a brief service with the American forces, Magsaysay was instructed to get back to Zambales, avoid capture, and organize an underground resistance. No better assignment could have been made.

In the long run the success of a guerrilla operation depends in a large part upon the degree to which the small forces actually in the field can depend upon the sympathetic support of those in the far larger countryside in which they work. In Zambales, that support for Magsaysay was unquestioned. He disdained to take any rank higher than that of captain, which he already had. He was in and of his own people. In Zambales he was "Monching," the affectionate diminutive of his name, Ramon. He was hidden out, time after time. The Japanese couldn't find him, even with a big

price on his head. His knowledge of those roads, those mountains, and those people paid a huge dividend.

He was not one of the more publicized leaders of the
resistance although he was constantly in touch with the American military command. He was in a good strategic spot
which flanked the Japanese in central Luzon, and lay south
of Lingayan Gulf. The Japanese had a right to assume, moreover, that his forces embraced quite a few veteran soldiers
who had managed to escape from Bataan to the north. He
was also in a position to furnish vital information on the
Japanese defenses of Lingayan Gulf, which he did.

What was of most importance, however, was that he and
his force symbolized the true resistance to Japan in western
Luzon. The area was never administered by Japan because
there was always "Monching" in the background. And the
idea of Japanese domination was never accepted because it
was always possible to resist, as he had shown.

At the end of the war Magsaysay served briefly as a sort
of military administrator for Zambales, and his immense
services to the cause of liberation were then first publicly
recognized. With the restoration of civil government it was
inevitable that he would be called upon. In the first election
he was presented as the candidate of Zambales for the House
of Representatives and he was elected almost without opposition. Thus his political career began.

A MAN WHO WAS "DIFFERENT"

It is hard to realize the impact of Magsaysay upon the
Philippine political scene without a better understanding of
just what he was and was not. The latter was especially important. Here was a man who seemed to have broken all
the accepted political rules and was still, obviously, a person

of enormous worth. He was the creation of new times and new conditions. To many he represented the idea of a new Philippines. To others he could be greeted only with dismay.

First of all, he was not a lawyer. For forty years almost every man chosen for high office in the Philippines had passed the bar examination. With that, of course, went the fact that he was in no sense a professional *politico*. He had no organization behind him, no family interest or obligation, no debts to pay. He was not even a graduate of the University of the Philippines. His degree was in commerce and his chief qualification for this was that he knew something about bus lines. More than that, he had worked with his hands. There were older men in the Philippine legislature who had planted rice, but their number was rapidly diminishing. There was even the question of blood. Most Filipino leaders, such as Quezon, had a strong Spanish admixture. Some, such as Osmeña, were part Chinese. The ruling political class was recognizably *mestizo*. Magsaysay was presumably pure Malay. This may not be accurate, for there was possibly some trace of Spanish blood on his mother's side, and her name, del Fierro, was Spanish. But Magsaysay was a Zambaleno, a Malay, and proud of it. He was not fluent in Spanish and apparently made no attempt to become so.

Magsaysay even looked a bit different. He was somewhat taller than the average Filipino but had a chunky frame. He had great physical strength and endurance. His eyebrows jutted and they were heavy. His face was craggy. He was often called the Philippine Abraham Lincoln, and his appearance had something to do with the designation. He liked to think of himself as a typical Filipino but he was certainly not quite that. Actually his differences from what Filipinos had come to expect from persons in public life were to become his greatest assets.

Perhaps the most important of these, as we shall see, was his reputation for an impregnable personal integrity. This might have been less important at another time. There had been and were many persons in Philippine public life who had been and were scrupulously honest. But Magsaysay came into positions of influence and authority at a time when the charges of corruption were most vehement and at a time when there was a public lack of confidence in the ability of those in power to resist temptation. There was no such feeling concerning Magsaysay. One well-known politician was heard in the lobby of the Manila Hotel to murmur, rather ruefully: "Every man has his price—except, of course, Monching."

On the other hand, his immense personal courage, and his deserved reputation for it, were not different from the great Filipino tradition, but they gave the tradition a fresh luster. Here, at last, was a man who could make personal some of the virtues that were usually held up as an ideal to be admired but not often to be realized. This courage was not an abstraction. It was a completely tangible element in the usually intangible thing called "the quality of leadership." Magsaysay knew this very well. An American newspaperman, a friend of Magsaysay, likes to tell a story on this point:

When I visited Magsaysay in 1951, the campaign against the Huks had just passed its peak. It was becoming clear that he would win, but the threats against his life had multiplied. Several assassination plots had been uncovered just in time.

But in the afternoon he would drive me back to the Manila Hotel in that jeep of his and then persist in standing on the front steps for fifteen or twenty minutes to conclude our conversation. I would ask him to come in. He would decline, saying that it would only be a minute. So he stood there. He was a perfect target, with that bright Aloha shirt, those khaki shorts, and light stockings. There were a hundred clumps of bushes around the hotel that could have hidden a rifleman. There was a clean shot straight across the Luneta. It would have been easy. I confess that I usually tried to sidle around until I got behind a pillar and even then I was afraid of a ricochet. Finally, I remonstrated with him.

"Look here," I protested, "you are target number one. Why do you needlessly expose yourself? In that outfit and on the steps of the hotel you are simply asking for it."

He chuckled for a minute (without changing his place on the steps) and then became intensely earnest. "Perhaps you don't entirely understand," he replied. "These people are crying for a leader. Some of them want me. But how can I be a leader unless they *know* that I am fearless?"

What I had first thought to be mere bravado turned out to be dedication to a people and its cause.

Events were to prove that the courage was moral as well as physical. Magsaysay drove in that jeep all over "Huklandia." He was later obliged to drive through the jungle of politics. He was to face assassination attempts of a subtler sort. He had to be "fearless."

When he went to the legislature he gravitated naturally to the correct spot. He became a member and later the chairman of the House Committee on National Defense. In the beginning this was not vital, but when the military forces proved their inability to cope with the Huk menace, their quality became a matter of national concern. Magsaysay was relentless in his criticism and because of his background his words bore weight. When it came to guerrillas he knew what he was talking about.

FIGHTING THE HUKS

At the most critical time President Quirino invited him to Malacañang and asked him to take the post of secretary of defense. Some of the accounts of their conversation are doubt-less apocryphal but the substance could hardly be doubted. Quirino is said to have asked Magsaysay, directly, if he could get rid of the Huk menace. Magsaysay is said to have replied:

"Yes, Mr. President, I can."

"What will you require?"

"An absolutely free hand."

This, presumably, was a basis for agreement, and in September, 1950, Magsaysay took over the defense portfolio. He was the cabinet officer charged with supervision of the armed services. More than that, he was the individual charged with ridding the country of the growing threat to good and free government. It was the biggest opportunity of his life.

The speed and vigor with which he acted came as something of a welcome shock even to those who knew him and trusted him. It was dismaying to those who had reason to fear him. On his first day in office the new secretary abruptly dismissed several very high-ranking Army officers. On his second day he sent some men, supposedly permanent "arm-chair fixtures," into the field. Thereafter he bombarded the whole Army command with a series of crisp, often curt, directives. Even more frequently he issued his orders in person.

There was a complete overhaul of Army dispositions and tactics. Units that had been in the field and had given less than a good account of themselves were recalled for fresh and strenuous retraining. Units that showed a disposition to fight received plenty of opportunity and encouragement. Here, at last, was a guerrilla fighter who knew how to fight with guerrillas against other guerrillas.

The barracks positions were quickly disposed of. Units were cut down in size and made—and kept—fully mobile. This had a double advantage. Before long many of the Army forces were able to move with a speed equal to that of the Huks. The element of surprise, upon which the Huks had always depended, now threatened them. They, also, could be surprised. But this depended, in turn, upon the ability to break up the system of forewarning that had been imposed upon the villages. It was necessary to regain the confidence of the people themselves and ridding them of the barracks burden was one way of doing so.

This was coupled with the most drastic orders against living off the country. Magsaysay had to wipe out the bad impression that had been made by the Constabulary and to a lesser degree by the Army. The rations of the Army were increased and soldiers were told to use them and nothing else. Any charges of looting were promptly investigated and the offenders summarily punished. The villagers had to be convinced that their real friends were the armed forces of their government and not the terrorists who had preyed on them. This took time, but eventually it was successful. The Huks began to get less help—and less information—from the villagers.

Magsaysay adopted an ingenious and effective method to dispose of the false claims of successes. There was no more firing into the air and a report of "hundreds killed and the rest dispersed." He equipped each unit with small cameras. No man, and no unit, could lay claim to honor, promotion, or award on the basis of having killed a Huk unless there was a photograph of the dead Huk to prove it. It seems simple, but it worked.

One of the most important things, also, was that Magsaysay literally and personally took the field. He took over a jeep, mounted a machine gun on the back of it, and went into action. He visited all his posts, often at night. There was no forewarning and no rigamarole of inspection. He went out to see that the job was done and to see the men who were doing it. The stories of those surprise visits rapidly grew into a legend, but there was some basis for it. They helped to enforce discipline, but, more important, they built morale. There were promotions on the spot as well as stinging rebukes. The soldier in the field had a powerful friend as well as a stern leader.

It may be well, at this juncture, to dispose of the other legend—that Magsaysay went out to "kill" Huks, and dispatched large numbers of them singlehandedly. He said repeatedly that this was not true. "As far as I know," he once remarked, "I have never killed a single Huk. That was not my job. There were others to do that. It was up to me to see that they got support and leadership."

On the other hand, there was the frequently repeated charge that Magsaysay was no better than his foes in his methods of operation. His was an "unethical" warfare, it was said, in which he had no hesitation to resort to ambush, deceit, torture, and his own private brand of terrorism. To a direct question on this point he replied with candor and vigor:

I had to fight fire with fire. No fighting is pretty and guerrilla fighting is probably the worst. Sure, we ambushed them whenever we had a chance. They were trying to ambush us. Sure, we deceived them, to the best of our ability. Torture? No, not to my knowledge and certainly not with my consent. I didn't want to get my information that way. But this much I can say. No man who honestly surrendered in the belief that he would receive fair treatment had reason to complain. We had hundreds of them and they were treated in the beginning as prisoners of war. Later we tried to do something good with them. But we never did lure any innocent man into a surrender trap by kind words and then cut his head off. That wasn't our way. I couldn't control every little squad in the field and there may have been cases of what you Americans call "excesses." They did not have my sanction. In fact, to cut down the chance of private revenge I tried to make it a practice to put men into action in provinces or barrios where they could not have had any family connections. I tried to tell them that this was not the time to settle private grudges. It was a time to fight for our country.

Magsaysay's men, as they began to call themselves, did fight, and they fought increasingly well. It was, as he said, no pretty fight, but it got results. The Huks soon began to realize that they were up against something different and confidence in their cause wavered. It was soon possible for Magsaysay to put into force the other side of his campaign, that of attraction, land resettlement, and genuine reform. This will be discussed in the next chapter.

A real turning point came not many weeks after Magsaysay went into action. It will be recalled that Christmas, 1950, was the date set for the capture of Manila by the Huks, and that Magsaysay took his office in the preceding September. What actually happened before that Christmas time was the largest single disaster for the rebels.

It has been observed that one of the strongest assets of the Huks was their well-developed intelligence network. This, in turn, was largely directed by an efficient politburo, in which each man had a specific function and in which some had specific areas of command. The politburo at this stage operated in and from Manila itself. It was small wonder that the Huks were confident that the city could be taken when most of their top leaders, except those who were actually commanding in the field, could live and operate in the capital with seeming impunity. Magsaysay knew that he would have to break that organization.

How he did so constituted one of the most dramatic and

even bizarre episodes of his career. It started with one of the
frequent plots to effect his assassination. He was invited to
a "discussion" with some Huk leaders, provided he would
come to a notorious Manila slum, late at night, unarmed,
and alone. He accepted the challenge, although he knew it
was part of a plan to kill him. He met one man only. The
assassins did not come on the scene. He was persuasive and
the man was won over to a rather timid cooperation in hope
of reward. Through information that he subsequently supplied, Magsaysay was able to find out more about the politburo and where and how they could be located.

It seems that messages were transmitted from one member of the group to another by means of a woman who delivered vegetables. One story has it that she was a young
girl, another that she was an old crone. When Magsaysay
was asked about it he merely laughed, shrugged his shoulders,
and said: "She delivered vegetables. We watched the basket,
not the woman." The woman was cautiously observed and
followed. Each house at which she called was noted. Then,
suddenly, Magsaysay struck. In a group of simultaneous raids
a large part of the politburo was captured.

Disorder and confusion ensued in the Huk camp. An attack on Manila was out of the question. The effect of this
coup, however, was larger than that. The Huks were not
again able to set up an efficient directing political organization. Their unity had been destroyed. More and more they
disintegrated into outlaw bands taking refuge in swamp or
mountain. Taruc's boast of 30,000 well-trained men under
arms became more and more hollow. Within a year, as
Magsaysay said, it was merely a question of "mopping up"
and saving as many men as possible from the ruins. By the
end of that year freedom of travel throughout almost all of
"Huklandia" had been restored. The villagers could go back

to their rice-planting without fear of forays. Manila heaved an immense sigh of relief and turned its attention more fully to politics.

There, too, Magsaysay was once more to play a decisive role.

THE CLEAN ELECTION

During this time, it should be emphasized, Magsaysay had enjoyed the complete and outspoken support of President Quirino. It was not always easy for the President to give it, since Magsaysay had a way of treading upon official toes and some of the toes that were hurt belonged to Quirino's close friends, associates, and supporters. There were rumblings that Magsaysay was getting too big for himself and should be put in his place. Quirino stood by him.

As the mid-term senatorial election of 1951 approached, the charges of corruption multiplied. The largest outcry evoked the "dirty" election of 1949 and insistently demanded that it must not be repeated. The National Committee for Free Elections became increasingly active. Press and radio trumpeted the cause of an honest ballot. Women's clubs were enlisted. Even such organizations as the Junior Chambers of Commerce took to the field—and the Junior Chambers, incidentally, did an excellent job. Day in, day out, it was hammered home to the public that this had to be the "clean" election.

Faced with this clamorous demand, President Quirino again called upon Magsaysay. He asked his Secretary of Defense to see to it that there was no obstruction to balloting, that returns be properly counted, ballot boxes safeguarded, and the public reassured. To such a challenge Magsaysay responded with enthusiasm. There was one body of men, now, upon whom he knew he could rely. He turned out the Army.

But this was something different from any previous army-controlled election. The troops were not put on station to see that any particular candidate was elected. They were instructed merely to see to it that every citizen had an unimpeded right to vote as he chose. Magsaysay even made some shifts in assignment so that officers would be taken out of areas or cities in which they might be put under political pressure. This time, there would be no goon squads.

The political circumstances should be kept in mind. Magsaysay was a Quirino appointee. Nominally, at least, he belonged to Quirino's Liberal party, although that had been unimportant in Zambales. But he threw the whole force of his organization and his personality into the election to assure the right of every man to vote against Quirino's party, if he so desired. Wherever it was feasible, soldiers patrolled the voting areas. Their use could be amply justified, if that were necessary, on the ground that they were guarding against any possible incursion of the Huks, who had urged a boycott of the election. Actually, they were on guard against any breach of order that would hinder the casting of ballots.

The result was spectacular. The election was the most orderly in years. There was a small clash in Cavite Province, always a hotbed of trouble, and half a dozen persons were killed. A mayor of a large provincial city was murdered, but it was quickly established that the motive was personal, not political. Two million voters went to the polls and cast their ballots without fear, obstruction, or intimidation. This was the "clean" election.

Press and radio also played an important part. One of the sources of trouble, and sometimes of dishonesty, had been the delay in reporting election returns. This time, communications media mobilized to get the returns from every important center within the first twenty-four hours. Magsaysay's troops kept the ballot boxes under guard, and the reporters and correspondents were on the job to see them opened.

The results were headlined in the Manila papers within those twenty-four hours. Quirino's party had suffered a devastating defeat. There were nine senators to be elected (at large) and all nine who won belonged to the opposition Nacionalistas. Mr. Laurel, beaten by Quirino in the 1949 presidential election, was sent to the Senate with a tremendous vote. Quirino's own brother, a Liberal, ran at the bottom of the list.

Politically, this election was important to the Philippines. It demonstrated that an entrenched party in power could be repudiated by a free electorate. It brought back a belief in the basic principles of democracy, which had been sorely shaken. It was only a senatorial election but it marked a turning point. Actually, in the public mind the question of who did or did not win in each senatorial contest was less important than the fact that the freedom to go to the polls without hindrance had been firmly reestablished.

It is curious and interesting that out of those circumstances Magsaysay once more gained stature. The party to which he belonged had been soundly thrashed. The President who had appointed him to his cabinet post had been, in the general view, severely rebuked, yet Magsaysay was not merely untouched but emerged stronger than ever. In the public mind the "clean" election was of his making. This was not literally true, since many persons and groups had contributed to it. But Magsaysay quickly came to stand as the symbol of that idea. Here was a new man, a new vigor, and a new hope.

It was natural that the opposition leaders would make

overtures to Magsaysay, and they did so even before the ballots were counted. He was urged to desert Quirino's Liberal party and to look forward to a presidential nomination within two years. He was reluctant. He was not a professional *politico* in any sense. He was not at all sure that he could obtain the sort of backing that he would require from the opposition Nacionalistas. He felt that he had a big job to do in the rehabilitation and resettlement of the Huks and he knew that he could not do it if he stepped out of office. He stayed in the cabinet.

Opposition to him was, by this time, steady even if quiet. He represented ideas that some of the older men could not understand, much less embrace. To many of them, politics had always been a game that was played according to well-accepted rules. Magsaysay seemed ready to break all of them. He was baffling.

An amusing example of this was afforded at President Quirino's birthday party, in Baguio, just after the election. An American reporter happened to be standing just behind President Quirino, out in the garden, and overheard a revealing conversation. An old-line, grizzled *politico,* veteran of many contests, came up to the President and after an exchange of pleasantries spoke his mind: "Sure, Mr. Presidente, I know that it *had* to be a clean election. But did it have to be so *damn* clean?"

The gulf between such an attitude and the point of view of Magsaysay is obvious. He had not compromised with the Huks; neither would he compromise on political principle. A thing was either clean or unclean in his mind. There was no middle ground. It is important, also, that more and more Filipinos were coming to hold and to express this view. Magsaysay was their logical choice for leadership.

THE INEVITABLE BREAK

Magsaysay's break with Quirino was slow, but inevitable. After the 1951 senatorial election the President had lost both face and power. Magsaysay, on the other hand, was stronger than ever. The land resettlement program, with which Magsaysay was successfully fighting the Huks, required government support and sizable appropriation. Magsaysay came to feel that he could depend upon neither. There was never an open break at this stage but Magsaysay became increasingly unhappy. He found himself obstructed, time after time, at little points. His recommendations were adroitly shunted aside. Sound programs were allowed to wither for lack of support. Magsaysay was often abrupt and outspoken. And Quirino and Magsaysay no longer spoke the same language.

It should be remembered also that Quirino through this time was a sick man. He had not enough physical strength to meet his problems, and certainly not enough to cope with a secretary of defense who was unbelievably robust. To that should be added the fact that Quirino knew, as everyone else in the Philippines knew, that Magsaysay's star was in the ascendant. A Magsaysay for President Movement had already been organized while Magsaysay was still an officer in Quirino's cabinet. The President's situation could not have been comfortable.

Quirino's stalwarts within the party did nothing to help him at this point. On the contrary they urged that he "cut Magsaysay down to size," reassert his own leadership, and sweep the polls at the election. Their advice was bad, on the score of the election, but it was even worse because it made Quirino feel that he could, and properly should, dispense with the services of the strongest man in his cabinet.

The final break came, ostensibly, on the question of a further amnesty for the Huks and for renewed negotiations with them. Magsaysay felt that this would be useless and pointless. The Huks were already very much on the run and there was no need to negotiate. But more than that, Magsaysay's program of rehabilitation for those who surrendered offered all the advantages of an amnesty, and it was working in spite of the lukewarm support accorded by the administration. In the end, Quirino went against Magsaysay's advice, and, indeed, over his head, in ordering a cease-fire and a period of negotiation. In February of 1953 Magsaysay handed in his resignation.

In the letter of transmittal, however, Magsaysay made it clear that a larger issue was at stake. He had lost confidence in, and become disgusted with, a government that he said was "full of crooks and grafters." Such a government, he felt, could not hope to deal with a Communist menace. On this point he was specific and blunt. He wrote to the President: "It would be useless for me to continue as Secretary of National Defense with the specific duty of killing Huks as long as the administration continues to foster and tolerate conditions which offer fertile soil for Communism. Merely killing dissidents will not solve the Communist problem. Its solution lies in the correction of social evils and injustice, and in giving the people a decent government, free from dishonesty and graft."

This was strong political medicine, and with it Magsaysay projected himself into the political arena. On the following March 9 he announced his attachment to the opposition Nacionalista party. In May his candidacy for President was joyfully proclaimed.

It was an odd political marriage of convenience. The hard core of the Nacionalistas was still the Laurel-Recto combination, and Magsaysay did not fit into their sort of pattern. Senator Laurel was quite frank about it. "The one thing we have to do," he said, "is to beat Quirino, and Magsaysay is the man to do it." Obviously Senator Laurel wished to avenge his defeat in the "dirty" election of 1949. He was undoubtedly also wise enough to know that the country was in dire need of a change in administration. Subsequently, Senator Laurel established his complete loyalty to Magsaysay. Unfortunately, Senator Recto did not.

At this point another strong personality was injected into the campaign, that of Ambassador Romulo. For some time he had been uneasy about representing, in Washington, an administration in Manila with which he was not in sympathy. In the face of the steady tirades about "graft and corruption" he had been obliged to be apologetic and explanatory. There was no specific point upon which Ambassador Romulo was not correctly sustained by his home government, but the ambassador was a special pleader for the cause of his own people and his pleas were being discounted by the stream of reports of maladministration in the Philippines.

Ambassador Romulo also knew that President Quirino was tired and sick. There was a chance, he felt, to revitalize the Liberal party under new leadership if another candidate could be presented. He himself had strong support in the university and newspaper circles in the Philippines and several "Romulo for President" clubs had been organized. Accordingly, in May, 1953, he went back to Manila, looked over the ground, and submitted his resignation as ambassador. He became a candidate for the Liberal nomination, in opposition to Quirino.

The Liberal convention was stormy from the outset. Romulo had reason to believe that he could count upon a majority of the delegates, provided they could vote in a secret ballot. This was because so many of the delegates were Quirino appointees or owed their various emoluments to the administration that they might well be afraid to stand up and be counted for fear of reprisal. The question of secret balloting, therefore, became the issue. When Romulo and the secret ballot were overruled he charged, naturally, that the convention was "rigged" for Quirino, and he and Quirino's own Vice President, Fernando Lopez, walked out. They formed a new Democratic party and took the field.

General Romulo soon realized that it was a lost cause. As an independent he could not begin to cope with the organized machinery of either the Liberals or the Nacionalistas. Another factor was even more important. He had felt all along that a change of administration was necessary. But he soon saw that his own candidacy would help, rather than hurt, Quirino. The young "Romulo for President" groups would not have voted for Quirino in any case. All he would do would be to draw off strength from Magsaysay, not Quirino.

On the basis of his own eloquent writing it is correct to say, also, that General Romulo's opinion and estimate of Magsaysay changed during this time. Up to this point, Romulo had had little occasion to come into contact with Magsaysay. He had felt, and had said, that Magsaysay had an inadequate background in education and experience to hold the highest office in the land. But Romulo soon realized that the support of a whole people was vastly more important than such considerations. There may have been some quiet meetings between the two men, although neither one has said so. If there were, Romulo could not have been unimpressed by the force and power of this crusader from Zambales. More than that, they were campaigning for exactly the same things, a change in administration, an end to this tale of graft and corruption, basic reforms in law and its administration, a resurgence of real democracy.

The outcome was logical. The Democratic party merged in a coalition with the Nacionalistas. Romulo became the campaign manager for Magsaysay.

ELECTION VICTORY

There had never been a campaign like that one in the Philippines. There may never be again. Magsaysay was of the people and he went to the people. He and his supporters went into the most remote villages. They explained what the right to vote actually meant. They explained, also, that these villagers could vote for a candidate who was one of them, who understood their needs and was sensitive to them. Magsaysay was not only the man who had beaten the Huks. He was the man who proposed to beat the landlord and the usurer, who was a fighter against hunger and want and despair. Here, at last, was the man who could personify hope.

The campaign combination of Magsaysay and Romulo was a good one. Magsaysay was superb in the villages, where he was obviously at home. Romulo, one of the most gifted orators that the Philippines has produced, was at his best with the large urban audiences, the larger the better. And the two were speaking the same political language.

But the campaign went far beyond personal appearances. The various groups that had mobilized behind free and fair elections back in 1951 came back as organizations working for Magsaysay. There was a People's Movement for Magsaysay, a Philippine Women for Magsaysay, the Students for Magsaysay, and dozens of little local groups. Always in the background was the party machinery but it seldom came to the surface. It was not necessary. This was a popular, not a party, movement.

The outcome was never in doubt. Magsaysay obtained the largest popular vote in Philippine history, and the widest margin of victory. A president had been elected not by one party or its machine, but as the representative of a whole people. Democracy had returned.

Eight

THE REBUILDING

President Magsaysay undertook to dramatize, from his first day in office, the advent of truly popular government in the Philippines. Smashing tradition, he called off the elaborate inaugural ball with all its trappings that were symbolic of an earlier period, and held a public reception instead. Malacañang Palace and its grounds were joyfully crowded. As an interesting sidelight it can be noted that the g was added to the spelling of the name. It was known as Malacañan during the whole of the American rule. The other, and older, spelling is in conformity with Tagalog pronunciation and local use. To many Filipinos this simple change symbolized that the Palace now belonged to the people. Magsaysay did everything in his power to make them feel just that.

The elaborate system of guards that had surrounded President Quirino was dismissed. Twenty-eight years earlier Governor General Davis had broken down the concrete barriers at the Palace gates to show that the Governor was accessible to the people. The public response was one of instant and warm approval. Magsaysay may not even have known of, or remembered, the Davis episode, but he got the same result, and on a far larger scale. The people thronged in to see him, and he could be seen.

One experiment along the line, however, proved to be impracticable. Magsaysay had announced that he intended to root out the well-publicized graft and corruption and to make the government truly the servant of the people. Accordingly he invited the people to send in their complaints and put the government-owned telegraph at their disposal. Any person who wished to present a case to the President could do so, free of charge. The result was natural: the telegraph lines were quickly jammed and the plan had to be called off. Many of the complaints were without merit or too trivial for high executive action. But an executive office was set up to receive and sift such complaints and was made available to the public.

A Presidential Complaints and Action Committee was established by Magsaysay. Its function was to hear grievances of all sorts and recommend remedial action where it was justified. The extent to which the people took advantage of this machinery is more important than the actual disposition of cases. In its first year of operation the committee heard 59,144 complaints, more than a thousand a week! Of these, 31,876 were settled by direct action. Another 26,780 were referred to various government departments to be followed up. At the end of that first strenuous year the committee had actually less than 500 cases still pending.

The effect on public morale was considerable. It had been made clear that the government was for the people, not against them. There was access to justice for even the smallest person. The idea of a truly democratic government was winning out.

LAND RESETTLEMENT

Meanwhile, the President, burdened with new executive responsibilities, tried to go ahead with certain specific projects that were designed to provide better living conditions for those in need. Most conspicuous of these was the land resettlement program, which had been of primary interest to his operations while he was secretary of defense.

He had felt that the best way to beat the Huks was to offer some concrete plan of rehabilitation to those who wished to get away from the conditions that the Huks had successfully exploited. Accordingly, at his urging provision was made, in the military budget for 1951, for the expenditure of certain residue funds for the use of land resettlement of Huks who surrendered and gave evidence of good faith. Out of this came the Economic Development Corps (EDCOR), a branch of the military service charged with the administration of land development projects for purposes of rehabilitation.

The obvious place to start was the island of Mindanao. It was underpopulated and underdeveloped. There had been some attempts, earlier, to move settlers from crowded areas in the other islands to the relatively virgin Mindanao territory. They had not been too successful. On the other hand, certain private economic ventures, particularly in the Bukidnon upland in the northern part of the island, had shown what could be done. The prospect was alluring. Here was Mindanao, with an area about that of the state of Indiana and a population of not more than half a million.

EDCOR set to work. The obstacles were enormous. In the first place there was a relatively unfriendly Moro population in Mindanao, not inclined to see an influx from the north. But that was only the beginning. In the areas chosen for resettlement there were few roads but plenty of forest and jungle. The land was totally different from that of the central Luzon coastal plain, from which most of the "converted" Huks were to be transported. Provision had to be made for tools, work animals, and in the beginning, even for basic rations, since the settlers could not expect to find easy means of subsistence. Land titles had to be established and the cadastral survey was years behind. And there was always the fact that the funds that could be made available were not adequate either for immediate needs or for the immense opportunity that was afforded.

Although this plan was conceived, originally, as a means of defeating the Communists on their own ground, it was to have, eventually, broader implications. In each of the resettlement areas there was always a nucleus of pioneers who were not Huks and had never been. They were carefully chosen ex-Army men, or persons and families from crowded areas who wished to make a move for the better. They were a stabilizing influence, since they had been carefully picked for their role. They may have had something to do with the fact that the desertion and defection rate was remarkably low. In spite of the hardships and handicaps, considerably less than 10 per cent of the settlers gave up.

When Magsaysay assumed the presidency, therefore, he was able to move with even greater confidence into the whole field of land resettlement, not merely as a means of fighting Huks but of providing better conditions for an agricultural population throughout the archipelago. Land resettlement ceased to be a military operation and became the function of the National Resettlement and Rehabilitation Administration. President Magsaysay pushed its program with exceptional vigor and got good results.

Magsaysay had hoped, in the beginning, to launch a frontal attack against the problem of tenant dependence. Under the Agricultural Tenancy Act the government had the authority to purchase large estates, break them up, and make them available for easy-term sale to farmers. In cases of absentee landlordism the government could even bring condemnation proceedings and force the sales. This program was not greatly effective, primarily because the government simply did not have the money to make the purchases. It was a factor in some cases, however, in improving landlord-tenant relationships.

On the other hand, the government had at its disposal a large amount of public land that could be made available for settlement. Qualified farmers had long been able to apply for land patents and move in as independent settlers. The Bureau of Lands functioned to receive applications and issue patents. With the advent of Magsaysay this process was greatly accelerated. More than 33,000 appplications were received in his first year in office. The Bureau, in turn, issued almost 30,000 land patents covering about 600,000 acres. This was more than twice the number that had been issued in the two preceding years combined.

For those, such as the regenerated Huks, who wished to move onto the land, or for others who wished to move from crowded areas to places more favorable, there was the Resettlement Administration that had taken over the operating lines of EDCOR. In that first Magsaysay year it opened several new resettlement projects and moved about 3,000 families onto some 65,000 acres of public land. In addition it allocated 25,000 acres to 1,700 landless families and helped them to move in as independent farmers outside the specific projects.

It is probable that the political and social impact of these operations was more important than its actual economic result. What Magsaysay was doing was to draw the last tooth of the Communists who had always promised, and never provided, "land for the landless." Now the land could actually be provided, and for free men.

But it should always be remembered that genuine "agrarian reform" is not merely a question of freeholding versus landlord ownership. Tenancy is a small part of the problem. Too many persons, in Asia and elsewhere, have been beguiled by Communist propaganda into the belief that land tenure is the be-all and end-all of land reform. It was relatively easy to dramatize this, by force, with the killing of landlords and the confiscation of property. This was the pattern in Red China, and it was apparently what the Huks proposed for the Philippines. But, as Red China has discovered, and as the Philippines could readily demonstrate, the murder of a few landlords did not even scratch the surface of the problem.

This is not to decry honest attachment to the land and pride in the soil. The ambition to own is very real and must always be taken into account. It can be an element of strength and stability in society. In Asia it has been almost instinctive and has been the greatest stumbling block to imposing programs of collectivization. Magsaysay was right to use this feeling as an effective weapon with which to fight Communists. He once said: "When the Filipino can look at his rice field and say, 'this is mine and no man and no government can take it away from me' we will have a happier family of rice-growers, and a richer and better society." Then he paused, and added: "And those Huks, or anyone like them, would never have a chance in the world."

CREDIT AND MARKETS

Merely owning the land, however, was not enough. It had to be productive and the men and women who worked it had to have an equitable return for their labors. Most of all, they had to get out of debt. Rural credit was, and still is, one of the most pressing problems in land reform. Punitive legislation alone was not sufficient to break the hold of the usurer.

If the victim did not complain, there could be no prosecution.

To meet this situation an Agricultural Credit and Cooperative Financing Administration had been set up in the Quirino administration. The farmer could go to this agency and obtain a loan at legal rate and free himself from the debt slavery that had been characteristic. In addition, through cooperative marketing he could be assured of a fair price for his product and be relieved of the strangle hold that the warehousing agent or middleman had exerted upon him.

President Magsaysay accelerated these operations. In his first year in office the government made available in rural credit approximately $9,500,000. That may not seem large by our standards of public expenditures but it was enormous in the Philippines. What was most important was not the volume of the credit but the fact that it was fully legal, at established and reasonable rates of interest, and could give the farmer the help that he needed when he needed it, without his having to mortgage his entire future and that of his children. This was the attempt to break that vicious circle of "in debt from birth to death."

The cooperative marketing idea was not new. It had been tried in a number of ways for many years. The history of cooperatives in the Philippines was no great encouragement. Several of them had been set up as "pilot plants," long before the Japanese invasion, but they had usually withered, after an auspicious start, within a few years. Postwar conditions, however, gave a fresh impetus to the cooperative idea. In the matter of work animals, for example, there was a compulsive need to share. There were not enough carabaos to go around. The government had put a rigid ban upon carabao slaughter but the national herd had not yet been rebuilt. Families joined, therefore, in the use of a carabao. This was not entirely strange, since in earlier and more prosperous days, there had been such a thing as a carabao herd that was used and shared by a whole village. The children had always cared for the animals, which were brought in to work as they were needed. There was individual ownership, to be sure, but there was collective use.

Cooperative marketing was somewhat different. It required an adjustment to a different scale of values. Village economy, based primarily on barter, was one thing, but pooling products for sale in a money market was quite different. With this in mind, the progress that was made was astonishing. Once confidence in the government was restored the farmers were ready to experiment. In the first year of Magsaysay's administration almost two hundred fifty farmers' cooperatives for marketing were set up. They enrolled more than one hundred thousand farmers.

It should be emphasized that there was never any idea of collectivizing Philippine agriculture. The very word was anathema to Magsaysay. "Cooperate, yes," he often said, "but collectivize, never!" The thing that was uppermost in the President's mind was the need to establish the dignity and security of the individual as a person and as a citizen. Government was there to promote that end but not to dictate what could or could not be done.

Next to rural credit in importance was the matter of transportation. The farmer's products were valueless, unless he could get them to market. The major highway network of the Philippines was fairly good once those five thousand bridges could be restored. But access to the main roads was woefully inadequate. Accordingly President Magsaysay emphasized the development of feeder roads and not merely the repair of the main arteries, which was already going forward. Several hundred miles of such roads were put through in Luzon, while the Mindanao projects required the construction of another one hundred fifty miles, merely as a start. The president, after his first year, estimated that his administration had brought well over a hundred communities that had previously been remote into complete accessibility.

THE USE OF WATER

Now came the question of the provision and use of water. It had, really, four phases. Flood control was imperative. Irrigation had to be provided and expanded. Water was the source of power for industrial development. Finally, pollution-free drinking water had to be provided for the barrios. The first three of these interlocked and overlapped. The fourth required special treatment. The new administration threw its full weight behind the projects that had already been initiated and began others of its own.

Two very large irrigation operations were in the construction stage, but work had lagged, to some extent, on both. It was necessary to get them back on schedule. This was not easy, since the difficulty often lay in the failure of small subcontractors to do the required work on time. In the state of the nation message at the end of his first year President Magsaysay reported, however, that work on both was going forward on schedule. They were somewhat different in scope and objective, but equally important.

The first was the Ambuklao project in central Luzon. This embraced the building of a series of four dams across the Agno River. The Agno is a turbulent stream, rising in the Benguet mountains and coming down into the rice lands of the coastal plain. It has a long history of disastrous flooding and the need for control was obvious. The Agno had to be turned into a friend instead of an enemy.

When the work is complete there will be a power installation at each of the dams. The output will not be massive, by our standards, but it will send cheap electricity into the whole of the northern part of the coastal plain. Magsaysay put it this way: "One of our big jobs is to get electric lights into every barrio in the Philippines. Ambuklao is a large step in that direction."

Of even greater importance is the function of this project in irrigation. Much of the rice land of central Luzon is dependent upon the seasonal monsoon rains. This has limited the land to one crop annually. The provision of a stable water supply will make it possible to bring in two crops a year, which can change the whole food-production pattern of the Philippines. The value of double-cropping has been so dramatically demonstrated in Formosa, where there is abundant rice for export, that the Philippines cannot fail to follow the example. But a year-round supply of adequate water is the first requirement. Ambuklao is designed to provide just that. Some American agronomists have gone so far as to state that the rice production of the Philippines can be almost doubled in any year when the right use of this water is made. This will mean, not so much rice for export, but more to eat for every Filipino and a lower price for rice.

The other big project is somewhat different in character. Its primary objective is not irrigation, but power. This is the Maria Cristina development in northern Mindanao, financed largely by private American capital. Some of it is already in operation, although it also fell behind schedule. Magsaysay tried, as best he could, to speed up its completion.

Maria Cristina is a magnificent waterfall, over which Lake Lanao drains into Surigao Strait. It has often been called the Niagara of the Philippines. It has been studied as a power source for more than thirty years. One objection to its development was based on the fear that its natural and scenic beauty would be destroyed. Fortunately, it has been possible to meet that objection. Maria Cristina is still as lovely as it was, but power is being generated. It is possible to get a penstock drop of about three hundred feet, which is ample. And it can be done without changing, in the slightest, the beautiful face of the fall or the various points of vantage from which it can be seen.

The power that is being generated is being used, at this time, primarily for the production of fertilizer. This is a quick way to amortize some of the investment. But the real reason for the Maria Cristina development is that it will eventually provide those electric lights for all of northern Mindanao, and will power the trans-Mindanao electric railway that will bring Cotobato and Davao into closer contact with the other islands and with Manila. Of further importance is the fact that the entire northeast tip of Mindanao is highly mineralized. Agusan Province has an immense residual iron deposit which has been estimated at ten billion tons. It has not been possible to work this resource because of lack of power. Maria Cristina can provide it. One waterfall can change the lives of many persons and perhaps the life of a nation. Magsaysay knew this.

Emphasis on the use of water resources was not confined, however, to these major projects. An effort was made to enlist the rural communities in joint efforts to provide a better water supply. With government aid eleven smaller irrigation projects were undertaken, covering about two hundred thousand acres. These were widely distributed, reaching into 27 provinces. An interesting procedure was adopted in some cases. Magsaysay used government funds to supply cement to community enterprises. The villages, in turn, were required to supply the sand, gravel, and labor. The result was to get a good permanent irrigation structure to replace the mud walls. Once again, the effort was cooperative, not "collectivized." And ninety such systems went into operation in that first year of rebuilding. Wherever it was possible pumps were put in to replace or supplement the old gravity installations.

Then came the problem of providing uncontaminated drinking water for the villages. When the Japanese were driven out, United States Army engineers estimated that more than 80 percent of the village water supply was polluted. In the campaign to restore the health service and to combat endemic parasitic disease and epidemic disease such as typhoid, it was necessary to give the villagers clean water to drink. It was relatively easy to meet a problem such as this in urban areas. Fifty city waterworks projects were laid out and completed. In the villages a different approach was required. The one good source of uncontaminated water was the artesian well. It was necessary to exploit it.

The water-table situation in the Philippines is similar to that which prevails in many parts of New England. At shallow levels there is a substantial water supply, most of it being run-off from the torrential monsoon rains. It can be tapped relatively easily by the dug well. But the shallow dug well had been a proved source of infection in village after village. At deeper levels, however, there is a uniform and stable water supply that can be tapped by drilling. There are two obvious advantages to drilling: the water is of better quality, and well heads can be completely sealed off with concrete so that surface contamination cannot take place.

With these factors in mind Magsaysay threw the whole weight of his administration behind an artesian wells program. Its objective, he said, was to put clean water into every barrio in the Philippines. Actually some work had been done in this field, chiefly under American pressure, before Magsaysay took office. In 1952, for example, 153 artesian wells were drilled. In 1953 the total number was raised to 256, and the roads began to be dotted with signs that said "Drinking Water Ahead." Now the pace was greatly accelerated. At the end of the first year of the new administration 1,300 new artesian wells had been installed.

At this point the government obtained the inspired support of private organizations. Under the initial leadership of a group of public-spirited Chinese residents of Manila, headed by Albino Sycip, Liberty Wells Association was formed. Each new well drilled was a monument to "liberty" and individuals were asked to contribute. Wells could also be designated as memorials to persons or families. The first Liberty Well was a memorial to General Wood. Groups and individuals in the United States also cooperated and the Liberty Wells Association was soon able to match the money outlay that the government could make.

Each one of those wells cost about $600. The Liberty Wells Association raised more than $300,000 in its first year. There was no costly campaign of promotion, for the program had such obvious merit that no pressure was required. There was strong editorial support in both the Philippines and the United States. Liberty Wells is still doing its part of the job and doing it well.

It will be some time before Magsaysay's dream of an artesian well in every barrio can come true. But the start that has been made is impressive. It is already reflected in a greatly improved public health position. The death rate in 1957 was less than 10 out of 1,000. Restoration of the prewar standard is not yet complete, since there is still a too high incidence of parasitic disease, but large gains have been made. In the long run, moreover, the political and social impact of a determined program of good water for the barrios

can be important. This is another of those points at which
the citizen can be convinced that those in authority are on his
side. The idea of government *for* the people still needs emphasis in Asia. Drilling a well is a good way to illustrate it.

ECONOMIC DIFFICULTIES

What has been set down here should have made it plain
that the new administration was in a strong political position
in so far as the people at large were concerned. There was an
air of confidence, of national pride, of steadfast expectation
of better days to come. A new Philippines was emerging
from past disasters.

There were, however, some cold and unpleasant economic
facts of which the villager, proud of his new well, would not
be fully aware. This government was not solvent. Tax collections had been improved, it is true, but the revenue was
not nearly equal to the enormous demands that were being
placed upon the young nation. There was substantial United
States assistance at many points, but it could not solve the
basic economic problem. The Philippines was still running at
a loss. Some of the export products had made a good recovery and reached prewar levels in value but not in volume,
because of higher prices. The war in Korea was a stimulant.
Yet the adverse balance of trade was still running in excess of
$50 million a year in spite of rigid import controls. The
balance of payments in the international field continued to
be adverse and reserves were depleted.

Magsaysay insisted that the domestic administrative budget
of the government must be brought into balance, and this
was done. The actual operating expenses were reduced to the
point that a surplus could be shown. Deficit financing, for
day-to-day operations, had been discarded. But this was only

a beginning. There were programs of amelioration and expansion that required financing. There were debts—national, provincial, and municipal—that had to be paid. When all obligations were taken into account the government was running in the red at the rate of at least $100 million annually, and probably more than that.

It was at this precise time, moreover, that the first restrictive measures of the Philippine Trade Act were to come into effect. The free market would be curtailed. Something, obviously, had to be done.

This was a point, fortunately, at which President Magsaysay did not have to start from scratch. Late in 1953, before he left his office, President Quirino had already urged upon the United States a restudy of the provisions of the Trade Act with a view to possible revision. President Eisenhower had expressed his sympathy and had stated that the United States would be glad to cooperate. Business groups, American and Filipino, both here and in the Philippines, had expressed their grave concern. What was needed was merely a mode of procedure.

General Romulo was again able to play an important part. After he had resigned his post under President Quirino and, then later, entered Magsaysay's camp, he had stated flatly that he would not accept any post, elective or appointive. He was trying, obviously, to stop any rumors that he had made a "deal" with Magsaysay and would get the inevitable reward. But his services were obviously needed and Magsaysay promptly made use of them. He sent Romulo back to the United States early in 1954 as his "personal envoy" to explore this problem of revising the Trade Act.

General Romulo's familiarity with the Washington scene immediately began to pay dividends. A resolution was shortly introduced in Congress to postpone the operative provisions

of the Trade Act—that is, the first imposition of tariffs—
which would have come into effect on July 4, 1954. The
Congress, just before that date, adopted the measure that
set a new date, January 1, 1956, pending a fuller explora-
tion of the whole question. The first breathing space had
been obtained.

As soon as Congress adjourned, the first conferences were
held in Manila in which members of Congress participated.
Those conferences resulted in a recommendation that there
be a formal approach to the question of revision of the Trade
Act and that the United States and the Philippines name suitable representatives to carry out the discussions. This was
done with commendable promptness on both sides.

President Eisenhower named James M. Langley, a newspaper publisher from New Hampshire, to head an American
study group. Mr. Langley was backed up by a formidable
body of economists and Far Eastern experts. His committee,
moreover, had the solid backing and invaluable help of the
Far Eastern section of the State Department.

President Magsaysay chose Senator Laurel to head the
Philippine delegation. It was a gracious gesture and it proved
to be a good choice. Senator Laurel was ingratiating and
disarming. He renewed old friendships at Yale, where he had
been graduated, made peace with General Douglas Mac-
Arthur who had brought him back for trial from Japan on a
collaboration charge, and headed the Philippine group with
dignity and assurance. The group was strong. It included,
first of all, Miguel Cuaderno, Governor of the Central Bank
of the Philippines, who was generally regarded in this country as one of the best economists in Asia. Alongside him was
Senator Gil J. Puyat, chairman of the Philippine Senate
Finance Committee, who represented the legislature's concern with anything that was discussed, since legislative ap-

proval would be required, both there and here. There were
other members of the legislature, both Senate and House, as
well as a number of persons recognized as economic spe-
cialists. It was interesting and important, however, that this
was not a partisan group. It could have been called "non-
party," but the term "multi-party" would have more accurately described it.

They began their discussion with the American panel on
September 20, 1954. They continued with relatively little
interruption until December 15, when their joint statement of
complete agreement was issued. All parties to the discussions
have testified that the atmosphere was always warm and cooperative. There seems to have been no desire to demand or
make undue concessions on either side. It was rather an attempt to come to grips with vital problems that affected the
welfare of both the Philippines and the United States.

The Philippine concern was obvious. It was necessary to
postpone the imposition of a trade restriction program that
would gravely hurt or possibly even paralyze export trade at
a critical time. In addition, the Filipinos felt that the so-called
parity provision was not parity at all, since it operated only
in favor of the Americans, and that the rigid pegging of the
peso to the American dollar, regardless of Philippine consent,
was also, in a way, a denigration of Philippine sovereignty.
What the Filipinos wanted was a re-negotiation of the trade-
access provisions and a redefinition of parity.

The Americans, on the other hand, wanted the Filipinos to
give up their 17 percent tax on dollar exchange, which
actually put a different value on the peso and acted to the
disadvantage of Americans doing business in the Philippines.
There was also the need to assure certain domestic American
interests that they would not be overwhelmed by preferential
imports from the Philippines.

Beyond these restricted points of view was the realization that there was a continuing need for close association between the United States and the Philippines. American assistance was clearly required and would be needed for some years. At the same time, it was also realized that there must be, eventually, some end to Philippine dependence upon the American market if the economic independence of the country was ever to be achieved.

In the end, there was a return to the previously established pattern of adjustment and change, but once more its operative dates were put off. Quotas and progressively imposed tariffs would continue to be the basic pattern of the trade relationship and the ultimate date of complete independence for the Philippines was then set for 1974.

On the question of parity, however, there was a substantial change. It was agreed that any concessions made to Americans in the Philippines must be on a strictly reciprocal basis and that similar benefits should accrue to Filipinos in the United States. This is good sense and good morals. The original parity provisions did not serve to stimulate the flood of American investment in the Philippines that had been hopefully expected but they did serve to give needless offense to the sensibilities of the Filipinos.

In a similar recognition of the self-respect that was involved in the exercise of sovereignty it was agreed to eliminate altogether the American control of the value of the peso. In the Trade Act of 1946 it had been stipulated that any change in the exchange rate of the peso or any restriction on the transfer of dollars could be made by the Philippine government only with the consent of the President of the United States. This provision was thrown out entirely, and at the same time the Philippines agreed to discard the exchange tax, as a reciprocal gesture. It is worthy of note, however, that thus far the Philippines has vigorously resisted any attempt to devalue the peso. It is no longer legally pegged to the American dollar through United States enactment. The Filipinos have, in effect, kept it pegged at two-to-one by their own freely taken action. Mr. Cuaderno, Governor of the Central Bank, is a "hard money" man.

In still another effort to meet this question of Philippine sovereign self-respect a substantial change was made in the structure of the quota system and in the plan for the eventual imposition of the American tariffs. In the Trade Act of 1946 rigid quotas had been fixed on seven Philippine products, and beyond their level, export to the United States was prohibited. In the new agreement a distinction was made between these "absolute" quotas and a new group of "tariff" quotas. The absolute quotas were retained only for sugar and cordage. In each case the levels were kept reasonably high. The tariff quotas were put on cigars, scrap tobacco, coconut oil, and pearl and shell buttons. They provided for a given volume that could be admitted to the United States duty free, but also provided that exports to the United States in excess of that volume could be made simply by paying the full American tariff in each case. The quota on rice was taken off altogether since it was meaningless. The Philippines had no surplus rice to send to the United States, and indeed, would be forced to buy rice from the United States rather than to sell.

The quotas, in turn, were to become the basis for the gradual imposition of the American tariffs. Instead of the progressive year-by-year imposition of a percentage of the American tariffs on all imports from the Philippines, which was the original pattern but which had already been somewhat modified, as we have noted, it was agreed that the volume of products, within the quota limits, that could be admitted duty-free should be progressively reduced on a percentage basis. The periods at which those reductions were to be made was changed from one year to three to simplify the operation. The net effect of these provisions was not materially different. By 1974 Philippine exports to the United States would be nonpreferential and the Philippine dependence upon the free American market would have been forced out of existence. But the method of bringing this about was felt to be more equitable under the new agreement. It gave a better period of adjustment and a chance to diversify markets while a part of the export product was still receiving favored treatment in the United States.

At the same time, to facilitate this readjustment, the ban upon the levy of export taxes by the Philippines was rescinded. This was another step in the direction of economic independence.

A clear summary of what was accomplished was made in a joint statement that was issued by Senator Laurel and Mr. Langley when the agreement was signed:

The United States Delegation and the Philippine Economic Mission, after less than three months of continuous negotiation, have reached agreement on a revision of the 1946 Trade Agreement to be recommended to the Congresses of their two countries. Notwithstanding honest differences of opinion between the Delegations on several of the issues involved, and despite their vigorous presentation by each side, agreement was reached in a relatively short period because of the spirit of friendship and goodwill which persisted throughout the negotiations.

The agreement reached underscores the desire of both nations to put their trade relationship upon a more normal and stable basis. This agreement:

1. Yields to the Philippines control over its own currency by eliminating Article V thereof;
2. Eliminates most absolute quotas on Philippine articles entering the United States;
3. Eliminates quota allocation limitations on Philippine articles subject to quotas in the United States;

4. Makes the enjoyment of parity rights by citizens of either country in the territory of the other reciprocal;
5. Makes imposition of quantitative restrictions on the products of both countries reciprocal;
6. Gives to citizens of either country the right to engage in business activities in the territory of the other on a reciprocal basis;
7. Provides security exceptions in the mutual interest of both countries;
8. Increases tariff preferences for Philippine articles entering the United States;
9. Decreases tariff preferences for United States articles entering the Philippines;
10. Eliminates the prohibition against the imposition of Philippine export taxes;
11. Provides for the elimination of the Philippine exchange tax and the dual rate of exchange it creates by substitution of an import levy to be progressively reduced and eliminated;
12. Permits the Philippines to ask the United States Congress for possible increases in the sugar quota when other nations are permitted to do so; and
13. Increases duty-free quotas on Philippine articles which are subject to declining duty-free quotas in the United States.

It is hoped that with these changes the Philippines will sooner succeed in attaining a better balanced economic status as a free nation. It is also hoped that these changes will further strengthen the friendly and mutually beneficial political and economic relations between the two peoples.

JOSE P. LAUREL, *Chairman*
Philippine Economic Mission
to the United States

JAMES M. LANGLEY, *Chairman*
United States Delegation for
Philippine Trade Negotiations

December 15, 1954

The required legislative approval was quickly given in the Philippines. In the United States the congressional processes moved more slowly but in the end, after some debate and some minor modifications, the revisions were approved. A better framework for Philippine-American trade relationships had been set up.

Both in Manila and Washington there was repeated emphasis upon the cordiality that had marked the negotiations. There was an atmosphere of goodwill throughout and it was felt that a new rapport had been established. Credit for this should go in the first place to the high quality of the men who sat down together to thresh out the problems. Senator Laurel, in several public appearances in the United States, made an excellent impression, and Mr. Cuaderno was respected everywhere as an outstanding economist. The American group, similarly, was highly praised by a number of officials and business men who testified in the congressional hearings to its thoughtful and thorough approach to the complicated questions that were raised.

What should not be overlooked is that some of the success in this meeting of minds should be attributed to the presence (in the background) of the personality of Ramon Magsaysay. His election had given a new confidence in the stability and security of the Philippine government. He had given the firmest support to the men who were representing that government. There was a new feeling of assurance that honorable commitments could be made and that they would be honorably respected. The revision of the Trade Act was not directly of Magsaysay's making. But the spirit in which it was done stemmed in no small part from him.

"PERSONAL" GOVERNMENT

This towering personality of Magsaysay had elements of both strength and weakness as far as government was concerned. The Filipinos had a real leader in whom they could repose love and trust. This was an element of great strength. But they also had a chief executive who found it difficult to adjust his office to the dreary routine of getting things done in the routine way. The Filipinos had chosen the right man at the right time but they had headed him straight into difficulty.

From the beginning, Magsaysay found it hard to leave a job to anyone else. He was quite willing to delegate authority and demand responsibility, in the military sense, but he could not divorce himself from the personal interest in every case that came to his attention. As a result he tried to do too much. He saw too many persons. He had asked for "bare feet in the Palace," which was all to the good. But there were too many of them. If he heard of trouble in a distant barrio he was inclined to take off on a moment's notice to see at first hand what the difficulty was. It was not that he did not trust subordinates. It was rather that he could not detach himself from any problem, however trivial, that might be raised. He soon found himself working on a twenty-hour-a-day schedule. He had enough physical stamina to take it but it was a strain on the nervous system.

More than that, he loathed the paper work, which is unfortunately part of any executive office. He was impatient of dreary detail; he looked for short cuts. Personal antagonisms were the inevitable result. He had a vision and a sense of mission and was likely to be abrupt with any person who seemed to stand in the way. That very quality made him loved by his people—and it made him highly respected in the United States—but it did not ease his way in the Philippine Congress.

The post-election honeymoon was soon over. Before he had served out his second year he was obliged to call the

Congress back into special session even to enact the necessary budget. At this stage he once laughingly remarked:
"You know, I think I could go to the country and get a
four-to-one majority for anything that I asked for; but I
have a dickens of a time getting a majority of one in the
Senate."

There were reasons for this. Most of the senior legislators
represented a political and social philosophy quite different
from that of the President. It was not that they were un-
progressive, but simply that they saw progress in different
terms. Much of Magsaysay's social program had to do with
reforms that dealt with land tenure and land use, but a considerable part of the support for his party and its leading
representatives came from the landlord class. It was small
wonder that some of the appropriation proposals met with
consistent resistance.

In addition, there was a strong group of producer interests
represented in the Congress, who felt that the import and
exchange controls were too rigid and worked to their
eventual disadvantage. They introduced legislation to modify
those controls. President Magsaysay, with strong support from
Mr. Cuaderno, informed the House that it could pass the
proposed bill if it liked, but that he would certainly veto it.
The measure was dropped, temporarily.

Some of the larger aspects of the Magsaysay policies came
under sharp criticism from Senator Recto. Vice President
Garcia, in his capacity also as Foreign Secretary, had issued
a policy statement that seemed to endorse an "Asia for the
Asians" outlook and was interpreted in some circles as unfavorable to the United States. President Magsaysay promptly
repudiated the announcement and had no difficulty in making
it plain that he and his Vice President were not at odds. But
Senator Recto took up the issue and began a series of at-

tacks upon the President on the ground that Magsaysay was
too pro-American. Mr. Recto urged a much greater degree
of both economic and political independence from the United
States than had obtained up to that point. In some quarters
it was charged that Mr. Recto was playing directly into
neutralist and Communist hands by his position. This was
certainly not his intention, but it was his intention to oppose the President on major matters of policy. The conflict
eventually became so sharp that Magsaysay refused to endorse Mr. Recto's candidacy for reelection to the Senate, and,
in effect, read him out of the party. Mr. Recto regained his
seat by a slim margin and subsequently entered the next
presidential campaign as the candidate of a new party.

Thus the road to recovery was painfully traveled. There
was obstruction at various points. There was always a per-
sistent lack of adequate funds to do the things that needed to
be done. There was some recovery in trade, and the operation of the revised Act began to diminish some of the dependence upon the United States. The building and rebuilding
boom continued. But reserves were still too low, and the
controls had to be kept. Magsaysay continued to be optimistic,
but he knew that he was grappling with big problems.

The greatest victory, however, had been won. There was
a new vitality in the political and social state. There was a
renewed sense of democracy and of government by consent.
There was a new pride in being a Filipino. Some of this was
translated, as we shall see later, into a fresh Philippine influence in foreign affairs. There was a sense that the Philippines, somehow, was coming of age. The growing pains were
unpleasant, but there was the knowledge that they reflected
growth.

Nine

THE PHILIPPINES
IN THE FREE WORLD

One of the most interesting, and in the long run perhaps very significant, aspects of the growth of the young Philippine state is its emergence on the world scene. At the same time that these domestic struggles were making the life of the republic precarious, the clear and certain voice of the Philippines was being raised in world councils. That there was an aspiration to leadership in East Asia was clearly apparent. It soon became plain, also, that the Philippines could speak with some authority on the position of the small nations, on the problems of a disappearing colonialism, and on the relationship between East and West.

Some of the vigor and independence of the Philippine positions and statements were, probably unconsciously, provoked by the attitude of the Soviet Union and the Communist satellites. It was the Communist party line that the Philippines was not truly independent and could act only as a puppet of the United States. It was in the interest of truth and the cause of freedom that the Filipinos stoutly resisted such an accusation. They undertook to make it unmistakably clear that they spoke, without hesitation, not as an American dependency of sorts, but as a free Asian people.

The Soviet attitude and propaganda line was clearly indicated. At the San Francisco meeting that set up the United Nations, Molotov angrily shook his finger at the Filipino delegation and asked, "Why are they here? Their country is not even independent." Technically, this was true. Philippine independence was not consummated until the following year. But the Philippines—and India, to which Molotov also objected—symbolized the emergence of these peoples as a new force in Asia, a force for freedom. There was confidence in those countries, and among most of the prospective members of the United Nations, that this free status was shortly to be achieved and that their voice should be heard.

It was true that on many subsequent occasions when there was an alignment of nations on an issue the Philippines could usually be found in the same camp as the United States. But this could have been expected. The structure of the two governments was similar and their aims were likely to be parallel if not identical. There was, however, no suggestion of coercion on the part of the United States. The Philippines was completely free to take its own courses of action and if these differed from those of the United States, as they sometimes did, there was neither criticism nor complaint.

Naturally, by far the largest sector of Philippine "foreign" relations after 1946 concerned relations with the United States. The association had been, and continued to be, so close that the word foreign may seem strange, but it is literally and technically correct. The most important problems that had to be solved concerned those relations with the United States, which had become, as far as the Philippines was concerned, a "foreign" power. We have already seen how some changes, especially in the economic field, were brought about in this Philippine-American relationship. They were the product of many men and many minds but the central policy that evolved was dictated by what Mr. Nehru once called "the hard logic of circumstances." The Philippines was free to contest with the United States at any given point, but neither Filipinos nor Americans could successfully contest with the cold facts in the case. This did not make the Philippines dependent upon the United States in determining courses of action. The Soviet charge was false.

Fortunately the Philippines had, in the United Nations, an excellent instrument through which to assert its independence and exert its influence. Fortunately, also, it had the right man for the job in General Carlos P. Romulo.

THE ROLE OF ROMULO

It is impossible to discuss the place of the Philippines on the world stage in the first decade of its independence without emphasis upon the role of Romulo and without repeated reference to him. In his various capacities as Resident Commissioner, "special envoy," Foreign Secretary, Ambassador to the United States, personal representative of President Magsaysay, and always chief Philippine represenative in the United Nations, Romulo was a central figure in most of the policy decisions that were made and most of the actions that were taken. In many ways he could and did represent the "foreign policy" of the Philippines. More than that, he could always make it clearly understood. He was, above all, articulate.

General MacArthur had recognized this quality. At the height of a successful career as a newspaper editor and publisher, Romulo was attached to MacArthur's staff, at the outbreak of the war, as an intelligence and public relations officer. When the fall of Bataan was imminent, General MacArthur gave him another and highly important assignment. He took him out of the Philippines and sent him to the United States to present the Philippine cause to the American people. MacArthur could not have chosen a better man.

Romulo had been educated partly in the United States, and had received his M.A. from Columbia. (He was later to be honored by so many American universities that someone laughingly applied to him the quip that was made about the late Dr. John Finley, saying that he "had more degrees than a thermometer.") He had been an international officer of the Rotary Club. He was one of the most eloquent speakers ever to have been developed in a veritable nation of orators. Most of all, he knew Americans and how to get along with them.

In those war years he was tireless. He wrote three books and many magazine articles. The largest part of his work, however, was on the platform. He made hundreds of addresses and went to every part of the country. He spoke to thousands of persons who had never seen a Filipino. He made friends everywhere, not merely for himself but for the Philippines. Without detracting in the least from his personal skills and accomplishments, it should also be said that he was speaking in a good cause. He was a champion of human liberty. He could make personal and vivid some of the abstractions for which his auditors might have been trying to find words.

These experiences were valuable to him when he took his place as a spokesman for free Asian peoples in the United Nations. He had headed a strong Philippine delegation to the Convention on Freedom of Information that was held in Geneva in 1948. In 1949 he was elected president of the General Assembly.

His tenure in that office was a triumph. All his forensic and parliamentary abilities were brought into play. The sessions were uniformly lively and it seemed to many persons that a new vitality had been brought into what had been routine meetings of a debating society. The General

Assembly is now recognized as a real force in the United Nations structure. Some of the credit for the gradual shift in emphasis in the operations of the organization should go to the effect of the personality of Romulo who made its deliberations often come really alive. But it should be noted that this was more significant than a personal victory for Romulo. His own prestige was unquestionably enhanced, but with that came a new stature for the small nations. One of their number could preside over the deliberations of the international organization and make a distinctive contribution to orderly process and free discussion. The United Nations had still to establish itself as a world body. What Romulo was able to do was a large step toward that end.

In the United Nations it was inevitable that some aspects of Philippine policy should be reflected in repeated clashes with the Soviet Union and the Communist satellites. This was not because the Philippines was aligned with any bloc, but simply because the Filipinos had espoused the cause of individual and national freedom, both for themselves and for others. Moreover, they were engaged, at home, in a struggle for survival against a Communist-led rebellion. Under those circumstances they could have little sympathy with most of the points of view set forth by the Soviet Union. In a large majority of the issues which were discussed in the United Nations, the Philippines could be expected to speak and vote against the Soviet Union. The forensic tilts between Romulo and Vishinsky (who was also no mean orator) became a recognized feature of the Assembly sessions.

A climax in this opposition of points of view came when the Communists invaded the Republic of Korea in July, 1950. The Philippines immediately became an outstanding spokesman in the United Nations for the Korean cause. But its support was more than merely verbal. When the Security

Council called upon member states to furnish what help
they could to the Koreans to halt the invasion, the Philippines was the first country to join the United States in the
offer of military assistance. In spite of the fact that the fight
against the Huks had reached a critical point and that the
Philippines might have said with good reason that no men
could be spared for another country, a military force was
promptly dispatched to Korea. General MacArthur was delighted to have Filipinos under his command again, and, as
he confidently expected, they gave an excellent account of
themselves. It was more than a token force.

In another sense, however, it was importantly a "token."
These were Asian troops fighting in behalf of fellow Asians.
They were the best possible answer to the reiterated Communist charge that there had been "imperialist" and "colonialist" intervention in Korea. It is true that the Filipinos
went to Korea at the behest of the United Nations. They were
acting in and through a world organization. At the same time,
both in Korea and in the Philippines, there was the feeling
that there was something rather special about this action. It
symbolized a union of free Asians in the fight against communism. President Syngman Rhee was quick to recognize
this fact and he spoke in the warmest terms of appreciation
of the Philippine assistance. There was a meeting of minds
as well as of troops.

The idea that the free Asian states should somehow unite
to defend themselves against Communist aggression was not
a new one in the Philippines. Especially was it not new to
Romulo. Even before the Korean invasion he had been hard
at work on plans and programs to bring the Southeast Asian
states together in a community of interest. Gradually some
of these plans took concrete form.

THE BAGUIO CONFERENCE

Early in 1950, in response to the insistent urging of Romulo, Philippine President Quirino extended an invitation to neighboring countries to come to the Philippines to discuss questions of common concern. Six countries responded favorably. They were India, Pakistan, Ceylon, Thailand, Indonesia, and Australia. Their representatives met with the Filipinos at Baguio in May of that year.

In the back of Romulo's mind there was undoubtedly the idea of the eventual formation of some sort of firm alliance. This proved to be quite impossible at that time. India and Indonesia accepted the invitation only on condition that political questions should not be raised and that there should be no thought of political commitments. Economic problems could be discussed if they did not too greatly overlap the political, but the emphasis was to be upon a "cultural" community of interest. As a result the meeting was frequently referred to as the "Cultural Conference."

This does not mean that it was without significance. A group of Asian states, and Australia, were brought together under Philippine leadership to explore matters of common concern. A first step was taken toward the establishment of some sort of unity of purpose. It should be remembered that each of these states, with the exception of Thailand, had been oriented for a long period toward one or another Occidental power. They had had closer relationships with Britain, The Netherlands, or the United States than with each other. In a sense, therefore, the Baguio Conference was part of the process of getting acquainted with neighbors who had long lived in the same community but had been on no more than nodding terms.

It was agreed in the conference that these nations should

continue vigorously to press for a better interchange of ideas
and a larger area of understanding. In one area there was
complete agreement, and curiously—in the light of the pre-
conference declaration that no political questions should arise
—this area was political. In the end, the conference members expressed themselves in full support of self-determination
for all nations. There had been considerable anti-colonial
overtones in a number of the speeches and discussions, as
could have been expected. But the idea of possible unity
against Communist imperialism and colonialism was never
allowed to come to the surface.

For its own reasons, some of which seem obscure, the
United States gave little sympathy or support of any kind to
this conference. Washington exhibited a decided coolness
toward the whole idea, when it was first broached, and subsequently made it plain that this was entirely a Philippine
affair, undertaken upon Philippine initiative and totally un-
related to the American interest in the Philippines or in
Southeast Asia. Some of this attitude may have come about
as a response to Philippine criticism of the defense measures
that the United States was taking in respect to the area.
Mutual defense agreements with Australia and New Zealand
were in process of construction at the time, and the groundwork was being laid for the eventual peace treaty and defense pact with Japan. The Philippines had been outspokenly
critical of the fact that these defense talks were going forward, among the Western powers, and that they directly
affected the area in which the Philippines was concerned
without any consultation with the Philippines. What the
United States was doing, in effect, was setting up a group of
bilateral defense agreements, whereas some of the Filipinos—
especially Romulo—were thinking in terms of regional defense. Apparently it was felt in Washington that the time

was not ripe to go into such planning and it may have been feared that the Asian conference at that stage might be an impediment to the actual programs that were going forward. It was not until four years later that this position was dramatically reversed.

It is doubtful, in any case, that strong United States support for this conference would have brought about the effective unity for defense that Romulo had in mind. But when, in 1954, the United States moved vigorously to create a unified defense organization for Southeast Asia the opposition of the neutralists had so greatly crystallized that its possibilities were limited.

MUTUAL DEFENSE PACT

Meanwhile, the United States had concluded a formal mutual defense pact with the Philippines in 1951. It provided that an attack on the Philippines would be considered a threat to the security of the United States, and that the latter would act in defense of the Philippines in accordance with "constitutional processes." The apparent limitation embodied in that last phrase was inserted because of some congressional opposition to military pacts that would be self-enforcing, on the ground that they would abridge the "sole" power of Congress to declare war. President Truman had been bitterly criticized in some quarters for his dispatch of troops to Korea without prior action of Congress. When Mr. Truman subsequently referred to the Korean conflict as a "police action" and not an act of war, his statement was greeted with open derision. But not all of the criticism of Mr. Truman was unfriendly. Many of the persons who were solidly in favor of what had been done in Korea felt that the method by which it was done was of doubtful constitutionality. Accordingly, the formula of "within constitutional processes" was evolved and was written into subsequent agreements.

In the case of the Philippines the argument was largely academic. The United States had, and expected to retain, substantial naval and air bases in the Philippines. The Philippines obviously could not and would not be attacked without an assault on those bases. That the United States would defend them was obvious, and in so doing it would be defending the Philippines. There were, moreover, other reasons for United States protection: the long association of the Philippines with the United States, the continuing interest of the United States in the young nation, and the manifest concern of the United States to prevent further Communist aggression in Southeast Asia.

Nevertheless, it was felt in the Philippines that this Mutual Defense Pact was too nebulous and that no steps had been taken properly to implement it. Accordingly, early in 1954 a joint Philippine-American defense council was set up to effect the proper implementation. When it met in Manila, prior to the larger Southeast Asia conference, the United States was represented by John Foster Dulles, Secretary of State. The Philippines was represented by Vice President Garcia, acting in his concurrent capacity of secretary of foreign affairs. The terms of the implementation were readily agreed upon and Mr. Dulles made the formal statement that the United States defense of the Philippines would be automatic. The question of the exact status of the American bases was not, however, solved at this point, and it continued to be, as we have noted, a troublesome problem. But the Filipinos felt that they had received fresh and much-needed reassurance.

This was the situation that obtained when the Manila Conference met in September, 1954. The United States had made defense commitments to the Republic of Korea, to Japan, to Nationalist China, to the Philippines, and to Australia and New Zealand. There had been, however, no regional commitment made by the United States or any other power. There were fingers on the hand but there was no palm.

Early in 1954 the French position in Indo-China deteriorated rapidly. The fall of the citadel of Dienbienphu was imminent. A conference at Geneva was called to discuss both the Korean impasse and the question of a settlement in Indo-China. Dienbienphu was taken by the Communists before it came into session. Mr. Dulles felt strongly that some sort of regional agreement on defense should be reached before any of the representatives went to Geneva, and he proposed such an alignment among the free powers. He met strong opposition, especially from Britain. It was felt by the British, and by some others, that the best policy was to wait to see what could be accomplished at Geneva before further pacts of any sort were made. The United States was an "observer," not a member of the conference at Geneva, and was not a signatory to any of the agreements that were reached.

At Geneva, the case of Korea was quickly disposed of. The free Koreans proposed, in full support of the position that the United Nations had repeatedly taken, that Korean unification be brought about through a free popular election under United Nations supervision. This was rejected out of hand by the Communists, and since there was no further valid basis for discussion the Koreans promptly and properly walked out of the negotiations.

In the case of Indo-China, a much more complex formula was argued and finally agreed upon by a majority. It was accepted that there should be a temporary partition between North (Communist) and South (free) Vietnam, and that in two years' time a popular election should be held to effect a unification. There was to be a complete cease-fire, and freedom of movement was to be granted to those who wished to go from one area to the other. France agreed upon a complete withdrawal of any claims to sovereignty, and prepared to take out her troops.

Significantly, the United States did not accept this "settlement." Even more important was its prompt rejection by the Vietnamese in the South. If that "settlement" were to be made, it was obvious that it would have to be imposed, and imposed to the Communist advantage. The actual threat of Communist aggression and expansion was heightened rather than lessened by the presumptive agreement at Geneva. It could take a legalistic form.

THE FORMATION OF SEATO

Two immediate effects of the Geneva fiasco were the speeding-up of plans for a regional defense conference in Southeast Asia and the establishment of some sort of mutual defense organization. Mr. Dulles renewed his proposals. At this point he received outspoken support from President Magsaysay and Ambassador Romulo. Magsaysay suggested Manila as the logical site for any such conference and prepared to issue the invitations that were needed. Romulo made a speaking tour in the United States urging that such a meeting be held and that it go even beyond the framing of a military alliance and proclaim a "Pacific Charter." The plans were debated briefly in Congress and received warm support.

When it came to actual participation in such a meeting, however, its proponents ran into strong and bitter opposition in Asia. Invitations were formally issued to all "threatened" states. They were indignantly rejected in India and

Indonesia, both on the ground that no threat existed and because of opposition to any such pacts or alignments. Burma and Ceylon followed India's lead. The proposed alliance or organization was openly anti-Communist and the neutralist movement had gained full momentum in these countries.

There was still another obstacle. Great Britain, France, Australia, New Zealand, and the United States were to be represented. They were not Southeast Asian nations, in any sense, but merely non-Asian powers who proposed to continue to exert some influence and even authority in the area. The cry of "neo-colonialism" was raised by the neutralists and the proposed meeting was stigmatized as a subterfuge to perpetuate alien rule in eastern and southern Asia. This cry was joyfully taken up by the Communists who, naturally, had every reason to oppose any strengthening of opposition to them.

In the end, therefore, the conference was considerably less "Asian" than might have been hoped and wished. From South Asia only Pakistan came quickly and boldly into the agreement. (This was to have increasing significance as time went on since Pakistan was also a part of the Baghdad Pact and thus became a bridge between the two ultimate defense commitments.) Thailand supported the plan from the beginning and gladly joined the conference. This was logical, since Thailand was most directly in the line of march of the southward Communist expansion. It seemed likely that Thailand might well be the one country most immediately in need of defense help. The Philippines was the third Asian state. Its membership and, in some respects, its leadership were inevitable. The idea of regional association had been pushed by the Philippines for some years. There was no mistrust of colonialism in the Philippines. The Philippines, also, could be a bridge. More than that, the Filipinos were just emerging from a desperate fight against Communist subversion and revolt and were keenly aware of the threat that some other Asian states seemed to ignore. Without the Philippines as a sort of center of gravity a Southeast Asia Treaty Organization would have been much more difficult, if not impossible. The very choice of Manila as the place for forming the organization was inevitable and significant.

At the same time, the participation of the non-Asian states was in each case logical. France had already renounced any claim to sovereignty in Indo-China but could not eschew a vital interest in the security of the area. Britain rightly represented Malaya, Singapore, North Borneo, Brunei, and Sarawak. Malaya had not then yet achieved independence and could not associate itself with the organization in its own right. Australia and New Zealand had had recent experience with a threat to their security from the Japanese advance through this very area. More than that, Australia was actually supplying some contingents of troops to fight the Communist terrorists in Malaya as a part of the Commonwealth obligation. The commitments of the United States were obvious. Also, it should be remembered, these non-Asian powers would be obliged to provide a substantial part of the physical and economic strength that would make Southeast Asia's defense possible. Pakistan, Thailand, and the Philippines readily recognized this and made no objection to the preponderance of non-Asian representation. It was, however, suggested that the treaty that was to ensue might more properly be called the Manila Pact than the Southeast Asia Mutual Defense Agreement. This was not a vital point of difference, and both terms were subsequently used.

Eventually, as we shall see, this non-Asian participation came to have great importance in another way. When agreements on broad policy apart from defense were reached, and when statements of intent and purpose were proclaimed, they represented a true meeting of Asian and non-Asian minds. East and West had been brought together to meet a common danger in a fashion somewhat different from anything that had happened previously, and their joint declaration of objectives was ultimately to be unique.

The ease and speed with which agreement was reached was astonishing. The conference was in session for only three days. A multilateral treaty was approved and a Pacific Charter promulgated. There were differences, but not dissension. An important point of discussion was the actual form that the organization established by the treaty should take. Britain, Australia, and—to a lesser extent—the Philippines felt that NATO provided a suitable model that might well be followed. This comprised the establishment of a central command with committed and disposable forces at any given time. The United States opposed this view, holding that the organization should be more flexible, with striking forces ready to go into action but without a "staff and command" structure. One reason for this was political. The logical place at which to set up a central command, such as existed in NATO, would have been Singapore. But this would have given fresh ammunition to those who were attacking the regional defense idea as a form of colonialism, since Singapore was unmistakably a British Crown Colony. At that time it was still hoped that some other Asian states might wish to join the alliance. A command post at Singapore might be a deterrent. It is also likely that the United States, with military units in many parts of the world, did not wish to commit further specific troops at any one point.

With good grace, the British, Australians, and Filipinos withdrew from their position and allowed the United States viewpoint to prevail. The central military authority of the organization became "consultative" rather than "command," and was merely one function of the secretariat of the organization. This secretariat was to be set up in Bangkok, not Singapore. Unquestionably, this decision had its military disadvantages, yet its political advantages may, in the long run, outweigh them.

What was thus agreed upon and established was perhaps somewhat less strong than the NATO commitments. In the treaty that was reached it was set forth that an aggressive threat in the area was a danger to all and that each should act, again "within constitutional processes," to assist in meeting the threat. It was not a firm "offensive and defensive" military alliance. It was an agreement that all these nations could act in harmony. Moreover, it was made plain that its protection could and would be extended to other states that wished to join. Subsequently this provision was extended to include free Vietnam as an area to which the defensive provisions of the organization applied, although the Republic of Vietnam, under the terms of the Geneva agreement (to which it was not signatory), could not presumably become an active member of the organization itself.

Thus SEATO was formed. It has often been asserted that there are no "teeth" in the organization. This criticism is short-sighted. Its members are firmly pledged to mutual assistance and it is extremely unlikely that the "constitutional processes" of any one of them will prevent the giving of such assistance. The organization has sometimes been derided as being a merely consultative body. But consultation in the cause of common defense is one of the things that is badly needed. It is well known that one of the reasons for the speed and success of the Japanese invasion of Southeast Asia was the lack of adequate prior consultation among those who were obliged to defend themselves. The danger to all had not been sufficiently recognized and there were no joint plans for meeting it. The Southeast Asia Treaty Organization provides the machinery through which to prevent a repetition of such a disaster. The consultations are going on continuously; they are discussions of the common threat and how best to meet it. More than that, they represent, as we have indicated, a meeting of minds between East and West and it is imperative that this meeting be a continuous process.

The Manila Conference did not stop, however, with a mere military alliance. It went into the political field and reached a declaration of joint purposes that may, in the long run, be even more significant than the military agreement. It wrote the Pacific Charter.

THE PACIFIC CHARTER

This was Romulo's special project and chief object of enthusiasm from the beginning. It was in no sense an improvisation. Three years before the meeting in Manila, Romulo had drafted the outline of such a charter on the back of a menu in a New York restaurant. The final document did not differ, materially, from that first draft. Six months before the Treaty Organization came into shape, Romulo and President Magsaysay went over the text of a proposed declaration of purposes to be delivered whenever such a meeting should take place, and Magsaysay made it public as an objective in Philippine policy. It was on the basis of this text that Romulo made his appeal to the American public. What was finally adopted was no essential deviation.

It was Romulo's position, strongly supported by Magsaysay, that military commitments alone were not enough to meet the Communist threat. It was felt that a clear declaration of good intent was necessary to offset the continuous barrage of Communist propaganda about colonialism. If Western powers and Eastern states could agree to such a declaration a firmer basis for any military alliance could be reached.

Actually, by this time, most of the "colonial" positions of the Western powers had already disappeared. France was in the process of getting out of Indo-China permanently. India, Pakistan, Ceylon, and Burma were no longer parts of a British Empire. The Dutch had transferred sovereignty in Indonesia. The Philippines had become independent. But the Communists continued to exploit the issue of colonialism as if none of these events had taken place. In some of the former colonies, moreover, they could always count upon whipping up enthusiasm by attacks on "imperialism" and thus sow the seeds of distrust of the motives of the free Western states that had formerly been colonial powers.

Accordingly, it was proposed in Manila that all the signatories to the treaty commit themselves to the principle of "self-government and independence" for all peoples. The British and Australians wisely suggested that this declaration be modified and limited to the independence of "all countries whose peoples desire it and are able to undertake its responsibilities." It was readily agreed that this was no more than common sense and there was no further obstacle to the adoption of a Pacific Charter. This is its final form.

The Delegates of the United States, Great Britain, France, Australia, New Zealand, Pakistan, Thailand and the Philippines,

Desiring to establish a firm basis for common action to maintain peace and security in Southeast Asia, and the Southwest Pacific,

Convinced that common action to this end, in order to be worthy and effective, must be inspired by the highest principles of justice and liberty,

Do Hereby Proclaim:

FIRST, in accordance with provisions of the United Nations Charter, they uphold the principle of equal rights and self-determination of peoples, and they will earnestly strive by every peaceful means to promote self-government and to secure independence of all countries whose peoples desire it and are able to undertake its responsibilities;

SECOND, they are each prepared to continue taking effective practical measures to insure conditions favorable to the orderly achievement of the foregoing purposes in accordance with their constitutional procedures;

THIRD, they will continue to cooperate in economic, social and cultural fields in order to promote higher living standards, economic progress and social well-being in this region;

FOURTH, as declared in the Southeast Asia Collective Defense Treaty, they are determined to prevent or counter by appropriate means any attempt in the treaty area to subvert their freedom or to destroy their sovereignty or territorial rights.

It was, and still is, Romulo's view that these political commitments may, in the long run, prove to be even more important than the military commitments of the Southeast Asia Treaty Organization. This may not be the case because, as we have pointed out, the "colonial" position was already abandoned, except by the Soviet Union and its many colonies. What Britain has done in Ghana and Malaya, and France in Morocco and Tunisia, and what both are trying to do in Cyprus and Algeria, gives the Pacific Charter something of an ex post facto air. At the time, however, this question of colonialism was very much alive and a clear commitment could do no harm.

Within only a few months this declaration of good purpose was to form the basis for the electrifying reply of General Romulo to Prime Minister Nehru at the later Bandung Conference. It was possible for him to defend the Southeast Asia Treaty Organization as a specifically "anti-colonialist" alliance that could protect Asian states against the spread of Communist colonialism. It is probable that the Pacific Charter played an important part in changing the ultimate tenor of the conference at Bandung; it certainly made possible the exercise of some of the Philippine leadership that was felt there.

THE BANDUNG CONFERENCE

In December, 1954, the prime ministers of India, Pakistan, Burma, Ceylon, and Indonesia issued invitations to twenty-four other Asian and African states to meet with them in a conference to discuss matters of common concern. The time was set for the subsequent April, and Indonesia was to be the host nation. The site of the conference was the beautiful mountain resort of Bandung, in Java.

This was presumably to be a meeting of the newly independent or emerging states from all parts of what had been the colonial world. The guest list was not quite inclusive. Israel, for example, was pointedly omitted because the Arab states would not have attended if Israel were represented. South Africa was not among the African nations invited because the conference obviously intended to bring up the question of racial discrimination there. Nationalist China was left out for two reasons: because of Premier Nehru's personal antipathy to President Chiang Kai-shek, and because Red China's Premier and foreign minister, Chou En-lai, was expected to be one of the lions of the gathering. Perhaps also in deference to Premier Chou, the free Republic of Korea was not invited (nor was the Communist regime in northern Korea). Vietnam, however, had delegations both from the free South and the Communist North.

In contrast to the Manila meetings, no Western power was

asked to take part. This conference was not intended to establish a better understanding between East and West, but rather to consolidate the non-Western groups. This fact has led to the frequent suggestion that the Bandung roster was made up on the basis of pigmentation, that is, that no "whites" were wanted. This is probably an oversimplification, although it is true that the conference agreed upon a strong protest against any form of racial discrimination. What is more likely is that the sponsors of the meeting wished to avoid, if possible, the clash between the free world and the Communist world. The Soviet Union was certainly an "Asian" power. The United Kingdom and France were certainly still powers. But Prime Minister Nehru and his associates had no intention of making this conference a battle ground between the two great ideologies.

Indeed, it quickly became apparent that one of the purposes in the minds of the inviting powers was to promote the cause of neutralism. Chou En-lai had just concluded his persuasive tour of India and some of the Southeast Asian states. The "five principles," chief of which was "peaceful coexistence," were much in the air. Premier Chou was scheduled for top billing at Bandung to preach his gospel. And he had the powerful support of Prime Minister Nehru.

It didn't work out that way. An unofficial steering committee including Mr. Nehru, Prime Minister U Nu of Burma, and Colonel Nasser of Egypt, with the prior blessing of Chou En-lai, had decided that there should be no opening policy statements in the conference. This was presumably to avoid the possibility of an early clash of opinion. When the delegates assembled, however, this plan was promptly overruled. The various states proposed to deliver their uninhibited declarations right from the start. Mr. Nehru retired from the discussion in an air of pique, and Chou En-lai went

into the background to exercise his personal charm as best
he could.

Sir John Kotelawala, Prime Minister of Ceylon, forthwith
broke the convention wide open. In a stirring address he
declared that the peoples who had suffered under any form of
subjection should rightly oppose all forms of subjection,
colonialist or Communist. This put a new light on neutralism.
The biggest gun of the neutralists was spiked at the outset.
If to be neutral was to be anti-Western, it had to be anti-
Communist as well. Sir John was followed in the same vein
by Iraq's foreign minister, Fadhel Jamali. South Vietnam's
Minister of Planning, Nguyen Van Thoai, took the floor to
sustain this point of view from the background of the experience of his own country. Prince Wan Waithayakon of
Thailand concurred. General Romulo followed with the
blunt declaration that "in our view a puppet is a puppet."
North Vietnam, and even Chou En-lai, could well have
winced.

In the end the neutralists lost ground, at least temporarily,
instead of gaining it at Bandung. The hard core of the
neutralist position is the assumption that the free world and
the Communist world, specifically the United States and the
Soviet Union, should be equated as equally dangerous. In
actual practice, however, there has been a reluctance to
assess the predatory character of the Communist drive for
domination. The fact that Western colonialism is largely a
thing of the past and that Communist colonialism is very
much a thing of the present and future seems to have been
lost upon some of the exponents of the "middle course."
The Bandung Conference served to bring some of these
aspects of the situation back into a better perspective and the
delegates were eventually persuaded to declare their opposi-

tion to aggression from whatever source. In their final communiqué the term "co-existence" does not appear, nor are the "five principles" mentioned. The declarations against racism and in favor of the principle of self-determination are moderate and sound.

Two things happened in the late stages of the conference that were to receive wide attention. Chou En-lai, outside the actual deliberations, made the statement that the Peiping regime was ready and willing to make a peaceful accommodation with the United States. This was apparently done for its effect upon the delegates, to convince them that it was Red China that was peace-loving and flexible and that it was the United States that was obdurate. The United States properly called for some concrete evidence that Premier Chou was actually setting forth a new policy line. Subsequent events have proved, clearly enough, that the Bandung statement was a mere propaganda maneuver.

The second development came when Premier Nehru broke his self-imposed silence with a frontal attack upon the Southeast Asia Treaty Organization. He declared that it had "diminished the climate of peace" that had been reached at Geneva, that it was in contravention of certain regional nonaggression agreements, that it violated the spirit of the United Nations Charter, and that it contributed to the international tension that he and others were trying to relieve. Mr. Nehru was actually restating positions that he had taken previously. He was opposed to regional pacts and alignments. He was opposed to commitments that were specifically anti-Communist, although he was vigorously fighting the Communists in his own country. He was opposed to the formal recognition of an acute danger of Communist aggression, holding that this constituted an alignment with one

world camp as against another. This was the neutralist position toward the newly constituted Southeast Asia Organization and the nations that had joined it.

This brought forth the most vigorous and eloquent address that was delivered at the Bandung Conference. General
Romulo took the floor, on behalf of the Philippines, to defend the Manila Pact, the membership of his country in it,
and the purposes for which it was reached. Point by point
he demolished the arguments that Prime Minister Nehru had
brought forward. He showed precisely how the Manila Pact
fitted into the United Nations framework. He was able to
cite the Pacific Charter as the very embodiment of the ideals
that Mr. Nehru himself supported and that had animated
much of the discussion at Bandung. It was an exposition of
Philippine policy, as it had been evolved over the years, that
was without precedent. Once more, the great lessons of human freedom were bearing fruit. General Romulo's summary
was masterful:

To sum up: The Manila Pact is a treaty of collective defense.
No aggressive purpose is written into it.

As for the Pacific Charter, we consider this to be a document
worthy of the best traditions of any civilized state in the world
today, whether Asian or non-Asian. This is the moral basis and
justification of the Manila Pact, and we stand on its principles,
proud and unflinching, in the sight of our friends and neighbors
in free Asia.

To all free Asians we say: "This is a treaty on which we can
all stand together, without vanity or invidiousness, but united
in the determination to preserve the peace and freedom of Asia."

To any potential aggressor or any power that intends aggression we say through this treaty: "We desire to live in peace
with you, but if you attack us we shall fight back with all our
strength."

Let me say to Premier Nehru in conclusion:

The empires of yesterday on which it used to be said that the sun never sets are departing one by one from Asia. What we fear now is the new empire of Communism on which we know the sun never rises. May your India, Sir, never be caught by the encircling gloom!

It was declarations such as this that prevented the Bandung Conference from becoming a mere anti-Western holiday. They were of further significance because they showed clearly how small countries such as the Philippines could make firm commitments to the free world and still maintain freedom of action and national self-respect. This was the central theme of the emerging Philippine policy and Bandung afforded an excellent opportunity to enunciate it.

On the other hand, the Bandung meeting did play an important part in the evolution of the Afro-Asian bloc that was to take shape in the United Nations. In spite of the condemnation of alignments that was heard frequently at Bandung, about twenty of the participants gradually came to accept a grouping on the basis of what were held to be common interests, and to vote accordingly when it came to a test. The impact of this bloc was subsequently to be felt in matters such as the Algerian dispute, the Suez crisis, and the continuing Arab hostility toward Israel. The Philippines did not associate itself, in any formal way, with this bloc. It retained complete freedom of action. Occasionally, when there was agreement on some particular issue, the Philippines might cast its vote on the same side as that represented by the bloc. More frequently, when the Philippines felt that some anti-Western positions of the bloc were playing into Communist hands, it voted in opposition. The Philippines was earnestly trying to bring the Asian world closer to the West, in a better understanding, feeling that its own experience justified the belief that this was right and wise. Its defensive alignment was specifically against the Communist danger. The West was not considered as a potential enemy. This was national policy of great magnitude.

THE INTERNATIONAL NEIGHBORS

While most of the Philippine positions were taken in and through the United Nations, to which the warmest possible support was given, there was a variety of problems to be solved and relationships to be established on a nation-to-nation basis. Sometimes, as in the case of Red China, the United Nations interest might determine the nation-to-nation policy. In other cases, while remaining within the framework of United Nations interest, policies had to be determined upon a somewhat different ground. It may be profitable to review, briefly, some of the problems and solutions in the developing relationships of the Philippines to its international neighbors.

RED CHINA. In the case of the most powerful of those neighbors, Communist China, the Philippines pursued a course strictly in accordance with the United Nations decisions, but took independent positions of strength and clarity. When free Korea was invaded the Philippines promptly provided a troop contingent. When the question of declaring Red China an aggressor was raised, the Philippines spoke and voted for the resolution. When the embargoes were imposed the Philippines was, and continues to be, scrupulous in observing them, in spite of some business pressures.

On the question of diplomatic recognition of the Peiping regime and of seating it in the United Nations as the representative of China, the Philippine course has been unequivocal. Since 1949, each successive Philippine administration has stated flatly that it had, at the time and under the existing conditions, no intention of recognizing Peiping. Similarly, in the repeated votes in the United Nations wherein the question of Peiping's representation in various bodies has been raised, the Philippine vote has been cast regularly against such an action. In these cases, the Communists—and occasionally some of the neutralists who had espoused Peiping's cause—naturally made the charge that the Filipinos were acting at the behest and under the direction of the United States. This is not true. The Filipinos had had their own experience with the Communists. Their national policy, domestic and foreign, was necessarily anti-Communist. This was good enough reason to avoid support of the Communist cause, in whatever form or place, without any urging from the United States. It is also probable that the strong position of the Catholic Church has, because of the pervasive religious bent of the Filipinos, given additional weight to the determination not to play into Communist hands. The Filipinos have had centuries of association with the Chinese. They have no desire for an association with the Red Chinese.

NATIONALIST CHINA. The association between Nationalist China and the Philippines has been continuously friendly, but occasionally complicated by local problems. There is, and has been for years, a strong Chinese community in the Philippines. At its upper levels it is conservative, productive, and valuable. (We have already noted its leadership in the Liberty Wells Association.) This community, also, is naturally anti-Communist, since it represents capitalism among the overseas Chinese. This group has been a good bridge between Manila and Taipei. Its loyalty to the Philippines and its contribution have never been questioned. It has also been loyal to the concept of a free China and has made its substantial contribution there as well.

The community of the "smaller" Chinese is in a less

favorable position. These people are merchants, proprietors of the market stalls and the corner *tiendas*. For years it was a common saying in the Philippines that if one wanted anything from a safety pin to a wagon wheel he could get it "at the Chinese." At the advent of the Commonwealth the Chinese actually controlled 80 percent of the retail trade in the city of Manila. Some Filipinos charged that they had obtained this favorable position by being willing to accept a lower standard of living, a smaller margin of profit, and a working time that no Filipino could possibly accept. This was only partly true. Chinese control of the large grocery stores that catered to Americans and upper-class Filipinos was attributable to sound and imaginative merchandising. In any case, there was Filipino resentment.

Over the years—and even over centuries—the Chinese merchant had always been regarded as fair game by those in authority. The Spaniards put a vicious head tax on him. During the American occupation, if the small Chinese proprietor wished to remain in business, he was frequently the target of a quiet shake-down by local politicians.

With the coming of Philippine independence, the government had a dual objective in approaching this problem. First, the new nation needed to establish uniformity of citizenship. It did not propose to recognize a permanently alien community within its midst. Second, it was felt that the Filipino proprietor could be brought more effectively into the field of small trade if he had more adequate protection from the competition of the Chinese. Accordingly it was proposed that all Chinese be registered, be made applicants for Philippine citizenship, and unless they obtained it be deprived of their trading privileges. It was not an easy thing to enforce. Many of the Chinese, or their parents, had entered the Philippines illegally—immigrant smuggling was an accepted fact of life—and could not establish a valid claim to citizenship. But, much more than that, the legislation plainly discriminated against an industrious community and was meant to do so, in the interest of a community that was possibly less industrious.

The first issue, however, was even more important. In following the American pattern the Filipinos had rejected the idea of duality of nationality or citizenship. The Overseas Chinese do not always concur in the forceful establishment of the uniform pattern. (The Republic of Vietnam has been faced with the same problem on an even wider scale and with deeper repercussions than has the Philippines.) The question will eventually be answered and the problem solved but it will require time and patience. Intermarriage is one solution. There are hundreds of thousands, perhaps even millions, of Filipinos who have some admixture of Chinese blood—and on the basis of the evidence the mixture is a good one.

Meanwhile, there have been occasional strains in the relationship between Manila and Formosa. These are unfortunate because the two countries are committed to the same cause and their defense is interdependent. It seems apparent, at this stage, that the United States will be obliged to offer what services it can to help in solving the problem. How much can be done remains to be seen.

JAPAN. No other one problem has produced more complications for the Republic of the Philippines than the reestablishment of normal relationships with Japan. The two countries have to live together in East Asia. They can be of value to each other. But the Philippines was invaded and all but destroyed by the Japanese, and the demand for adequate reparation was logical. What was not logical was the first level at which the Filipinos made their claim. They set the value of damage, for which they should be recompensed, at $8 billion. There was no possibility that the Japanese, also with a shattered economy, could pay this much. The only chance was that the United States, already giving substantial assistance to Japan, would through increased grants to Japan, funnel through this channel of reparations what the Filipinos had demanded. The Americans could hardly be expected to do this. It would have been far better for the United States to give what it could to the Philippines in the form of direct aid.

Moreover, there was the fact that in many Filipino—and in many American—minds there was the strong conviction that the Japanese should themselves accept the moral responsibility for what they had done and not merely be rescued from the consequences of their acts through the generosity of the United States. This became the first basis of reparations discussions between the Philippines and Japan, and the first hurdle was topped when the Japanese agreed to accept such a moral responsibility. After that it became a question of determining, through negotiation, just how much Japan was willing to pay and in what form.

No agreement had been reached when the powers met in San Francisco in 1951 to consummate the peace treaty with Japan. The Philippines signed the treaty, but with the strong reservation that the reparations problem had not been solved. The implication was clearly that the treaty would not be ratified in the Philippine Senate unless and until this question was cleared up. General Romulo made a strong statement to the effect that the Philippines might be ready to forgive but that it would not be easy to forget.

Negotiation between Manila and Tokyo continued, somewhat spasmodically, for almost four years. Two presumptive agreements were repudiated in Manila on the ground that their provisions were inadequate. Eventually an agreement was signed and ratified in both capitals, and the Philippine Senate then ratified the peace treaty with Japan.

The final figure is about three quarters of a billion dollars. Only a small part is in actual cash payment. A supply of goods and services makes up the bulk and a part of the services is the undertaking of salvage operations to finish the cleaning-up of Manila Bay and some other harbors. The remainder takes the form of Japanese capital investment in Filipino-controlled enterprises in the republic. Some such operations may, in turn, supply certain needed raw materials to Japan. Others will be in the field of manufacture. This last phase is interesting and unusual, in that the Japanese have agreed to invest in certain Philippine productive units that are intended to be in direct competition with Japan itself. The Japanese are thus contributing toward making a break in what was an accepted economic pattern and a desirable one from the Japanese point of view.

Prior to the war economic interchange between the two countries was based largely upon a supply of Philippine raw materials to Japan and Philippine importation of Japanese manufactured goods. The raw materials that Japan wanted were iron and manganese, lumber and abacá. The methods of obtaining them varied. Iron could be had by outright purchase. Manganese was produced by operating companies that were actually Japanese-controlled, until the Filipinos enforced the provisions of their own constitution, when it came into effect. Lumber was obtained on a purchase basis, in the main, but there were some logging concessions granted to Japanese-controlled operators. The Japanese imports of Philippine hardwoods were disadvantageous to the Philippines because Japan did not buy milled lumber or processed wood products. Instead, the Japanese actually rafted Philippine logs all the way to Japan, milled them, and then returned wood products to the Philippine market at a lower cost than local producers could meet. This meant, in effect, that the timber resources of the Philippines were being depleted to the advantage of the Japanese middlemen and manufacturers, and that the Filipinos lost on two counts.

It was the abacá situation, however, that really fixed a spotlight on some aspects of Japanese-Philippine trade relations that were disadvantageous to the Philippines. In this field there was, decades ago, outright physical penetration of the archipelago by Japanese growers. The Japanese never did purchase the end product of Manila hemp, finished cordage, in the Philippines. Instead, they sent in their own settlers to grow the abacá plant and ship an unfinished product to Japan. Until this peaceful Japanese invasion, the production center of abacá in the Philippines had been the southeastern part of the island of Luzon. The Japanese went to southern Mindanao and virtually took over the province of Davao. As early as 1925 they were producing more than half of the abacá of the Philippines.

More than 50 percent of the agricultural land in Davao was in Japanese hands and a large part of it had been obtained illegally. It was a simple matter for a Japanese agent of a "development" company to go through a marriage ceremony of sorts with a Bogobo woman from the hinterland, register a land holding in her name, and then send the poor illiterate creature back to the bush. An abacá plantation could thereafter be operated on behalf of an ostensible Filipino landholder who would never see the land or obtain anything from it. The dummy corporation technique was also widely used.

Illegal landholding was only the beginning. The Japanese were good cultivators and had solid financial backing if they needed it. Much more, they could use productive techniques that were far in advance of the conventional Philippine mode of operation. Instead of the laborious toxying and stripping by hand that the Filipinos used to produce the long white fibers of the inner plant, the Japanese put in machine decorticators, cut their abacá plants into four-foot lengths, and turned the fiber out by the bale. These could not meet the specifications of the American market—which was based on the refraction of light by the finished fiber—since the bales were made up in part of the "streakies" that come from the outer part of the plant. But there was no difference in tensile strength and the Japanese were not interested in the American market in any case. They were interested in getting the raw material for marine cordage into Japan.

After the war, the Japanese developments in Davao were taken over as alien property. Their final disposition has not yet been settled. They will not go back into Japanese hands, the Filipinos are sure. What will be done with them in Filipino hands remains to be seen.

While the Japanese were taking these raw materials out of the Philippines they were sending back a veritable flood of inexpensive manufactures. Most important of these was textiles, and a Japanese trade slogan was "an undershirt for every Filipino." The undershirt could be had in the local Japanese-owned bazaar for about a dime. The Filipinos had their own beautiful textiles—*piña, jusi,* and *sinimay*—but these were handmade and could not compete with the product of the advanced Japanese spinning and weaving. The influx of Japanese textiles became so acute that in 1934 the then secretary of state, Cordell Hull, negotiated a gentleman's agreement with Japan to limit its shipments to the Philippines. As far as Japan was concerned the agreement was more honored in the breach than in the observance. The textiles continued to come in, but were labeled as originating in Hong Kong or Shanghai rather than in Japan.

There were other items of importance. Japan could put rubber-soled shoes on the Philippine market at fifteen cents a pair. They weren't very good shoes, but they were shoes. Filaments for electric lights could be purchased in the United States by Japan, put into cheap bulbs, and sold in Manila at one fourth the price of an American lamp. They weren't very good bulbs, but they were electric lights. A Japanese-made bicycle was certainly not as good as the British or American product (even if it did sometimes carry a conspicuously forged label), but it could be had for one third of its American or British inspiration. Flashlights, toys, paper products, costume jewelry, pencils, finally even Japanese beer—"brewed especially for the tropics"—were poured into the Philippine market.

A good case can be made for the supplying of low-cost consumer goods to an underdeveloped buying market. The Japanese met a specific need in the Philippines and knew how to exploit the need. The longer-range view is that economic stability and development should come first, even if immediate market advantage has to be sacrificed. Governor Murphy, in a conference with some Filipino leaders when the gentleman's agreement was under negotiation, put it this way: "It may be better to pay a dollar for an American undershirt and have the dollar, than to try to pay a dime for a Japanese one and not have the dime."

It is certain that the Japanese will again make a determined bid to get the best possible market for diversified low-cost consumer goods in the Philippines. The Filipinos, however, are making a vigorous effort to build up their own manufacture in many of these fields. They propose to compete with Japan rather than to be exploited. At the same time, with any progressive diminution of the American market for Philippine products, Japan becomes a natural and valuable export outlet for the Philippines. It is highly significant that in the past five years the decline of proportional Philippine exports to the United States has been almost exactly matched by a proportional increase in exports to Japan.

The Philippine-Japanese relationship is now stable. But the Filipinos still have quite a few memories and they have had some experience with the Japanese economy. It is possible that the future relationship can be worked out to the advantage of both countries, but this will require statesmanship of a high order.

KOREA. The fact that the Philippines so quickly embraced the cause of Korean freedom made a friendly association between the two republics almost automatic. There are no questions in dispute between the two governments and there has been a pleasant interchange of official visits. Korean President Syngman Rhee has recently proposed a general Pacific defense alliance among the free nations. If this could be brought about, such a plan would undoubtedly have Philippine support. At the moment the relationship between the two countries is perhaps not as close as might be desired, considering that they are working toward the same ends. There is no present obstacle, however, to development of an even more friendly association to the advantage of both.

INDONESIA. Relations between the Philippines and Indonesia may well be described as diplomatically correct, if something less than cordial. There has been only one specific question of consequence that has been raised and it was treated with dignity on both sides. The Philippines had occasion to protest against a considerable influx of Indonesians who were being smuggled illegally into the southern islands. It is not a new problem—the Chinese used that route for

years. It is hard to do very much about it. The most southerly
tip of the Sulu archipelago in the Philippines is only four
miles from Borneo, and the Moro vintas are swift and sea-
worthy. When the protest was made, the Indonesian government stated promptly that it did not condone this violation of
Philippine immigration laws and would do whatever was in
its power to stop it. The exchange of views was entirely
proper. And both the Filipinos and the Indonesians know
that if an Indonesian wants to get out of Borneo or Celebes
into Jolo or Sulu he will do so. The fact that the Indonesian
does want to get out may have some significance. The numbers involved are minor.

In the larger view, the differences between Manila and
Jakarta are more important. The outlook of the two governments is different, and at some points they are almost
diametrically opposed. The Filipinos have had little sympathy
with the "guided democracy" of Indonesian President
Sukarno. They did not like his willingness to accept Communist support for his government nor his insistence that
the Communists should be represented in the top councils of
the state. Similarly, as General Romulo made plain at
Bandung, they have little patience with neutralism, or with
the Indonesian distrust of the motives of the United States.

Thus, while the Philippines warmly espoused the cause
of Indonesian independence, it is not sympathetic toward
some of the directions that have been taken by President
Sukarno, and has declared a firm "hands-off" attitude on
the question of New Guinea. Accordingly, there is little
likelihood that there will be a closer *rapprochement* between
Indonesia and the Philippines in the near future. There is,
of course, no economic compulsion toward such an association. As raw material producers—in the field of coconuts for
example—the two states are competitive rather than com-

plementary. Trade between these two great contiguous archipelagos is almost negligible.

In some other areas, however, they have a community of interest and experience that could be shared to the advantage of both. For example, in the public health field they face much the same problems and each has made some important contributions. They could well pool some resources. The Philippines could certainly be of help in sharing some of its experiences in the evolution of a truly democratic state, but this will not be possible so long as there is a consistent Indonesian distrust of Western influence. This highly desirable interchange has not yet been achieved. It represents an opportunity as well as a difficult problem in policy.

INDIA. What has been said about Indonesia applies also, to some extent, to Philippine relations with India. Here, also, there is no economic inducement to close association, and there is wide divergence on the question of neutralism and relationship with the Western world. The relation, once more, is correct and something less than cordial. As the Bandung Conference illustrated, the Filipinos do not accept the thesis that Prime Minister Nehru—or his deputy, Mr. Krishna Menon—can bespeak the "Asian mind." The Philippines does not accept the challenge to its right to enter into whatever alliances it deems proper. It does not accept the bogeyman of imperialism as the prime target at which all the shooting should be done. It does not accept the idea of fruitful co-existence with the Communists.

Many persons have suggested that there is, at bottom, a personal contest between Prime Minister Nehru and General Romulo to come out as the real spokesman for the new Asia. This, also, is oversimplification. The new Asia is extremely complex. The idea of an "Asian mind" is as ridiculous as would be the idea of a "Western hemisphere

mind." That one man should expect to appear as the mouthpiece of half a billion persons in twenty-five different political
structures and in stages of development that range from the
Stone Age to the Atomic Age, is sheer nonsense. General
Romulo and Prime Minister Nehru represent two quite different approaches to the problems of the emergent Asia.
Each is eloquent and persuasive. These differences in approach are not likely to be quickly composed. Until they are,
Indian-Philippine relations will remain correct and something less than cordial.

VIETNAM.   One of the most interesting—and heartening
—developments in the growing foreign relations of the Philippines, is an increasingly warm association with the free Republic of Vietnam. The two countries face each other directly,
across the South China Sea. They are of similar, if not
identical, Malay origin. It is logical and desirable that they
should be deeply friendly. There was an important trade
association in the past. Saigon, with a regular rice surplus, was
the point to which the Philippines usually turned first when
there was a need to import food. There was not, however,
any close cultural association with the then French colony,
and no political association at all.

That has been changed with the advent of Vietnamese
independence, for the Philippines has had an opportunity to
demonstrate its interest and goodwill toward its harassed
neighbor. When the Geneva partition of Vietnam resulted in
a tremendous influx of refugees from the Communist North
to the free Republic, a major health problem was created.
The Filipinos recognized this and promptly organized and
sent to Vietnam teams of doctors and nurses to help out.
This action had an immediate impact on the Vietnamese out
of all proportion to the very sound help that was given. It
was a gesture of real friendship from a neighboring Asian
state. It will be long remembered.

The Philippines was also able to be of help in quite a different way. When Vietnamese President Ngo Dinh Diem undertook to set forth a constitution for the free republic, he thought naturally of the Philippine history and background in this field. Accordingly he asked President Magsaysay to send over a Filipino who was familiar with the problem of constitution-drafting, to help the Vietnamese in their work. President Magsaysay chose a young lawyer and former newspaperman, Juan Orendain, who had been closely associated with the drafting of the Philippine Constitution, and sent him to Saigon. This may be one of the reasons that the Vietnamese Constitution bears some strong resemblances to the Philippine Constitution and, in turn, to that of the United States.

The fact that there is a strong Christian influence among the Vietnamese and that the President himself is a devout Catholic also furnishes a bond at this time. It is part of a process of laying the foundation for strong and valuable international friendship.

"SHOWCASE OF DEMOCRACY"

In its relation to the rest of East Asia the Philippines has often been referred to, both in the United States and in the Philippines, as the "showcase of democracy." Some Filipinos are proud of the appellation; others resent it on the ground that there is no need to be a "showcase" for anything. It cannot be denied that the Philippines occupies an unusual position. It is by far the most westernized of the Asian states. It has taken over its political institutions almost entirely from Western models. Its social institutions, especially in the villages, are often essentially Asian; its metropolitan communities, on the other hand, are truly cosmopolitan. East and West have met and mingled in the Philippines to an extraordinary degree.

It is for this reason that some Filipinos, such as General Romulo, feel that their country has a distinct mission as an international interpreter. It can tell the Occident some of the things that it needs to know about the Orient and do so with sympathy and good grace. On the other hand, by example more than by precept it can show the Asians what can be taken from the Western world and used in Asia to good advantage. This is where the "showcase" concept arises. The cause of freedom and democracy in Asia can be promoted if the Philippines remains its exemplar.

It is this genuine mixing of the ideas of East and West, also, that makes the idea of "Asia for the Asians" unpalatable to many thoughtful Filipinos. And when such a slogan is used to express an attitude that could be construed as anti-American it is doubly unpalatable. Now and then, and here and there, an individual Filipino may try to make political capital out of shouting a chauvinistic defiance of the mighty United States. His words are meaningless. The Philippines will continue to be pro-American in many important aspects, just as the United States will continue to be "pro-Philippine." Each needs the other.

The degree to which the Philippines has already been able to make its influence felt in the free world is one of the most gratifying things on the Asian scene. This is a demonstration that freedom can speak with authority in its own right when it has been rightly achieved and stanchly defended. To this extent the Philippines cannot escape the role of "showcase," in all its relations with other countries. The Filipinos therefore must accept the responsibility of making good on that which is shown.

Ten

AFTER MAGSAYSAY

Early in the morning of March 17, 1957, President Magsaysay was killed. His plane, en route to Manila, crashed into a mountainside on the island of Cebu.

In the early reports of the disaster there were suggestions of sabotage. A man of Magsaysay's character makes bitter enemies. A long and careful investigation by both Philippine and American military and intelligence agencies discredited these reports. There was clear evidence of mechanical failure. The plane had turned back once, for engine repair, before the fatal flight. Magsaysay, who had braved death a thousand times, was the victim of accident.

The Philippines was stunned with shock and grief. One newspaper said, "This is the blackest day in our history." The public outpouring of sorrow was without precedent in the Philippines. When the Palace grounds were open to the public, as Magsaysay lay in state, literally hundreds of thousands of persons poured in. Dozens of persons fainted in the streets. Some deaths from shock were reported. Later, more than a million Filipinos lined the long road to the cemetery.

Among the politically minded there was a consciousness of the loss of a great leader at a critical time. Many felt that it might be irreparable. But the national feeling went deeper than that. Filipinos in every station of life—especially the most humble—felt that they mourned a close, warm, personal friend. No other Filipino had been able to identify himself so closely with the interests of the "little man." He repre-

sented aspiration and achievement to all those who needed
hope. Much more than that, he was no mere remote champion
of good causes, but a man who made his people feel that he
spoke for them, personally and individually. Other men had
been honored, respected, applauded, and often enthusiastically
followed. Magsaysay was loved.

This sense of shock and grief was not confined to the
Philippines. It echoed throughout the world. Magsaysay had
become something of a symbol of the new Asia that was
coming into being. He had been the living answer to cynics
and skeptics. In the United States, for example, there was
much talk of the need to bring "democracy" to other peoples.
Magsaysay was the best proof that it could be done. His
death, therefore, was regarded as a loss to the whole cause
of human freedom. An American attitude was reflected by
The New York *Times,* which said editorially:

The tragic death of President Ramon Magsaysay has taken
from the Philippines, and the Filipino people, a great leader. His
greatness lay, in part, in the very fact that he was so much of
those people. He was no stranger to the most intimately human
problem in the lives of the simplest of the folk he led. He was
in and of his country as the truly great so often are.

With good reason the Filipinos have often called him "Our
Abraham Lincoln." They have recognized those same homely
virtues, that massive integrity, that humble warmth of heart
that make a man able to lead because he is both honored and
truly loved. On our part, remembering, we can understand the
shock and grief that encompass the Philippines and can extend
our expressions of sympathy in a loss that we likewise share.

As Ambassador Romulo has pointed out, it is not only the
Philippines but the whole free world that has been bereaved.
Here was a living symbol of that freedom and of the worthy
fight to make it secure. His life helped to ennoble the good cause
that we and the Filipinos have been glad to share. We understood each other because of our joint and mutual devotion to
that cause. Let us, therefore, not forget—he was one of our

leaders too. And because he belonged also to us, and to all free men, we likewise mourn.

Too often, perhaps, the narrative of his struggle and eventual triumph has been told in the terms of the conventional "success story." This falls short of the great truth. His was not so much the triumph of a man as it was the vindication of an ideal. We are obliged to believe that virtue, honor, courage, steadfastness and great compassion can win the field against the enemies of the human spirit. Without that belief the ashes of the world's sorrows would be too bitter to bear. Ramon Magsaysay taught us that our belief and our hope were not vain. He made victory real and personal for all of us.

His legacy is a challenge. It is just that to his own people. It is also a challenge to us to understand and to help. We need to give our encouragement and our prayers to Vice President Garcia, who succeeds him. His burden is heavy and we should try to lighten it if we can.

Our friends in the Philippines will be right if they enshrine the memory of Magsaysay in the same glorious panel that has the names of Bonifacio and Rizal. Here, also was a great fighter for freedom in its truest and broadest sense. Here is a national "hero" and a national "leader" who is worthy of the highest honor and whose virtues should command emulation.

But that honor can be paid, justly, only in the deeds of the living. It is only as his vision is fulfilled that he will have received the tribute that is his due. A great leader has been lost. Those who have followed him can show, now, how great and good, in time of crisis, that leadership was.

There were no immediate political problems as the result of Magsaysay's death. Vice President Garcia, acting in his concurrent capacity as foreign secretary, was in Australia at a meeting of the Southeast Asia Treaty Organization when the tragedy occurred. Within six hours of the receipt of the news he was flying back to Manila. He was sworn in as the chief executive without delay.

In some Asian newspapers there were expressions of surprise and gratification that the presidential succession had

taken place without incident. Apparently some sort of collapse or coup had been expected. Obviously, this idea did
not even occur to the Filipinos. What some of their Asian
neighbors called a "triumph of peaceful democracy" was
accepted as a matter of course. It was not the first time.
After all, President Quezon had died in office and the succession of Osmeña was taken for granted. President Roxas
had died in office and Quirino was sworn in without question.
The importance of this case, and the emphasis upon it, lies
only in the fact that it again illustrates the degree to which
constitutional processes had become a fixed part of Philippine political society. Even the loss of a Magsaysay could
not shake that. Any attempt by a "usurper" to take over the
reins would have been not merely resisted but hooted at.

Nevertheless, President Garcia was in an extremely difficult position. He was stepping into the shoes of a man who
had been a national hero in the best sense. No one could
replace Magsaysay and it was not easy to succeed him. Garcia
recognized this fully.

"I felt at first," he said later, "as if I were in a small room
and that all four walls had suddenly tumbled in upon me. I
had to get out, or suffocate, but no one knew better than
I how hard that might be. I was grateful that everyone understood the situation in which I was placed and tried to help."

Garcia's personality is completely different from that of
Magsaysay. For one thing, he is twelve years older; he was
sixty-one in November, 1957. In spite of his reputation as an
orator many Americans have found him shy, almost diffident.
He is quiet, composed, gracious, and urbane. He has none of
Magsaysay's magnificent flamboyance. He is (and this is not
said unkindly) essentially a group man rather than an in-
dividualist. He prefers to persuade rather than to compel.

His scholastic record was brilliant. He was interested in

the classics and also in poetry, which he wrote with zest and profusion. (In the last campaign, his speeches were often interrupted by the shouted demands that he recite one of his poems that had become a great favorite among the Visayans.) He turned to law, where he succeeded with distinction, and then to politics. He sat in the pre-Commonwealth National Assembly as a loyal follower of Quezon, and then was three times elected governor of his native province, Bohol. His service there was marked chiefly by his unremitting demand for a better network of roads for the island. Subsequently he went to the Philippine Senate, where he served three consecutive terms, interrupted only by the Japanese occupation. Four years in succession, Philippine newspapermen voted him the "best" Senator.

He was chosen as Magsaysay's running mate in 1953 for two reasons. First, it was felt that his long political experience would serve as a proper balance to the inexperience of Magsaysay. Second, he had a record of anti-Japanese guerrilla activity that fitted well into the Magsaysay pattern. He had withdrawn from the Senate when the Japanese came in, gone back to Bohol, and organized a resistance government. The Japanese put a price on his head but could not collect.

In addition, he had considerable experience in foreign affairs, which Magsaysay had not. He was a member of the Philippine delegation at the formation of the United Nations. He was a recognized leader in the foreign affairs field in the Senate, where he was an active proponent of the idea of some sort of Southeast Asian mutual defense agreement. This was eventually to emerge as SEATO, in whose formation he played an important part.

Finally, he was a party "regular" who had never deviated from the Nacionalistas and who was a good vote-getter. In the 1953 Magsaysay landslide, Garcia ran a half million votes ahead of the Liberals' vice-presidential candidate. His choice as the logical nominee was vindicated.

When he took over as President he spoke with humility and restraint. His administration, he said, would be devoted to the Magsaysay principles and to the steadfast effort to put them into practice. He asked for no changes in the executive organization. He urged the legislature to support him and invoked the support of the people and of Divine Providence.

IMPORT CONTROLS

It was soon clear that he would need all the help he could get. The country was faced with the hard fact that its expenditures had exceeded its revenues in the preceding year by several hundred million pesos. The legislature was obliged to be economy-minded. At the same time, import and exchange controls that were designed to reduce the unfavorable trade balance were becoming increasingly unpopular. President Garcia therefore faced a two-pronged opposition in the legislature. First was a movement to cut into appropriations, and the Magsaysay projects were quick to suffer. Second was a drive to ease the import and exchange controls, which brought the most severe test of the President's position.

In fairness to Garcia it should be pointed out that these were not problems of his own making. He inherited them. Had Magsaysay lived, he would himself have been obliged to face the same situation. Not even the power of his personality could have brought about the miracle of providing enough money to go around. The various projects for economic development, land resettlement, social amelioration, and expansion of public services were all sound in themselves. But in sum they represented an outlay of money that simply was not there. When some of the younger men in the administration resigned in protest over the curtailment of appropriations for specific projects, they were protesting (and should have realized it) not against Magsaysay or Garcia or the legislature but against the economic facts in the case.

The question of import and exchange controls was also not new, and it was on this subject that Garcia was eventually able to demonstrate that he proposed to follow the Magsaysay example. His doing so was to pose some political as well as economic problems.

Imports had been under relatively rigid control for more than five years. Luxury goods were presumably banned altogether, although it was obvious in one trip through the Manila shops that the ban was being systematically evaded. Prices on all imported commodities, however, were forced up and remained up. At the same time, materials brought in under certificates of necessity—and there *was* necessity for an expanding industrialization—were purchased at the legal peso rate of two to a dollar, which was unrealistic in the light of the fact that there was a black-market rate of anywhere from three to four. The Philippines had the legal right, under the modified trade act, to change the peso rate if it wished, but the administration and the Central Bank were rigidly opposed to any devaluation.

In view of this situation, a proposal was made in the Philippine Senate to modify import and exchange controls in favor of those individuals or organizations that actually produced for export and were thus earning foreign exchange. It would have provided that such exporters could obtain uncontrolled import licenses and exchange permits up to certain percentages of the amounts that they actually produced and exported. It was urged that such a course would stimulate the exports that the Philippines obviously needed and would also make the peso rate more realistic.

The proposed legislation was not new. The Senate had adopted a similar bill in the preceding year. At that time Magsaysay had killed the proposal by decisive action. He sent word to the House that it was useless to adopt the measure since he would veto it in any case. His opposition, he stated, was based on the fact that it discriminated in the matter of imports between the large operator and the "little man." A producer for export could get import and exchange preference; others could not. In a sense, Magsaysay's position was based upon moral rather than economic grounds, but it was fully sustained by the Central Bank.

After Magsaysay's death the Senate revived the bill and passed it. The House, after a stormy debate, also acted favorably. The issue was thus put up to President Garcia. He could sign the bill, veto it, or allow it to become law without his signature. The latter course was urged upon him by many prominent political and business leaders.

A tense period followed. The question had become not merely economic but political. Garcia had already become a candidate for reelection. His veto of the measure would probably alienate some considerable campaign support from those who might contribute to party funds. The "producers for export" represented some of the largest monetary interests in the Philippines. On the other hand, Garcia had pledged himself to follow out the Magsaysay policies and Magsaysay had stated flatly that he would veto such a course.

On the last day permissible under the law Garcia acted. He vetoed the bill. In a short statement he returned directly to the Magsaysay argument. He declared that the proposal would help the few against the many, the rich against the poor. He repeated his support of a policy of maintaining a firm currency, and he did not have to elaborate this by the re-

minder that the governor of the Central Bank had un-
equivocally declared that he would resign forthwith if the
measure became law. That had been well publicized. But
Garcia put both of these arguments on a broad base when
he said simply that under the existing unfavorable trade-
balance conditions any relaxation of the import controls
ought to be out of the question. He was on firm economic
ground, as later events proved.

How much he suffered politically by his action cannot be
established. Undoubtedly he suffered the loss of some campaign contributions, but his Nacionalista party was well-
organized and well-financed in any case. Additional funds
would not have made much difference. Counterbalancing such
a putative loss was the fact that Garcia had established himself as a man of political courage in the Magsaysay tradition.
This was the subject of laudatory comment in both the
Philippine and the American press. It seems probable, in the
light of the election result, that Garcia won more votes than
he lost by demonstrating that he could resist pressure.

OUTLAWING THE COMMUNISTS

At another point Garcia was able to follow through on a
Magsaysay policy against a considerably more subtle opposition. The legal status of the Communist party had been a
moot question in the Philippines for twenty-five years. The
party was declared illegal in the early thirties, then rein-
stated. After the war, it was again temporarily recognized
and the Communists actually elected members to the Congress, although the Congress refused to seat them. There
were periods of "amnesty" throughout the Hukbalahap rebellion, in which the question of the legality of the Com-

munist party, was always an issue. Magsaysay had finally succeeded in outlawing the rebellion itself, but the party was not formally outlawed in the statutes of the Philippines.

Magsaysay had taken the position that there could be no equivocation on this point. It was the Communist party, in his view, that had inspired and directed a revolt against the authority of government in the Philippines and against the liberty of Filipinos. He held, therefore, that it was an instrument of subversion and rebellion and should have no claim to political recognition under the law. He urged the Congress to adopt legislation that would make this clear once and for all.

After Magsaysay's death, Garcia espoused this cause. A Congressional Committee on Anti-Filipino Activities had brought in a strong report condemning the Communist organization altogether and Garcia warmly endorsed it. He pressed for legislative action.

There was no vigorous open opposition in the Congress. The Communist cause was unpopular and it would have been political suicide for any member of the Congress to defend it. But there was a strong undercurrent of mistrust. It was suggested that if the Communist party were really a political instrument and not merely an alien conspiracy an act outlawing it would violate the constitutional guarantees of free speech and free association. Some groups and individuals in the United States, sensitive to any transgression of political and individual rights, actually circularized Filipinos with the warning that a problem of this sort should be approached with caution. Such an attitude need not have been Communist-inspired. There is still a sharp division of opinion in the United States on the question of where "party" ends and "conspiracy" begins.

There was also the familiar argument that direct legislative action would "drive the Communists underground." Magsaysay had snorted at this misgiving and retorted: "Where do you think they are now?" But the uneasiness prevailed. A campaign in the field against the Huks was one thing. A formal vote by the Congress establishing a legal position was another.

President Garcia threw his full weight behind the bill to outlaw the party. He was gratified and reassured by the warmth of Congressional support. Opposition evaporated and the bill was enthusiastically adopted.

Nevertheless, President Garcia felt that it was necessary to set forth the precise reasons for his support of the measure. He signed the bill on June 19, 1957, and when he did so he issued a formal statement giving his reasons. It is one of his better state papers. It says:

I have signed into law the bill outlawing the Communist Party of the Philippines.

With this law, our people have not only officially made the fight against Communism a matter of national policy but we have also acquired a potent weapon in the fight against subversion.

Successful as we have been in breaking the backbone of armed Communist resistance, we find ourselves seriously handicapped in countering effectively the more insidious activities of Communists who have ostensibly forsworn violence and sought expediently the protection of the very laws of the land which they seek to destroy.

Thus, even with our success in the military field the Congressional Committee on Anti-Filipino Activities, after conducting the most comprehensive and authoritative study ever made on the problem of Communism in our country, concluded that Communism remains a real and continuing threat to the national security. It is to the credit of this Committee that the bill outlawing the Communist Party was conceived and recommended. It is, likewise, to the credit of the champions of civil rights in Congress that necessary safeguards were made such that the legitimate exercise by citizens of their rights shall remain inviolate. What the present law punishes is not dissent nor heresy but subversion and conspiracy.

Communist sources, as well as the evidence of our own experiences, establish the fact that the objectives of Communism are the destruction of our social, political and economic system, and their replacement by a foreign and godless ideology guided and directed from abroad. These same sources, as well as our experience, establish the Communist means of achieving these objectives as including armed force, sabotage, espionage and the many sinister forms of subversion. Far from contenting itself with seeking victory, as do other political minorities, by legal democratic process, Communist doctrine flatly denies the possibility of legal success and prescribes criminal conspiracy as its orthodox tactic.

Under the circumstances it is clearly the right and the duty of this Government to invoke the police powers of a sovereign state to protect itself and the institutions entrusted to its care from criminal attack.

The passage of this law reaffirms the position which our Government has taken, and will take, vis-à-vis Communism: A firm, unequivocal, and uncompromising stand against freedom's most odious and implacable foe.

In this vigorous and reasoned counter offensive to Communist aggression, I feel that we are serving the cause of the free world as well as our own best interests. If our neighbors can derive benefit or guidance from our experiences and approach, we will have made a substantial contribution to the peace and security of this area.

I assure lovers of freedom and democracy's friends everywhere that during my incumbency as President of the Republic of the Philippines, I shall not only see to it that the anti-Communist program of my illustrious predecessor, Ramon Magsaysay, will remain intact, but I shall also push it through with the same dedication and with unrelenting vigor.

President Garcia's assurance that what the law proposed to punish was not dissent but subversion was well received. It was a reaffirmation of the defense of human rights, but it was also a recognition of the fact that these rights could be challenged and violated by those same persons and organizations that insisted upon enjoying and invoking their protection. From this point of view the action that was taken was in defense of freedom and was not an impairment of it.

In any case, it is difficult to see how the Filipinos, with due respect to legal niceties, could logically have taken any other position. They had met Communist subversion, not as some vague ideological threat, but as a matter of life and death. They had seen villages looted and burned. They had seen their kinfolk abducted and killed. They knew, from experience, that the "new order" that had been preached was not an order under law but a rule of violence. That established government in the Philippines must outlaw such a "party" was inescapable. It had long since outlawed itself.

POLITICS, NOT POLICY

In an informal conversation with a newspaperman afterward, President Garcia said:

It was soon clear enough that our major concern in the next months would not be policy, but politics. This is only natural. A line of policy had been established under Magsaysay and I had said that I would follow it. I did, to the best of my ability. The only really serious challenge to it came on that matter of import controls and it is well known what I did.

There were occasional flare-ups of opposition on the ground that we were being too "pro-American" and should pursue a more independent course. I did not believe that this was true. We were expressing ourselves firmly on the matter of the bases. On the economic side we were certainly in no position to try to break away from our ties to the United States. Besides, I put down most of these "firm declarations" as merely pre-campaign speeches, made for effect, and I think I was right.

On the political side, the problem was really relatively simple. After Magsaysay's death a number of persons came forward, each asserting that he was the logical successor. I was one of them, of course, and I felt that I had the most valid claim. With a few exceptions, and everyone recognized them, there was no question of upsetting or greatly changing policies. It was rather only a matter of what particular person would be chosen to carry them out. For that reason, it became a campaign of persons rather than of issues.

This campaign of persons, however, had some strong reverberations. Legislative business ground to a virtual standstill. There was a widespread tendency to put off everything until "after the election." It can now be asserted, with the advantage of hindsight, that this period of drift was disadvantageous. The Philippine economy was deteriorating, but new and firm measures to meet a potential crisis were not likely to be introduced in the middle of a hot political campaign. It was hard to assert leadership when the identity of the person who would eventually assume the burden was much in doubt.

THE CANDIDATES

In the Philippines, nominations in the conventions are by a two-thirds vote. In the June, 1957, convention, Garcia was the easy and overwhelming choice of the Nacionalistas. He had, as he said, the most valid claim. He was the titular head of the party. He had been Magsaysay's Vice President and Foreign Secretary, and whatever differences they may have had were amicably composed. He was a party regular and a good vote-getter.

There was something deeper at stake. Garcia had pledged himself to carry out the Magsaysay policies. He had attempted to do so. If the Nacionalistas discarded him they would be, in the popular view, repudiating the heritage of Magsaysay. No party in the Philippines could do that and win. To

Garcia's credit it must be stated that he did not campaign on this ground. He did not plead his case as the "heir apparent." He undertook to act in his own right. But the convention knew that the shadow of Magsaysay would eventually dominate the election and that the choice of a candidate other than Garcia was out of the question.

The nomination of a vice-presidential candidate posed quite a different problem. It should be noted, at once, that in the Philippines president and vice president run independently of each other. Each must be elected alone, not as part of a ticket.

Among the Nacionalistas, the leading contender for the vice-presidency was Jose P. Laurel, Jr., Speaker of the House and son of the man who had been the "puppet" president under the Japanese. He represented no part of the Magsaysay tradition. He was a young, able, rising politician with the ability to put some important organizational machinery at the disposal of the party in a number of critical districts.

It is necessary to take a closer look at Mr. Laurel, because what he was and what he stood for were to become critical issues in the ensuing campaign. He was first of all a lawyer. He had four degrees in law, only one of them honorary. He had been a teacher of law from his graduate school days. He was the author of books on the relation of the judicial branch to the other branches of government, on the law of elections, and on constitutional government. At the same time, following in his father's footsteps, he was also a politician. Just before the war he was elected to the House of Representatives, where he was its youngest member. He remained in the House when it became the Japanese-controlled "National Assembly." In 1943 he went to Tokyo as a delegate to Japan's "Greater East Asia Conference," and remained there for the rest of the war. It was suggested that he was something of a hostage in the hands of the Japanese since his father had been induced to serve as the "puppet" president in the Philippines. After the war he went back to the House, in 1946, and served there continuously until 1957. He ran first as an independent and later as a Nacionalista.

In the legislature his preoccupation, again, was with the law. He was Chairman of the Committee on Revision of Laws, a member of the Electoral Tribunal, and three times the Philippine delegate to international parliamentary conferences. Because of his own skill as a parliamentarian he became the minority floor leader during the Quirino administration, and when the Nacionalistas came into power with the Magsaysay victory in 1953 he was unanimously chosen Speaker of the House.

In the latter part of his service there he began to take positions that were regarded as increasingly anti-American. He came to the United States, for example, and made several public addresses in which he stated that if the United States could not accommodate itself to the Filipino point of view on matters such as the sovereignty over military bases, the Philippines should be ready and willing to "go it alone." Such statements were discounted in the United States as a bid for political publicity at home on the ground that Mr. Laurel was "fearless," but they did not help his cause in the Philippines. Among many Filipinos there was no intention of "going it alone," and President Magsaysay had repeatedly stated that a cornerstone of his policy was continued association with the United States in the closest possible understanding. Laurel's "fearless" statements backfired.

At the same time some sections of the Philippine press and the political opposition began a not-too-dignified campaign of sniping at the Speaker. The question of collaboration was repeatedly, if indirectly, raised. Coupled with it was an attack, chiefly by insinuation, on Mr. Laurel's personal and private life. He was pictured as something considerably less than a national hero, while the domestic virtues of some of his opponents were conspicuously praised.

These various factors obviously influenced the convention. Laurel led on every ballot but he was never close to the required two-thirds majority for nomination. Eventually the convention gave up. It placed the vice-presidential nomination in the hands of a committee, agreeing to be bound by the committee's choice. The committee, apparently having in mind Mr. Laurel's control of so much provincial political machinery through the power of patronage, decided to make him the nominee. Garcia and Laurel, a not-too-happy combination, became the ticket.

Like the Nacionalistas, the opposition Liberal party had little difficulty in choosing its presidential candidate but incurred considerable discussion about the running mate. The logical man to head the ticket was Jose Yulo. His nomination was taken for granted even before the convention met, as soon as he had indicated that he would accept it. He had been Quirino's unsuccessful candidate for the vice-presidency in 1953; after his defeat he had retired from the political scene but was readily persuaded to return to it.

In some sections of the Philippine and American press Mr. Yulo was frequently called a "sugar baron." This was misleading. He married, in 1922, a woman whose family had some sugar holdings. After the war Mr. Yulo acquired, in his own right, some valuable sugar properties. But he was first and always a lawyer and a good one, and he was a "self-made" man. He was orphaned in childhood. He specialized in corporation law and even as a very young man built up a strong practice. His abilities were recognized in the United States, also, and he was admitted to the American bar by

the United States Supreme Court. Even before the inaugura-
tion of the Commonwealth he entered the government as
Secretary of Justice, a position he held from 1934 to 1937.
In 1939 he turned actively to politics, ran for a seat in the
House, and was elected. The House, in turn, promptly made
him Speaker by unanimous vote.

He remained in the "puppet" government during the Japanese occupation and was named Chief Justice of the Supreme
Court. His friends say that he was anything but an enthusiastic collaborator and that he did all he could secretly to
assist guerrilla activities. President Manuel Roxas cited his
case as a good argument for a general amnesty after the war.
Mr. Yulo joined the Liberal party of President Roxas and
held several appointive government offices, before turning
back to law and business.

Mr. Yulo was certainly not in the Magsaysay tradition.
He represented big law and big business. On one point, however, there could be no question: he was firmly identified as
pro-American. Also, there was no question of his position
in the party. With the death of Quirino, Mr. Yulo, as the last
vice-presidential candidate, was the titular head of the
Liberals. Actually, he was even more than that. He was their
one big hope.

Shortly before the election, a visiting American reporter
who had had no previous experience with Philippine problems was chatting with a genial Filipino fellow newspaperman in the lobby of the Manila Hotel, trying, as he said,
"to get his facts straight." "Now, let's see," he said, "Yulo
is head of the Liberal party; is that right?" The Filipino
laughed. "Don't be silly," he replied. "Joe Yulo *is* the Liberal
party."

This was an exaggeration, but it is illustrative of how some

Filipinos were thinking. The Liberal party, as a party, had lost much ground during the Quirino administration, as shown by its subsequent defeat. Its only strength, at this juncture, lay in the concentration upon individuals and personalities rather than upon mere party machinery. The Liberals, as Liberals, would not be returned to office. Mr. Yulo, as a person, might be elected. (It may be wise to explain that the term "Liberal" is a party designation, not a description of policy. Actually, the "Liberals," as a party, were strictly conservative in outlook.)

It was probably this need to concentrate upon personality rather than upon party that caused the Liberals to light upon their candidate for vice president, Representative Diosdado Macapagal. He was an individual in his own right, not a "party" man. It is likely, also, that the worth of continuing the Magsaysay concept and tradition was recognized. Macapagal fitted that tradition perfectly.

He came from a very poor family in central Luzon—poorer probably than Magsaysay's. By undisputed merit, and by his own efforts, he went up through the public school system (with jobs on the side) until he was graduated with a Bachelor of Laws degree from the University of Santo Tomas. He took the bar examination and topped the field. Within the year he had his master's degree, and before the war served as a legal assistant in the office of the President of the Commonwealth. During the Japanese occupation he went "underground" and had no part of the "puppet" administration.

With the advent of the Republic, in 1946, he quickly assumed important offices. He was named chief of the law division in the Department of Foreign Affairs. He was the chief negotiator with Britain on the return of the Turtle Islands to Philippine sovereignty. He served briefly in the

Philippine Embassy in Washington and returned to Manila
to become Counselor on Legal Affairs and Treaties in the
Foreign Office. At that point he went into politics.

In 1948 he ran for Congress from his native province of
Pampanga, was easily elected, and remained in the House
until 1957. The House promptly made him its chairman of
the Foreign Affairs Committee, and in that capacity he carried
out a variety of assignments. He was a delegate to the Southeast Asia Conference of 1950, and delegate to the United
Nations in the same year. Subsequently he was chairman
of the Philippine delegation to the United Nations General
Assembly at its Paris meeting in 1951. He helped to negotiate
and sign the Philippine-American Mutual Defense Pact and
the Japanese Peace Treaty. He was a member of the Philippine mission that accomplished the basic revision of the
Trade Act of 1946. He was increasingly making himself felt
to be a spokesman for the Philippines in foreign affairs.

This was not, however, what was ultimately to make him
so important to the Liberal party, to the truly "liberal" cause,
and to the Philippines. In spite of the Magsaysay landslide
in 1953 Macapagal was reelected from Pampanga, although
the other victorious candidate was a Nacionalista. But once
back in the House, Macapagal quickly became identified
with some of the most important things that Magsaysay
wished to do. The specialist in foreign affairs became a leading protagonist of domestic reform. He wrote the Minimum
Wage Law, and tried, unsuccessfully, to put through a five-
day work week law. (It was subsequently adopted under
other sponsorship.) He was co-author of the Agricultural
Credit Law. He helped write the Rural Health Law. He
was closely associated with the drafting and the adoption
of the laws establishing rural banks, the communal fund for

irrigation, barrio autonomy in local matters, land redistribution, and construction of feeder roads.

Magsaysay found himself with a strong supporter from the ranks of the nominal opposition. Macapagal brought his legal skills to bear in the actual drafting of legislation, and rendered important service in this. He not only helped to sustain the Magsaysay ideas but aided in giving them practicable form. This was "loyal" opposition in the best sense.

Because of this background, Macapagal was an ideal co-candidate for Yulo. This was not "big business," nor neglect of the common man. It was technical skill applied for the national cause and applied in the name of the citizen. This was quickly recognized; Macapagal was chosen as the Liberal vice-presidential candidate and enthusiastically entered the campaign.

Another candidate now entered the presidential field, who could claim, with some merit, to represent the Magsaysay tradition and to have inherited the Magsaysay mantle. He was Manuel P. Manahan, a crusading young newspaperman who had been close to Magsaysay and was certainly imbued with the Magsaysay ideals.

Manahan's wartime record was admirable. He was imprisoned once by the Japanese for his resistance operations but managed to obtain his release and became more active than ever. He was the prime mover in the publication of the underground newspapers *The Liberator* and *Free Philippines.* This service was subsequently recognized by the Philippine government when it decorated him with the Legion of Honor, Officer Rank.

During the Liberation period he continued, briefly, to publish *Free Philippines,* and then set up three separate newspapers of his own, in English, Tagalog, and Spanish. He

was an outspoken critic of maladministration in government
and a champion of the rights of the oppressed. He held, as
did Magsaysay, that the one effective way to defeat the Communists was actually to do for the poor people what the
Communists only promised. He was instrumental in bringing about the surrender of Luis Taruc, the Huk leader.

When Magsaysay left the Quirino administration, Manahan
was among the first to come strongly to his support. With
some other like-minded young men he organized M.P.M.,
the Magsaysay for President Movement. He resurrected his
paper, *Free Philippines,* to present the Magsaysay cause in
the name of freedom. He was eloquent and persuasive and
undoubtedly made his contribution to the victory of Magsaysay in 1953.

Magsaysay had a job waiting for him. A Presidential Complaints and Action Commission was being set up to hear the
grievances of the common people. As has been noted, it
actually handled many thousands of complaints and did
so with distinction. Magsaysay made Manahan the chairman
of this commission. Thus he was identified, officially, with
the cause of the common man. In 1955 a major earthquake
hit Lanao Province in Mindanao. Manahan was named to
head the relief work. Finally, after complaints of corruption
on the waterfront had swelled to an uproar, Magsaysay named
Manahan the Commissioner of Customs, with orders to "clean
house." In less than a year this mission was carried out.
Smuggling rings were broken up. Customs collections rose
significantly. Seizures of illegal shipments of gold and currency reached more than a million pesos. The customs service
regained the respectability that it had enjoyed more than
a quarter of a century earlier under Guillermo Gomez, another man who had "cleaned house." But Manahan's pub-
lishing ventures had languished without his supervision. He

was bankrupt. He resigned from government service and took a job as business manager of a strong daily newspaper.

Upon Magsaysay's death, some of the young men who had founded the original Magsaysay movement became convinced that neither of the leading parties was willing or able to carry out the Magsaysay policies. Accordingly, they formed a new party of their own, the Progressive party, and Manahan was a logical candidate. The party had no money, no provincial organization, no history. But Manahan quit his job to become its presidential candidate. No one had ever suggested that he was deficient in courage.

The presidential field was filled by two further candidates, neither of whom wished any identification with the Magsaysay tradition. The first was Senator Claro M. Recto, long known as "the Oppositionist," who had been a declared opponent of the Magsaysay policies. The second was Antonio Quirino, younger brother of the late President Quirino, whom Magsaysay had so decisively defeated in 1953.

Senator Recto was usually credited with having the best legal mind in the Philippines. He had presided over the convention that drafted the Philippine Constitution. He had been a member of the Philippine Supreme Court. He had been chosen to go to the International Court of Justice at the Hague. He was the author of a number of books that were required reading for any aspiring young jurist. He had served the Japanese in the "puppet" administration and had subsequently brought forward the most cogent legal defense for the collaborators.

In the Senate he had always been a sharp and shrewd critic of the majority, even when he was a member of it. He thought and acted independently. After the amnesty, and then the death of President Roxas, the "Laurel-Recto Axis" became the heart of the revived Nacionalista party in the legislative branch. When Magsaysay stormed onto the scene, that was changed. The patient Laurel proved flexible. Recto did not.

By 1955 Recto's opposition to Magsaysay had become so insistent that the President virtually read him out of the party. Recto ran successfully for reelection to the Senate as an independent. His opposition to Magsaysay did not diminish and was especially vehement in the field of foreign affairs, in which Recto repeatedly declared that Magsaysay and most of his fellow countrymen were far too subservient to the United States and should embark upon a more independent course. He was joined in this opposition by one other senator, Lorenzo Tañada, who had headed his own independent Citizens' party, but later merged it with the Nacionalistas.

Toward the end of 1956 it became evident that the Liberals had no intention of opposing the reelection of Magsaysay in the ensuing year. Recto challenged this position on the ground that it meant the end of the two-party system for the Philippines. Accordingly, he joined forces with Senator Tañada to form a new opposition party which was called the Nationalist-Citizens party. At the time of Magsaysay's death this party had already taken the field with Recto and Tañada as its candidates. With Magsaysay gone and the Liberals again in opposition, its position was obviously stronger. Many Filipinos thought that Recto had a good chance to win.

On the other hand, the candidacy of the fifth aspirant, Mr. Quirino, was not taken seriously at any time. He headed a small splinter wing of the old Liberal party that still championed the policies of his brother. He had a small personal following in a few districts. He was expected to run last—and he did.

THE CAMPAIGN

There has not thus far been a more protracted, many-sided, ardent, or confused political campaign in the Philippines than that of 1957. Every barrio was plastered with posters. The newspapers thrived on political advertisements. The radio stations were swamped with demands for time. Much more, the candidates "went to the country" in the Philippine equivalent of whistle-stopping. Several came down with laryngitis. President Garcia had to go into a hospital to rest his throat two days before the election. Gil Puyat, who topped the senatorial poll by a wide margin, could not speak above a whisper. Manahan made nineteen speeches in two days.

From the outset it was emphasized that this was to be a clean, free, and orderly election. After the experiences of 1949, 1951, and 1953, no party could afford to be compromised. The old National Movement for Free Elections, which had policed the polls in 1953, had been disbanded, but its place was taken by the official National Commission on Elections. This body could hear complaints, pass judgments, and, if necessary, recommend prosecutions. It was nonpolitical and highly respected. It heard hundreds of complaints, especially on such matters as allocation of radio time or volume of newspaper advertising, but there was actually little ground for any criminal action. There were party machines at work and obviously a large amount of money was spent, but there was little transgression of the law. The Commission did, however, restrain government agencies that distributed relief goods or food supplies from any activity for a period before the election. By law in the Philippines, public works are suspended for a two-month period before any election. It was necessary to waive this ruling in a few critical cases, but in general it was followed. Too much money was spent in the campaign, obviously, but the expenditures were not misused.

The same thing was true, in the main, on the presentation of issues. There was less mud-slinging than might have been expected. There were some whispering campaigns that were not above reproach, but the tone of the contests remained on a fairly high level. One reason for this was that most of the candidates wished to invoke the Magsaysay image and it could not be demeaned. As Philippine election campaigns go, this one was certainly "clean."

President Garcia's line of campaign was obvious. He could stand on his record—and it was a good one. He was the "logical successor," and proposed to continue in that role. His party was obliged to call off some of its more enthusiastic and less discreet supporters in the lower echelons and advise them to concentrate on local, not national, contests. At the outset, it seemed that the Garcia-Laurel ticket could not possibly lose. The party was in power and its machinery was intact. This estimate was later to be revised.

After the first few weeks it appeared that the strength of Laurel's political following might have been overestimated. All the sampling—and there was much of it—showed Laurel running consistently behind the ticket. Two weeks before the election, President Garcia was quite frank about it and stated that he would probably have to win by a margin of 800,000 votes to carry Laurel in with him. Not many persons believed that he could command that much of a majority. Some of Laurel's friends felt that the President had shown less than enough enthusiasm for his running mate and that his estimate was unfair. In any event, it was honest and realistic, as events proved.

Most of the relative weakness that was shown by Laurel

must be attributed, however, to the strong and popular campaign of his opponent for the vice-presidency, Macapagal. Just as Laurel ran consistently behind Garcia in the samplings, so did Macapagal run consistently ahead of the Liberal presidential candidate, Yulo. Like Garcia, Yulo conducted an essentially conservative campaign. He was presented to the voters as a man of the proper legal and economic ability to steer the Philippines through the critical times that were obviously ahead. The fact that he was well-liked in the United States was not minimized, and this always contained the implication that if further American help were needed Yulo would be able to obtain it.

Toward the end of Yulo's campaign an unfortunate note was injected. Some of his enthusiastic supporters, by means of word of mouth and some newspaper advertising, undertook to portray Yulo as the favored candidate of the Church. There was a hot retort from those who insisted that the separation of church and state was being violated by such campaigning. The Apostolic delegate eventually issued a statement that the Church was taking no position whatever on any candidacy. This was right and wise, but the issue was there, nevertheless. Whether it hurt or helped Yulo in the end cannot be established.

Macapagal, meanwhile, could and did campaign on his record of support for the essential Magsaysay legislation. This was not disloyal to his Liberal party since, as has been noted, the Liberals had decided not to contest Magsaysay's reelection. Macapagal gave the impression of being a quiet and earnest, rather than a flamboyant, campaigner. His speeches were fully reported in the press, and they were usually thoughtful and to the point. He was establishing himself as a personality.

The degree to which this was a campaign of personalities,

and the extent to which it was dominated by the shadow
of Magsaysay, was well illustrated by the spectacular gains
of Manahan in the last few weeks before the election. In
July he had been considered a complete outsider. In the first
week of November some Manila papers were cautiously
speaking of the "remote possibility" of a Manahan "landslide." He had gone to the barrios to campaign and had
been wildly acclaimed in many of them. His political opponents charged that he was capitalizing upon his physical
resemblance to Magsaysay—and there was some. But he
was also capitalizing upon his established association with
the revered leader, his representation of the whole spirit of
young reform, and his freedom from any sort of political
ties and obligations. With a better and bigger political organization, he would have proved to be formidable indeed.
The last weeks of the campaign were marked by wholesale
defections of both Nacionalistas and Liberal groups to the
Manahan camp.

Senator Recto conducted the one real "opposition" campaign. He injected—or tried to inject—the issue of nationalism into most of his speeches. He had spoken at one time
of "Asia for the Asians," but obviously felt it wiser to narrow this down and speak of "the Philippines for Filipinos."
He repeatedly denied that he was anti-American, pointing
out that his two daughters were married to Americans. But,
he insisted, he was "pro-Filipino." In the context of economic and political relations with the United States this could
have, however, only one meaning. Recto was urging courses
of action that would, in time and as quickly as possible,
diminish the closeness of the ties with the United States.

In the earlier stages of the campaign Recto had some
strong support, particularly among the so-called intellectuals.
His own great ability was readily recognized. His courage

as an oppositionist was admired. But among the rank and file his brand of nationalism seemed to fall on deaf ears. This was not an issue in the campaign, and Recto could not make it so. The history of the Philippines and its relation to the United States was against him.

THE ELECTION

On election day, November 12, a typhoon swept across central Luzon. Some communication lines were damaged and it was feared that the storm might keep enough persons away from the polls to affect the results. This fear proved to have been unfounded, although the total vote was somewhat reduced. About five million persons went to the polls, representing slightly more than 70 per cent of those eligible. The Commission on Elections asked permission to authorize a special election at a later date for those who had been prevented from voting by the typhoon. The Supreme Court denied this request on the ground that there was no provision in law for the holding of delayed elections. It was also noted that only 18,000 persons were affected.

Similarly, the preelection fears of widespread election-day violence were shown to have been groundless. During the latter part of the campaign there were sporadic outbursts at different points and several persons were killed while others were injured. There was anxiety, therefore, over the danger of an election that might not be peaceful and orderly. President Garcia issued the sternest of warnings and instructions for tightened police security. The election was peaceful, but not unmarked by tragedy. On the morning of election day the Provincial Commander of Constabulary in Cavite and five of his men were ambushed and killed. The first reaction was that this might touch off a wave of election violence.

It was soon shown that the killing was an act of wanton banditry with no political implications. Election day just happened to be chosen by the bandits as the time for their outrage, but a gallant and competent young officer lost his life.

Early returns quickly established the election trend. President Garcia was running solidly ahead of Yulo, but both were strong. There was little likelihood that Garcia would have that 800,000-vote margin that would be required to help Laurel. Early editions of some Manila papers called it a "Garcia landslide." This was a substantial exaggeration.

There could, however, be no gainsaying the strength of Macapagal. After a brief flurry in which Laurel seemed to be overtaking him, the Liberal candidate for vice president began to draw away steadily in spite of the fact that Laurel showed surprising strength. Under other conditions Laurel might well have won. But Macapagal was not merely beating Laurel. He was outpolling both Yulo and Garcia by a considerable margin. It became apparent that the Phillipines would face the situation of having a president of one party and a vice president of another.

When the election returns were certified to the House on December 10, these figures, almost complete, were given:

For President		*For Vice President*	
Garcia	2,072,257	Macapagal	2,189,197
Yulo	1,386,829	Laurel	1,783,012
Manahan	1,049,420	Araneta	375,090
Recto	429,226	Tañada	344,685
Quirino	60,328		

The implications of these returns were obvious. The opposition candidate for the vice-presidency had drawn a bigger popular vote than either of the candidates for president. Laurel's final strength represented a lost cause. The fact that Manahan could attract more than a million votes had significance for the future. Recto's poor showing was the Filipinos' answer to the plea for a "new nationalism."

It was Macapagal, however, who was put in the spotlight. His election was something new in Philippine politics and it posed some problems.

Before the election, when Laurel's vulnerability was becoming increasingly recognized, and even exaggerated, President Garcia was asked what he would do in the event that he were returned as president and found himself with a vice president from the opposition. His reply was cautious but not unconstructive.

"We are both reasonable men," he said. "We are both devoted to our country. It should not be too difficult to reach the proper accommodation."

Actually, the President's hand was greatly strengthened by his party position. The Nacionalistas came out well in the senatorial elections and maintained their firm majority. In the Lower House, the term "landslide" was really appropriate. The Nacionalistas could count on more than three fourths of the contested seats. Garcia had all the legislative support, from the party point of view, that any president could ask.

On the other hand, it was clear that Macapagal, a candidate from the opposition, had what is called a "popular mandate." The people of the Philippines clearly wanted him to be the vice president, with the obvious implication that if anything happened to President Garcia, Macapagal would be the next chief executive. Garcia's immediate problem was how to fit Macapagal into the machinery of government. The vice presidents, and the vice governors before them, had always served in some executive capacity. Under the American administration the Vice Governor had been, ex officio, Secretary of Public Health and Instruction. Garcia himself had served, under Magsaysay, as Secretary of Foreign Affairs. But at this point Garcia had an experienced and well-liked foreign secretary in Felixberto Serrano, and it would have seemed unreasonable to replace him. For the time being the problem had to be left in suspension, with confidence in Garcia's statement that he and his Vice President were "reasonable men."

In some ways, the election of Macapagal strengthened the position of the government as a whole. It was the final and completely indisputable answer to the question of whether there could and would be a "free" election. When a people can choose a president from one party and a vice president from another, they are manifestly not subject to manipulation or coercion. This, once more, was "government by consent of the governed." The image of Magsaysay may have helped Macapagal. The practice of democracy made his election possible.

During this period of feverish political activity the economic position of the Philippines, as has been observed, continued to deteriorate. Imports continued to exceed exports by about $25,000,000 monthly. The flight of capital continued, sometimes taking the form of undervaluation of export shipments. As a result, by December the reserves position of the Philippines was critical. The official dollar reserve dropped below $150 million. The currency issue that this presumably sustained was more than $400 million. There was already price inflation in the Philippines, with the retail index standing at 340 against the pre-war norm (1938–41). Currency inflation was an obvious threat.

In December, the Governor of the Central Bank, Mr. Cuaderno, was in the United States exploring the possibility of further economic help and how it could justifiably be used. But it was apparent that the basic action had to come in and from the Philippines. President Garcia had stated that he proposed, after the election, to take "drastic" measures, if they were necessary, to set the Philippine economy back upon a firm basis. The measures were necessary, and they were taken.

On December 8, the Central Bank issued an order that was designed to put all imports under the most rigid control. No letters of credit for the import of any nonessential consumer goods would henceforth be issued. Cash deposits of 100 percent would be required for credit for the import of essential consumer and producer goods. For semi-essential consumer goods and nonessential producer goods, a cash deposit of 200 percent would be required. Barter agreements were brought under more strict supervision. Dollar remittances were temporarily suspended, pending clarification. The basis for this action—and it was sound—was to check the flood of imports by drying up the sources of credit. It was the sternest measure that a Philippine government had taken, but it was imperative.

President Garcia then met with his cabinet and the Monetary Board and drew up a seven-point "austerity" program. He took this to the country in a radio broadcast in which he called for popular support and willingness to make sacrifices. He explained the difficult position in which the government had been placed by the excess of imports and noted that, for the time being, the very program of industrialization upon which such high hopes were based was in itself a drain upon reserves until self-sufficiency could be established. He pledged vigorous measures on the part of the government and urged that they be understood and sustained by popular approval and renewed effort.

First of all, he said, the government would tighten up its controls to prevent the abuses that had arisen from the over-shipment of exports under license, and from underpricing. Second, the regulations in respect to barter shipments would be more closely enforced. Third, the government's own imports would be closely restricted to essential items; and fourth, the government would undertake to reduce its rice imports to a minimum. Fifth, the people would in turn be asked to cooperate in overhauling the local transportation systems to reduce the importation of gasoline and spare parts. (These systems were notoriously wasteful.) The sixth point was a proposed revision of the tax system to obtain a more equitable distribution of the burden and to achieve more effective collection from those with ability to pay. Finally, he expressed the hope that the people would cooperate in a new campaign to intensify food production in each category. This was tied to the determination of the government to reduce rice imports, if possible, but that could be done only if rice cultivation were intensified and if it were supplemented by other food products such as fish, corn, and vegetables.

How far the Filipinos could or would respond to such a program was problematical. The soundness of the reasoning behind it was undeniable. But such things as dollar reserves, balance of payments, or excess of imports have little meaning to the man in the village. It is the hard task of President Garcia to translate into the simplest terms for his people situations, problems, and possibilities that are enormously complex.

A new administration is thus taking shape with an unusual burden to be carried. Much of the glorious enthusiasm of the Magsaysay days has evaporated. It is true that a new day has dawned, but it is not entirely sunlit. There must be "austerity" in the Philippines, and austerity is seldom popular; it sits uneasily upon the light-hearted and warm-hearted Filipino.

Freedom, the Filipino has a right to believe, has come to stay. But the fruits of freedom must be earned.

Eleven

THE OUTLOOK

What is the outlook for the Philippines? Friends of the Filipinos, students of history, lovers of freedom, are asking that question with justified concern. If this "great experiment" fails, much will fall with it. If it succeeds, a new victory in a long struggle will have been won, and won on an important field.

The role of prophet is hazardous, often unrewarding. Happily, in the case of the Philippines some elements in the situation are so clear, some trends so firmly established, that at least some of those hazards can be reduced. International cataclysm would change those elements and trends. Short of that, certain patterns of thought and behavior seem likely to be followed. Certain factors—economic and political ones in particular—are clearly evident, and will continue to play their decisive role unless total upheaval supervenes.

ECONOMIC

What, then, is the outlook? On the economic side, the short-term view is bad, the long-range view good.

Unpleasant as it is, the fact must be recognized that the Philippines faces rough going, economically, for some time to come. An attempt is being made to change the total economy. This is not an easy, nor is it a short-term, process. As an exporter of raw materials or semi-finished products—chiefly sugar, coconuts, and hemp—to a protected market, the Philippines could prosper. But this was not an independent economy. The protected market is to be gradually withdrawn, according to the terms of the 1946 Trade Act and its subsequent amendments. Philippine production will have to become competitive, not "colonial."

This poses two problems. First, the permanent weight of agricultural production (the exports to the protected market were largely agricultural) must be shifted to sustaining crops, rather than money crops. In blunter terms, the Philippines must be prepared to feed itself instead of relying upon food imports that are paid for by those money crops. This requires, immediately, a substantial increase in the production of rice, but that production must also be reinforced by greater diversification of the agricultural economy, including such things as dairy products, vegetables and fruits, flour sources other than rice, coffee, tea, spices, and meats. It also requires a badly needed increase in the use of the great fish resources of the archipelago through improved methods of catch, preparation, refrigeration, and distribution.

The rice problem can be solved through an extensive expansion of irrigation that will make double-cropping possible in already productive areas, and will bring in some other lands that are now marginal. This will, however, be a long and expensive process. The Agno River project ought to double the rice output of central Luzon, but only one of its four dams has been completed, and that at a high cost. The supplementary problem involved in diversification can be solved only through processes of education and experiment. These cannot come about overnight. Meanwhile, rice will continue to be threefold overpriced in the Manila market, and canned and powdered milk will be imported, along with wheat flour, sardines, and celery.

The second problem is the establishment of an industrial

base sufficiently broad that the bulk of consumer goods can be produced locally, rather than imported and paid for out of those same money crops. It is hoped that eventually there will be large manufactures for export, and thus further earnings, but this is not the immediate problem. What industrialization must do now is give the Filipino a chance to produce at home rather than to buy abroad.

In the various efforts to change economic patterns throughout the world both the term and the idea of "industrialization" have been much abused. It has been held up as the panacea for all ills. In cases such as those of Japan, India, or Java, it has been proclaimed as the only way to escape intolerable population pressure on the land. In the Soviet Union and in Communist China it has been instituted by coercion, both to obtain a productive independence from non-Communist countries and to create the dogma-required urban industrial proletariat at a cost of unimaginable human suffering. In the planning for some "underdeveloped" countries it has been made a catch-all, and has been too often represented as a cure-all. It can present as many problems as it solves.

The case of the Philippines is illustrative. Since the Liberation more than eight hundred new Philippine "industries" have been established. Almost all of them had to depend, in the beginning, upon imports of machinery from abroad. Many, if not most, of them had to depend, and are still depending, upon imports to supply their basic materials. The function of the new industries has generally been packaging, processing, and assembling. There are exceptions, of course, and some operations, as has been noted, have been designed specifically to make use of available materials. All these operations have given employment and lent impetus to the whole process of recovery. But they have only scratched the surface of the problem and in some ways have intensified it.

Now, there is a lag. The new industries are not yet fully prepared to supply consumer needs and are importing materials to gain their own headway. Meanwhile, the very consumer goods that these industries hope eventually to supply must continue to be imported. It will take time, not only to reduce this gap, but also to supply, from local sources, much of this raw material that is now being brought in and whose import has contributed to the unfavorable trade balance that has been the crux of the financial crisis.

Until the Philippines attains complete self-sufficiency in food, and until the process of industrialization has been better geared to available raw materials, the Filipinos are in for a bad time. They will be helped by their continued export of the money crops, even under the restrictions that exist. They will probably continue to be helped by the United States, especially in investments that can speed up some needed projects. But continuation of the "austerity" that President Garcia has proclaimed will be required. There will not be famine, but the price of rice will remain too high. There will not be national bankruptcy, but some of the ice upon which the government will be obliged to skate will be uncomfortably thin. Our assistance will be needed.

In contrast to this immediately grim prospect, the long-range economic picture is bright. There is no dearth of resources. There is already a highly developed, if too much concentrated, agricultural production. There need be no population pressure on the land if there is any sort of adequate redistribution of population, since many areas are not yet even explored, much less settled. The archipelago as a whole is not over-populated. The potential mineral wealth is very great.

Some time will be required to bring many of the favorable factors into play. Power and irrigation projects go slowly, but their effect will eventually be felt. Feeder roads cannot be built overnight, but there is already a continuously expanding network of communication that will bring every producer into immediate contact with his market. In some cases, "development" means hacking away at a jungle. In many more, it means simply using already proved skills to obtain better distribution of the products of toil. More effective use of the great marine resources is a good illustration of this.

Similarly, the application of imagination and skill can make wide and profitable use of what is now either waste or merely potential. For example, the residue of sugar cane, bagasse, is still being used in many places simply as fuel. It is a possible source of cellulose products with a wide range of uses. The same thing is true of abacá waste. Good pioneer work has been done in this field, and offers room for great expansion. This is true for fibers in general, and it is important because the Philippines has for years relied upon imports of yarns, cottons, newsprint, and paper products of all sorts. The use of some local fibers, such as the world-famous *piña,* made from the pineapple, is well-established. But there is a place for much further development in this field. In spite of its renowned versatility, bamboo is not nearly as widely used as it can be, and it is abundant. There are tough grasses, such as cogon, that are now merely a menace but that can be transformed into a rich asset. These things are emphasized because they lie within the real Philippine life-pattern. *Piña, jusi,* and *sinimay,* all closely identified with the very life of the Filipino; they are fibers and textiles from his own soil. His village house is made of nipa and *swali,* plus the inevitable bamboo. The *bali-buntal* straw hat has no superior. Such things are not usually thought of as national resources or elements in wealth, but they can be. Before the war, Indo-China had a significant foreign trade in rattans, and "Hong Kong chairs" are a fixture on the American market.

The engineering of waste is still in its infancy in the Philippines. It has a favorable climate in which to grow.

It is in the field of mineral resources that the Filipinos can most confidently look to the future. The archipelago is a chain of volcanic islands, each with its mountainous back-bone. Their mineral wealth was known even in the days of Magellan. It has only begun to be developed. Arthur Fischer, the great director of the Bureau of Forestry in the Philippines for more than a quarter of a century and the man who did more than any other to establish the value and use of the superb Philippine hardwoods, once said:

Some day, I suppose, they will cut down most of these noble trees. Unless there is a sound replanting, the Philippine mahogany, the *narra, ipil, akle, camagon,* and *apitong* will be a thing of the past. It takes a century for such a tree to grow. But in the meantime, Filipinos, and those who are interested here, will come to realize that this whole archipelago, from stem to stern, is a potential mine. It is highly mineralized from the northern tip of Luzon to the south end of Mindanao. They will use mahogany to shore up mine shafts. The wealth is there, and men will go after it.

The lament for the trees is justified. The appraisal of mineral wealth has been repeatedly confirmed.

Before the Second World War the Philippines was second only to California as a gold producer under the American flag. Iron was being shipped to Japan. An immense chromite deposit was being worked in Zambales. Manganese was taken from Busuanga. Copper was mined at Lepanto, and silver was a by-product. Lead and zinc were coming out of Masbate.

And the geologists and explorers continued to insist that only the surface had been scratched. The whole northeastern end of Mindanao was an iron formation. Next to it lay huge deposits of nickel. It was no wonder that there was a mining boom in the thirties.

The boom collapsed because it was premature and often characterized by dishonest practices. The mineral wealth was still there. The real producers kept on producing, and they are still doing so.

To all this has now been added the prospect of striking oil in the Philippines. Small deposits were explored and worked for a number of years in Cebu and on the Bondoc Peninsula. Their yield was not significant but their indications were provocative. There were proved oil resources in the Indonesian archipelago, in Sumatra, and in Borneo. It was reasonable to assume that oil deposits occurred in the north of the volcanic crescent, and could and would be found in the Philippines. The small workings seemed to confirm this.

In 1957 three American companies, working with the Philippine government, began large-scale drilling operations at what seemed to be the most favorable location, the Cagayan Valley in northern Luzon. There was no quick oil strike, but there was no loss of confidence. The geologists and the engineers were convinced that the oil was there, that it was only a problem of getting down to it at the right places. By the end of the year they were still drilling and still hoping. A substantial part of the Philippine future rests upon their judgment and their hopes.

President Garcia is clear-headed, but optimistic, about these developments. In a recent discussion he said:

Our real economic future, of course, lies in our mineral wealth. Some of it will be noncompetitive. Some of it can be put on the market favorably. Our problem is only how to use it to the best advantage.

Now, naturally, when we get oil from Cagayan, many of the big questions will be answered. We will have the fuel that we need. Perhaps we can export, but that is not the first thing. We can develop a variety of enterprises here without being dependent upon imports. We can supplement our hydroelectric power sources with more thermal plants. We can use what may eventually be a surplus of energy to raise our whole standard of living. And we will have the by-products.

We can't eat gold and we can't drink oil. But if we have the minerals and have the fuel we can prosper. This ought to be our future.

Some of the President's confidence is shared. American interests have just started a large oil refinery on the Bataan Peninsula, facing Manila Bay. They hope, and expect, eventually to get their raw materials from the Philippines rather than import them. They are looking, also, to a happier future. The choice of Bataan as a site was dictated, undoubtedly, by business reasons. The emotional overtones, however, can hardly be denied. This, again, is victory.

POLITICAL

If this economic picture seems complex and cloudy, the political picture, on the other hand, is simple and clear. The outlook is exceptionally bright.

The Preamble to the Jones Law set forth the establishment of a "stable" government as a condition requisite for Philippine independence. It can now be said, with confidence, that the Filipinos are living under the most stable free government in Asia.

This stability consists in the recognition and use of the working instruments of a political democracy. A constitution is honored and upheld. The functions of each branch of government are defined and generally understood. The responsibility of that government to the electorate is vigorously defended. There is freedom to oppose, freedom to change, freedom to direct. Sovereignty resides in the people, and they are able to determine its use.

These statements could not have been made with the same assurance seven years ago. Democratic representative government seemed, for a time, to hang in the balance. But a change has been wrought, partly by the towering personality of Magsaysay and even more by a growing sense of political maturity, integrity, and independence of thought. In a sense, there has been a political rebirth in the Philippines. Any reversal, now, seems unlikely, and in the light of the steadily increasing political self-consciousness of a growing electorate, almost impossible.

Even the death of Magsaysay, tragic as it was, seems to have served a noble purpose in the end. What followed has proved that this was not "the end of the world" as far as political freedom was concerned. The institutions of government, and of freedom, could remain intact, even if a peerless leader were lost.

Thus, while the ensuing election may have seemed to some persons to be an almost sacrilegious turning away from great purposes to political trivia, it served an important end. It showed that men could decide without being "led." It showed that the right to dissent from a majority was intact. The fact that it was a "free" election had a far wider significance than any little question of "goon squads" at the polling booths. It was "free" in the much larger sense that the public could choose, on its own judgment of merit, those who should be placed in high office. The choice of a vice president from the opposition party may pose some temporary political problems. In the longer-range view it has demonstrated, as few things could, and has vindicated beyond question, the principle that Filipinos are and will be under a government that derives its just powers from the consent of the governed.

Interesting things lie ahead. This election marked the significant rise of a group of younger men who were not identified with the older Philippine political history. The Philippines has had its "Old Guard" (in the same sense that we use the term) for some time. It is now getting its share of the "Young Turks."

This development is good. It is probable that by the next presidential election, four years hence, some of the elder statesmen who have exercised influence for so long will have gladly retired from the scene. Their places will be taken by younger men who are not necessarily persons of more ability, but are less bound by certain ties to the past. It is unlikely that these "Young Turks" will be "revolutionary." Some of the ablest of the younger group are among the conservatives.

It does seem reasonable to suggest, nevertheless, that there will be a sharper definition of "conservative" and "liberal." This could be a sound basis for the growth of a real and effective two-party system for the Philippines. It would avoid the perils of fragmentation into a variety of splinter parties. It would provide a continuous and effective—and loyal— opposition.

This most recent election demonstrated clearly that these younger men, in government or out, will make their weight increasingly felt. This, also, is a good thing. In government, they can give a fresh vitality to some institutions that have grown tired and old. Outside, they can be the constant and vigilant monitors who insist that all the people be heard. In both roles they will represent the growth that ought to be expected. They have already given evidence that confidence in them will not be misplaced.

★   ★

One cannot escape the feeling that in some ways, in the Philippines, the wheel has come full cycle. For more than half a century dedicated men, Filipinos and Americans, have dreamed of the day when this people could be truly free. They have worked toward that end, sometimes at cross-purposes, sometimes in conflict, sometimes in doubt. Now the dream is becoming reality. Their faith and their labor have not been in vain.

There is now, in the Philippines, a free people. They are sovereign in their own right. They are independent. Much more than that, they can claim and enjoy the defense of their liberties. They can be free.

The way has not been easy in the past. It will not be easier in the future. There is no royal road to freedom, there or here. Quezon said that there were "dangers and disadvantages," but that they would be faced. They must still be faced, because they are still there. This is a beginning and not an end.

Some things, however, have been established. The Filipino has a right to live under a government of his own choosing. He can change that government if he wishes, because it is of his own making. It belongs to him. He can be free in his speech, his worship, his assembly, his movement, and his right to dissent. He can confidently expect a better world because he has the right to make it.

The Filipino is free, also, to sustain his close and affectionate association with those who have been his friends. The severing of political bonds has left, mercifully, no legacy of bitterness, either there or here. If the United States had a mission, it can still be carried out in the form of a deeper friendship. The Filipino loves freedom, as do we. It is our unbreakable bond.

There are many statues of national heroes in the Philippines. There have been many classrooms adorned with pictures of American heroes. This is as it should be. And some day in the Philippines, not far from the monuments to Rizal, Mabini, and Bonifacio, not far from the classrooms that have had their pictures of Washington and Lincoln, Filipinos and Americans will unite to erect a fresh and imperishable monument—to Thomas Jefferson.

Appendix A

ORGANIC ACT OF THE PHILIPPINE

ISLANDS, THE JONES ACT

CHAPTER 416—An Act to declare the purpose of the people of the United States as to the future political status of the people of the Philippine Islands, and to provide a more autonomous government for those islands.

Whereas it was never the intention of the people of the United States in the incipiency of the War with Spain to make it a war of conquest or for territorial aggrandizement; and

Whereas it is, as it has always been, the purpose of the people of the United States to withdraw their sovereignty over the Philippine Islands and to recognize their independence as soon as a stable government can be established therein; and

Whereas for the speedy accomplishment of such purpose it is desirable to place in the hands of the people of the Philippines as large a control of their domestic affairs as can be given them without, in the meantime, impairing the exercise of the rights of sovereignty by the people of the United States, in order that, by the use and exercise of popular franchise and governmental powers, they may be the better prepared to fully assume the responsibilities and enjoy all the privileges of complete independence: Therefore

BE IT ENACTED BY THE SENATE AND HOUSE OF REPRESENTATIVES OF THE UNITED STATES OF AMERICA IN CONGRESS ASSEMBLED, That the provisions of this Act and the name "The Philippines" as used in this Act shall apply to and include the Philippine Islands ceded to the United States Government by the treaty of peace concluded between the United States and Spain on the eleventh day of April, eighteen hundred and ninety-nine, the boundaries of which are set forth in Article III of said treaty, together with those islands embraced in the treaty between Spain and the United States concluded at Washington on the seventh day of November, nineteen hundred.

Sec. 2. That all inhabitants of the Philippine Islands who were Spanish subjects on the eleventh day of April, eighteen hundred and ninety-nine, and then resided in said islands, and their children born subsequent thereto, shall be deemed and held to be citizens of the Philippine Islands, except such as shall have elected to preserve their allegiance to the Crown of Spain in accordance with the provisions of the treaty of peace between the United States and Spain, signed at Paris December tenth, eighteen hundred and ninety-eight, and except such others as have since become citizens of some other country: PROVIDED, That the Philippine Legislature, herein provided for, is hereby authorized to provide by law for the acquisition of Philippine citizenship by those natives of the Philippine Islands who do not come within the foregoing provisions, the natives of the insular possessions of the United States, and such other persons residing in the Philippine Islands who are citizens of the United States, or who could become citizens of the United States under the laws of the United States if residing therein.

Sec. 3. That no law shall be enacted in said islands which shall deprive any person of life, liberty, or property without due process of law, or deny to any person therein the equal protection of the laws. Private property shall not be taken for public use without just compensation.

That in all criminal prosecutions the accused shall enjoy the right to be heard by himself and counsel, to demand the nature and cause of the accusation against him, to have a speedy and public trial, to meet the witnesses face to face, and to have compulsory process to compel the attendance of witnesses in his behalf.

That no person shall be held to answer for a criminal offense without due process of law; and no person for the same offense shall be twice put in jeopardy of punishment, nor shall be compelled in any criminal case to be a witness against himself.

That all persons shall before conviction be bailable by sufficient sureties, except for capital offenses.

That no law impairing the obligation of contracts shall be enacted.

That no persons shall be imprisoned for debt.

That the privilege of the writ of habeas corpus shall not be suspended, unless when in cases of rebellion, insurrection, or invasion the public safety may require it, in either of which events the same may be suspended by the President, or by the Governor General, wherever during such period the necessity for such suspension shall exist.

That no ex post facto law or bill of attainder shall be enacted nor shall the law of primogeniture ever be in force in the Philippines.

That no law granting a title of nobility shall be enacted, and no person holding any office of profit or trust in said islands shall, without the consent of the Congress of the United States, accept any present, emolument, office, or title of any kind whatever from any king, queen, prince, or foreign State.

That excessive bail shall not be required, nor excessive fines imposed, nor cruel and unusual punishment inflicted.

That the right to be secure against unreasonable searches and seizures shall not be violated.

That slavery shall not exist in said islands; nor shall involuntary servitude exist therein except as a punishment for crime whereof the party shall have been duly convicted.

That no law shall be passed abridging the freedom of speech or of the press, or the right of the people peaceably to assemble and petition the Government for redress of grievances.

That no law shall be made respecting an establishment of religion or prohibiting the free exercise thereof, and that the free exercise and enjoyment of religious profession and worship, without discrimination or preference, shall forever be allowed; and no religious test shall be required for the exercise of civil or political rights. No public money or property shall ever be appropriated, applied, donated, or used, directly or indirectly, for the use, benefit, or support of any sect, church, denomination, sectarian institution, or system of religion, or for the use, benefit, or support of any priest, preacher, minister, or other religious teacher or dignitary as such. Contracting of polygamous or plural marriages hereafter is prohibited. That no law shall be construed to permit polygamous or plural marriages.

That no money shall be paid out of the treasury except in pursuance of an appropriation by law.

That the rule of taxation in said islands shall be uniform.

That no bill which may be enacted into law shall embrace more than one subject, and that subject shall be expressed in the title of the bill.

That no warrant shall issue but upon probable cause, supported by oath or affirmation, and particularly describing the place to be searched and the person or things to be seized.

That all money collected on any tax levied or assessed for the special purpose shall be treated as a special fund in the treasury and paid out for such purpose only.

Sec. 4. That all expenses that may be incurred on account of the Government of the Philippines for salaries of officials and the conduct of their offices and department, and all expenses and obligations contracted for the internal improvement or development of the islands, not, however, including defenses, barracks, and other works undertaken by the United States, shall, except as otherwise specifically provided by the Congress, be paid by the Government of the Philippines.

Sec. 5. That the statutory laws of the United States hereafter enacted shall not apply to the Philippine Islands, except when they specifically so provide, or it is so provided in this Act.

Sec. 6. That the laws now in force in the Philippines shall continue in force and effect, except as altered, amended, or modified herein, until altered, amended or repealed by the legislative authority herein provided or by Act of Congress of the United States.

Sec. 7. That the legislative authority herein provided shall have power, when not inconsistent with this Act, by due enactment to amend, alter, modify, or repeal any law, civil or criminal, continued in force by this Act as it may from time to time see fit.

This power shall specifically extend with the limitation herein provided as to the tariff to all laws relating to revenue and taxation in effect in the Philippines.

Sec. 8. That general legislative power, except as otherwise herein provided, is hereby granted to the Philippine Legislature, authorized by this Act.

Sec. 9. That all the property and rights which may have been acquired in the Philippine Islands by the United States under the treaty of peace with Spain, signed December tenth, eighteen hundred and ninety-eight, except such land or other property as has been or shall be designated by the President of the United States for military and other reservations of the Government of the United States, and all lands which may have been subsequently acquired by the government of the Philippine Islands by purchase under the provisions of sections sixty-three and sixty-four of the Act of Congress approved July first, nineteen hundred and two, except such as may have heretofore been sold and disposed of for the benefit of inhabitants thereof, and the Philippine Legislature shall have power to legislate with respect to all such matters as it may deem advisable; but acts of the Philippine Legislature with reference to land of the public domain, timber, and mining, hereafter enacted, shall not have the force of law until approved by the President of the United States: *Provided,* That upon the approval of such an act by the Governor General, it shall be by him forthwith transmitted to the President of the United States, and he shall approve or disapprove the same within six months from and after its enactment and submission for his approval, and if not disapproved within such time it shall become law the same as if it had been specifically approved: *Provided further,* That where lands in the Philippine Islands have been or may be reserved for any public purpose of the United States, and, being no longer required for the

purpose for which reserved, have been or may be, by order of the
President, placed under the control of the government of said islands
to be administered for the benefit of the inhabitants thereof, the order
of the President shall be regarded as effectual to give the government
of said islands full control and power to administer and dispose of
such lands for the benefit of the inhabitants of said islands.

Sec. 10. That while this Act provides that the Philippine government shall have the authority to enact a tariff law the trade relations
between the islands and the United States shall continue to be governed exclusively by laws of the Congress of the United States: *Provided,* That tariff acts or acts amendatory to the tariff of the Philippine Islands shall not become law until they shall receive the approval
of the President of the United States, nor shall any act of the Philippine Legislature affecting immigration or the currency or coinage
laws of the Philippines become a law until it has been approved by
the President of the United States: *Provided further,* That the President shall approve or disapprove any act mentioned in the foregoing
proviso within six months from and after its enactment and submission for his approval, and if not disapproved within such time it
shall become a law the same as if it had been specifically approved.

Sec. 11. That no export duties shall be levied or collected on exports from the Philippine Islands, but taxes and assessments on property and license fees for franchises, and privileges, and internal taxes,
direct or indirect, may be imposed for the purposes of the Philippine
government and the provincial and municipal governments thereof,
respectively, as may be provided and defined by acts of the Philippine Legislature, and, where necessary to anticipate taxes and revenues, bonds and other obligations may be issued by the Philippine
government or any provincial or municipal government therein, as
may be provided by law and to protect the public credit: *Provided,
however,* That the entire indebtedness of the Philippine government
created by the authority conferred herein shall not exceed at any one
time the sum of $15,000,000, exclusive of those obligations known as
friar land bonds, nor that of any Province or municipality a sum in
excess of seven per centum of the aggregate tax valuation of its property at any one time.

Sec. 12. That general legislative powers in the Philippines, except
as herein otherwise provided, shall be vested in a legislature which
shall consist of two houses, one the senate and the other the house of
representatives, and the two houses shall be designated "The Philippine Legislature": *Provided,* That until the Philippine Legislature as
herein provided shall have been organized the existing Philippine Legislature shall have all legislative authority herein granted to the govern-

ment of the Philippine Islands, except such as may now be within the exclusive jurisdiction of the Philippine Commission, which is so continued until the organization of the legislature herein provided for the Philippines. When the Philippine Legislature shall have been organized, the exclusive legislative jurisdiction and authority exercised by the Philippine Commission shall thereafter be exercised by the Philippine Legislature.

Sec. 13. That the members of the senate of the Philippines, except as herein provided, shall be elected for terms of six and three years, as hereinafter provided, by the qualified electors of the Philippines. Each of the senatorial districts defined as hereinafter provided shall have the right to elect two senators. No person shall be an elective member of the senate of the Philippines who is not a qualified elector and over thirty years of age, and who is not able to read and write either the Spanish or English language, and who has not been a resident of the Philippines for at least two consecutive years and an actual resident of the senatorial district from which chosen for a period of at least one year immediately prior to his election.

Sec. 14. That the members of the house of representatives shall, except as herein provided, be elected triennially by the qualified electors of the Philippines. Each of the representative districts hereinafter provided for shall have the right to elect one representative. No person shall be an elective member of the house of representatives who is not a qualified elector and over twenty-five years of age, and who is not able to read and write either the Spanish or English language, and who has not been an actual resident of the district from which elected for at least one year immediately prior to his election: *Provided,* That the members of the present assembly elected on the first Tuesday in June, nineteen hundred and sixteen, shall be the members of the house of representatives from their respective districts for the term expiring in nineteen hundred and nineteen.

Sec. 15. That at the first election held pursuant to this act, the qualified electors shall be those having the qualifications of voters under the present law; thereafter and until otherwise provided by the Philippine Legislature herein provided for, the qualifications of voters for senators and representatives in the Philippines and all officers elected by the people shall be as follows:

Every male person who is not a citizen or subject of a foreign power twenty-one years of age or over (except insane and feeble-minded persons and those convicted in a court of competent jurisdiction of an infamous offense since the thirteenth day of August, eighteen hundred and ninety-eight), who shall have been a resident of the Philippines for one year and of the municipality in which he shall offer to vote for six months next preceding the day of voting, and who is comprised within one of the following classes:

    (a) Those who under existing law are legal voters and have exercised the right of suffrage.

    (b) Those who own real property to the value of 500 pesos, or who annually pay 30 pesos or more of the established taxes.

    (c) Those who are able to read and write either Spanish, English, or a native language.

Sec. 16. That the Philippine Islands shall be divided into twelve senate districts, as follows:

First district: Batanes, Cagayan, Isabela, Ilocos Norte and Ilocos Sur

Second district: La Union, Pangasinan, and Zambales

Third district: Tarlac, Nueva Ecija, Pampanga, and Bulacan

Fourth district: Bataan, Rizal, Manila and Laguna

Fifth district: Batangas, Mindoro, Tayabas, and Cavite

Sixth district: Sorsogon, Albay, and Ambos Camarines

Seventh district: Iloilo and Capiz

Eighth district: Negros Occidental, Negros Oriental, Antique, and Palawan

Ninth district: Leyte and Samar

Tenth district: Cebu

Eleventh district: Surigao, Misamis, and Bohol

Twelfth district; The Mountain Province, Baguio, Nueva Vizcaya, and the Department of Mindanao and Sulu.

The representative districts shall be the eighty-one now provided by law, and three in the Mountain Province, one in Neuva Vizcaya, and five in the Department of Mindanao and Sulu.

The first election under the provisions of this Act shall be held on the first Tuesday of October, nineteen hundred and sixteen, unless the Governor General in his discretion shall fix another date not earlier than thirty nor later than sixty days after the passage of this Act: *Provided*, That the Governor General's proclamation shall be published at least thirty days prior to the date fixed for the election, and there shall be chosen at such election one senator from each senate district for a term of three years and one for six years. Thereafter one senator from each district shall be elected from each senate district for a term of six years: *Provided*, That the Governor General of the Philippine Islands shall appoint, without the consent of the senate and without restriction as to residence, senators and representatives who will, in his opinion, best represent the senate district and those representative districts which may be included in the territory not now represented in the Philippine Assembly: *Provided fur-*

ther, That thereafter elections shall be held only on such days and under such regulations as to ballots, voting, and qualifications of electors as may be prescribed by the Philippine Legislature, to which is hereby given authority to redistrict the Philippine Islands and modify, amend, or repeal any provision of this section, except such as refer to appointive senators and representatives.

Sec. 17. That the terms of office of elective senators and representatives shall be six and three years, respectively, and shall begin on the date of their election. In case of vacancy among the elective members of the senate or in the house of representatives, special elections may be held in the districts wherein such vacancy occurred under such regulations as may be prescribed by law, but senators or representatives elected in such cases shall hold office only for the unexpired portion of the term wherein the vacancy occurred. Senators and representatives appointed by the Governor General shall hold office until removed by the Governor General.

Sec. 18. That the senate and house of representatives, respectively, shall be the sole judges of the elections, returns, and qualifications of their elective members, and each house may determine the rules of its proceedings, punish its members for disorderly behaviour, and, with the concurrence of two-thirds, expel an elective member. Both houses shall convene at the capital on the sixteenth day of October next following the election and be organized by the election of a speaker or a presiding officer, a clerk, and a sergeant at arms for each house, and such other officers and assistants as may be required. A majority of each house shall constitute a quorum to do business, but a smaller number may meet, adjourn from day to day, and compel the attendance of absent members. The legislature shall hold annual sessions, commencing on the sixteenth day of October, or, if the sixteenth day of October be a legal holiday, then on the first day following which is not a legal holiday, in each year. The legislature may be called in special session at any time by the Governor General for general legislation, or for action on such specific subjects as he may designate. No special session shall continue longer than thirty days, and no regular session shall continue longer than one hundred days, exclusive of Sundays. The legislature is hereby given the power and authority to change the date of the commencement of its annual sessions.

The senators and representatives shall receive an annual compensation for their services, to be ascertained by law, and paid out of the treasury of the Philippine Islands. The senators and representatives shall, in all cases except treason, felony, and breach of the peace, be privileged from arrest during their attendance at the session of their respective houses and in going to and returning from the same; and for any speech or debate in either house they shall not be questioned in any other place.

No senator or representative shall, during the time for which he may have been elected, be eligible to any office the election to which is vested in the legislature, nor shall be appointed to any office of trust or profit which shall have been created or the emoluments of which shall have been increased during such term.

Sec. 19. That each house of the legislature shall keep a journal of its proceedings and, from time to time, publish the same; and the yeas and nays of the members of either house, on any question, shall, upon demand of one-fifth of those present, be entered on the journal, and every bill and joint resolution which shall have passed both houses shall, before it becomes a law, be presented to the Governor General. If he approves the same, he shall sign it; but if not, he shall return it with his objections to that house in which it shall have originated, which shall enter the objections at large on its journal and proceed to reconsider it. If, after such reconsideration, two-thirds of the members elected to the house shall agree to pass the same, it shall be sent, together with the objections, to the other house, by which it shall enter the objections at large on its journal and proceed to reconsider it. If, after such reconsideration, two-thirds of the members elected to that house shall agree to pass the same, it shall be sent, together with the objections, to the other house, by which it shall likewise be reconsidered, and if approved by two-thirds of all the members elected to that house it shall be sent to the Governor General, who, in case he shall then not approve, shall transmit the same to the President of the United States. The vote of each house shall be by the yeas and nays, and the names of the members voting for and against shall be entered on the journal. If the President of the United States approve the same, he shall sign it and it shall become a law. If he shall not approve same, he shall return it to the Governor General so stating, and it shall not become a law: *Provided,* That if any bill or joint resolution shall not be returned by the Governor General as herein provided within twenty days (Sundays excepted) after it shall have been presented to him the same shall become a law in like manner as if he had signed it, unless the legislature by adjournment prevent its return, in which case it shall become a law unless vetoed by the Governor General within thirty days after adjournment: *Provided further,* That the President of the United States shall approve or disapprove an act submitted to him under the provisions of this section within six months from and after its enactment and submission for his approval; and if not approved within such time, it shall become a law the same as if it had been specifically approved. The Governor General shall have the power to veto any particular item or items of an appropriation bill, but the veto shall not affect the item or items to which he does not object. The item or items objected to shall not take effect except in the manner heretofore provided in this section as to bills and joint resolutions returned to the legislature without his approval.

All laws enacted by the Philippine Legislature shall be reported to the Congress of the United States, which hereby reserves the power and authority to annul the same. If at the termination of any fiscal year the appropriations necessary for the support of government for the ensuing fiscal year shall not have been made, the several sums appropriated in the last appropriation bills for the objects and purposes therein specified, so far as the same may be done, shall be deemed to be reappropriated for the several objects and purposes specified in said last appropriation bill; and until the legislature shall act in such behalf the treasurer shall, when so directed by the Governor General, make the payments necessary for the purposes aforesaid.

Sec. 20. That at the first meeting of the Philippine Legislature created by this Act and triennially thereafter there shall be chosen by the legislature two Resident Commissioners to the United States, who shall hold their office for a term of three years beginning with the fourth day of March following their election, and who shall be entitled to an official recognition as such by all departments upon presentation to the President of a certificate of election by the Governor General of said islands. Each of said Resident Commissioners shall, in addition to the salary and the sum in lieu of mileage now allowed by law, be allowed the same sum for stationery and for the pay of necessary clerk hire as is now allowed to the Members of the House of Representatives of the United States, to be paid out of the Treasury of the United States, and the franking privilege allowed by law to Members of Congress. No person shall be eligible to election as Resident Commissioner who is not a bona fide elector of said islands and who does not owe allegiance to the United States and who is not more than thirty years of age and who does not read and write the English language. The present two Resident Commissioners shall hold office until the fourth of March, nineteen hundred and seventeen. In case of vacancy in the position of Resident Commissioner caused by resignation or otherwise, the Governor General may make temporary appointments until the next meeting of the Philippine Legislature, which shall then fill such vacancy; but the Resident Commissioner thus elected shall hold office only for the unexpired portion of the term wherein the vacancy occurred.

Sec. 21. That the supreme executive power shall be vested in an executive officer, whose official title shall be "The Governor General of the Philippine Islands." He shall be appointed by the President, by and with the advice and consent of the Senate of the United States, and hold his office at the pleasure of the President and until his successor is chosen and qualified. The Governor General shall reside in the Philippine Islands during his official incumbency, and maintain his office at the seat of government. He shall, unless otherwise herein provided, appoint, by and with the consent of the Philippine Senate, such officers as may now be appointed by the Governor General, or such as he is authorized by this Act to appoint, or whom he may hereafter be authorized by law to appoint; but appointments made while the senate is not in session shall be effective either until disapproval or until the next adjournment of the senate. He shall have general supervision and control of all of the departments and bureaus of the government in the Philippine Islands as far as is consistent with the provisions of this Act, and shall be commander in chief of all locally created armed forces and militia. He is hereby vested with the exclusive power to grant pardons and reprieves and remit fines and forfeitures, and may veto any legislation enacted as herein provided. He shall submit within ten days of the opening of each regular session of the Philippine Legislature a budget of receipts and expenditures, which shall be the basis of the annual appropriation bill. He shall commission all officers that he may be authorized to appoint. He shall be responsible for the faithful execution of the laws of the Philippine Islands and of the United States operative within the Philippine Islands, and whenever it becomes necessary he may call upon the commanders of the military and naval forces of the United States in the islands, or summon the posse comitatus, or call out the militia or other locally created armed forces, to prevent or suppress lawless violence, invasion, insurrection, or rebellion; and he may, in case of rebellion or invasion, or imminent danger thereof, when the public safety requires it, suspend the privileges of the writ of habeas corpus, or place the islands, or any part thereof, under martial law: *Provided,* That whenever the Governor General shall exercise this authority, he shall at once notify the President of the United States thereof, together with the attending facts and circumstances, and the President shall have power to modify or vacate the action of the Governor General. He shall annually and at such other times as he may be required make such official report of the transactions of the government of the Philippine Islands to an executive department of the United States to be designated by the President, and his said annual report shall be transmitted to the Congress of the United States;

and he shall perform such additional duties and functions as may in pursuance of law be delegated or assigned to him by the President.

Sec. 22. That, except as provided otherwise in this Act, the executive departments of the Philippine government shall continue as now authorized by law until otherwise provided by the Philippine Legislature. When the Philippine Legislature herein provided shall convene and organize, the Philippine Commission, as such, shall cease and determine, and the members thereof shall vacate their offices as members of said commission: *Provided,* That the heads of the executive departments shall continue to exercise their executive functions until the heads of departments provided by the Philippine Legislature pursuant to the provisions of this Act are appointed and qualified. The Philippine Legislature may thereafter by appropriate legislation increase the number or abolish any of the executive departments, or make such changes in the names and duties thereof as it may see fit, and shall provide for the appointment and removal of the heads of the executive departments by the Governor General or within one of the executive departments under the supervision and control of the Governor General. There is hereby established a bureau, to be known as the Bureau of Non-Christian Tribes, which said bureau shall be embraced in one of the executive departments to be designated by the Governor General, and shall have general supervision over the public affairs of the inhabitants of the territory represented in the legislature by appointive senators and representatives.

Sec. 23. That there shall be appointed by the President, by and with the advice and consent of the Senate of the United States, a vice governor of the Philippine Islands, who shall have all of the powers of the Governor General in the case of a vacancy or temporary removal, resignation, or disability of the Governor General, or in case of his temporary absence; and the said vice governor shall be the head of the executive department known as the department of public instruction, which shall include the bureau of education and the bureau of health, and he may be assigned such other executive duties as the Governor General may designate.

Other bureaus now included in the department of public instruction shall, until otherwise provided by the Philippine Legislature, be included in the department of the interior.

The President may designate the head of an executive department of the Philippine government to act as Governor General in the case of a vacancy, the temporary removal, resignation, or disability of the Governor General and the vice governor, or their temporary absence, and the head of the department thus designated shall exercise all the

powers and perform all the duties of the Governor General during
such vacancy, disability or absence.

Sec. 24. That there shall be appointed by the President an auditor,
who shall examine, audit and settle all accounts pertaining to the
revenues, and receipts from whatever source of the Philippine government and of the provincial and municipal governments of the Philippines including trust funds and funds derived from bond issues; and
audit, in accordance with law and administrative regulations, all expenditures of funds or property pertaining to or held in trust by the
government or the Provinces or municipalities thereof. He shall perform a like duty with respect to all government branches.

He shall keep the general accounts of the government and preserve
the vouchers pertaining thereto.

It shall be the duty of the auditor to bring to the attention of the
proper administrative officer expenditures of funds or property which,
in his opinion, are irregular, unnecessary, excessive or extravagant.

There shall be a deputy auditor appointed in the same manner as
the auditor. The deputy auditor shall sign such official papers as the
auditor may designate and perform such other duties as the auditor
may prescribe, and in case of the death, resignation, sickness, or
other absence of the auditor from his office, from any cause, the
deputy auditor shall have charge of such office. In case of the absence
from duty from any cause of both the auditor and the deputy auditor
the Governor General may designate an assistant who shall have
charge of the office.

The administrative jurisdiction of the auditor over accounts whether
of funds or property, and all vouchers and records pertaining thereto,
shall be exclusive. With the approval of the Governor General he
shall from time to time make and promulgate general or special rules
and regulations not inconsistent with law covering the method of
accounting for public funds and property, and funds and property
held in trust by the government or any of its branches: *Provided,* That
any officer accountable for public funds or property may require such
additional reports or returns from his subordinates or others as he
may deem necessary for his own information and protection.

The decisions of the auditor shall be final and conclusive upon the
executive branches of the government, except that appeal therefrom
may be taken by the party aggrieved or the head of the department
concerned within one year, in the manner hereinafter prescribed. The
auditor shall, except as hereinafter provided, have like authority as
that conferred by law upon the several auditors of the United States
and the Comptroller of the U. S. Treasury and is authorized to com-

municate directly with any person having claims before him for
settlement, or with any department, officer, or person having official
relations with his office.

As soon after the close of each fiscal year as the accounts of said
year may be examined and adjusted the auditor shall submit to the
Governor General and the Secretary of War an annual report of the
fiscal concerns of the government, showing the receipts and dis-
bursements of the various departments and bureaus of the government
and of the various Provinces and municipalities, and make such other
reports as may be required of him by the Governor General or the
Secretary of War.

In the execution of their duties the auditor and the deputy auditor
are authorized to summon witnesses, administer oaths, and to take
evidence and, in the pursuance of these provisions, may issue sub-
poenas and enforce the attendance of witnesses, as now provided by
law.

Sec. 25. That any person aggrieved by the action or decision of the
auditor in the settlement of his account or claim may, within one
year, take an appeal in writing to the Governor General, which appeal
shall specifically set forth the particular action of the auditor to which
exception is taken, with the reason and authorities relied on for re-
versing such decision.

If the Governor General shall confirm the action of the auditor,
he shall so indorse the appeal and transmit it to the auditor, and the
action shall thereupon be final and conclusive. Should the Governor
General fail to sustain the action of the auditor, he shall forthwith
transmit his grounds of disapproval to the Secretary of War, together
with the appeal and the papers necessary to a proper understanding
of the matter. The decision of the Secretary of War in such case
shall be final and conclusive.

Sec. 26. That the supreme court and the courts of first instance
of the Philippine Islands shall possess and exercise jurisdiction as
heretofore provided and such additional jurisdiction as shall hereafter
be prescribed by law. The municipal courts of said islands shall possess and exercise jurisdiction as now provided by law, and the chief
justice and associate justices of the supreme court shall hereafter be
appointed by the President, by and with the advice and consent of the
Senate of the United States. The judges of the court of first instance
shall be appointed by the Governor General, by and with the advice
and consent of the Philippine Senate: *Provided,* That the admiralty
jurisdiction of the supreme court and courts of first instance shall
not be changed except by Act of Congress. That in all cases pending

under the operation of existing laws, both criminal and civil, the jurisdiction shall continue until final judgment and determination.

Sec. 27. That the Supreme Court of the United States shall have jurisdiction to review, revise, reverse, modify, or affirm the final judgments and decrees of the Supreme Court of the Philippine Islands in all actions, cases, causes, and proceedings now pending therein or hereafter determined thereby in which the Constitution or any statute, treaty, title or right, or privilege of the United States is involved, or in causes in which the value in controversy exceeds $25,000, or in which the title or possession of real estate exceeding in value the sum of $25,000, to be ascertained by the oath of either party or of other competent witnesses is involved or brought in question; and such final judgments or decrees may and can be reviewed, revised, reversed, modified, or affirmed by said Supreme Court of the United States on appeal or writ of error by the party aggrieved within the same time, in the same manner, under the same regulations, and by the same procedure, as far as applicable, as the final judgments and decrees of the district courts of the United States.

Sec. 28. That the government of the Philippine Islands may grant franchises and rights, including the authority to exercise the right of eminent domain, for the construction and operation of works of public utility and service, and may authorize said works to be constructed and maintained over and across the public property of the United States, including streets, highways, squares, and reservations, and over similar property of the government of said islands, and may adopt rules and regulations under which the provincial and municipal governments of the islands may grant the right to use and occupy such public property belonging to said Provinces or municipalities: *Provided,* That no private property shall be damaged or taken for any purpose under this section without just compensation, and that such authority to take and occupy land shall not authorize the taking, use, or occupation of any land except such as is required for the actual necessary purposes for which the franchise is granted, and that no franchise or right shall be granted to any individual, firm, or corporation except under the conditions that it shall be subject to amendment, alteration, or repeal by the Congress of the United States, and that lands or right of use and occupation of lands thus granted shall revert to the governments by which they were respectively granted upon the termination of the franchises and rights under which they were granted or upon their revocation or repeal. That all franchises or rights granted under this Act shall forbid the issue of stock or bonds except in exchange for actual cash or for property at a fair valuation equal to the par value of the stock or bonds so issued; shall forbid the declaring of stock or bond dividends, and, in the case of public service corporations, shall provide for the effective regulation of the charges thereof, for the official inspection and regulation of the books and accounts of such corporations, and for the payment of a reasonable percentage of gross earnings into the treasury of the Philippine Islands or of the Province or municipality within which such franchises are granted and exercised: *Provided further,* That it shall be unlawful for any corporation organized under this Act, or for any person, company, or corporation receiving any grant, franchise, or concession from the government of said islands, to use, employ, or contract for the labor of persons held in involuntary servitude; and any person, company, or corporation so violating the provisions of this Act shall forfeit all charters, grants, or franchises for doing business in said islands, in an action or proceeding brought for that purpose in any court of competent jurisdiction by any officer of the Philippine government or on the complaint of any citizen of the Philippines, under such regulations and rules as the Philippine Legislature shall prescribe, and in addition shall be deemed guilty of an offense, and shall be punished by a fine not more than $10,000.

Sec. 29. That, except as in this Act otherwise provided, the salaries of all the officials of the Philippines not appointed by the President including deputies, assistants, and other employees, shall be such and be so paid out of the revenues of the Philippines as shall from time to time be determined by the Philippine Legislature; and if the legislature shall fail to make an appropriation for such salaries, the salaries so fixed shall be paid without the necessity of further appropriations therefor. The salaries of all officers and all expenses of the offices of the various officials of the Philippines appointed as herein provided by the President shall also be paid out of the revenues of the Philippines. The annual salaries of the following named officials appointed by the President and so to be paid shall be: The Governor General, $18,000; in addition thereto he shall be entitled to the occupancy of the buildings heretofore used by the chief executive of the Philippines, with the furniture and effects therein, free of rental; vice governor, $10,000; chief justice of the supreme court, $8,000; associate justices of the supreme court, $7,500 each; auditor $6,000; deputy auditor, $3,000.

Sec. 30. That the provisions of the foregoing section shall not apply to provincial and municipal officials; their salaries and the compensation of their deputies, assistants and other help, as well as all other expenses incurred by the Provinces and municipalities, shall be paid out of the provincial and municipal revenues in such manner as the Philippine Legislature shall provide.

Sec. 31. That all laws or parts of laws applicable to the Philippines not in conflict with any of the provisions of this Act are hereby continued in force and effect.

Approved, August 29, 1916.

Appendix B

PHILIPPINE INDEPENDENCE ACT,

THE TYDINGS-McDUFFIE ACT

AN ACT To provide for the complete independence of the Philippine Islands, to provide for the adoption of a constitution and a form of government for the Philippine Islands, and for other purposes.

Be it so enacted by the Senate and House of Representatives of the United States of America in Congress assembled,

CONVENTION TO FRAME CONSTITUTION FOR PHILIPPINE ISLANDS

Section 1. The Philippine Legislature is hereby authorized to provide for the election of delegates to a constitutional convention, which shall meet in the hall of the house of representatives in the capital of the Philippine Islands, at such time as the Philippine Legislature may fix, but not later than October 1, 1934, to formulate and draft a constitution for the government of the Commonwealth of the Philippine Islands, subject to the conditions and qualifications prescribed in this Act, which shall exercise jurisdiction over all the territory ceded to the United States by the treaty of peace concluded between the United States and Spain on the 10th day of December 1898, the boundaries of which are set forth in article III of said treaty, together with those islands embraced in the treaty between Spain and the United States concluded at Washington on the 7th day of November 1900. The Philippine Legislature shall provide for the necessary expenses of such convention.

CHARACTER OF CONSTITUTION—MANDATORY PROVISIONS

Sec. 2. (a) The constitution formulated and drafted shall be republican in form, shall contain a bill of rights, and shall, either as a part thereof or in an ordinance appended thereto, contain provisions to the effect that, pending the final and complete withdrawal of the sovereignty of the United States over the Philippine Islands—

(1) All citizens of the Philippine Islands shall owe allegiance to the United States.

(2) Every officer of the government of the Commonwealth of the Philippine Islands shall, before entering upon the discharge of his duties, take and subscribe an oath of office, declaring, among other things, that he recognizes and accepts the supreme authority of and will maintain true faith and allegiance to the United States.

(3) Absolute toleration of religious sentiment shall be secured and no inhabitant or religious organization shall be molested in person or property on account of religious belief or mode of worship.

(4) Property owned by the United States, cemeteries, churches, and parsonages or convents appurtenant thereto, and all lands, buildings, and improvements used exclusively for religious, charitable, or educational purposes shall be exempt from taxation.

(5) Trade relations between the Philippine Islands and the United States shall be upon the basis prescribed in section 6.

(6) The public debt of the Philippine Islands and its subordinate branches shall not exceed limits now or hereafter fixed by the Congress of the United States; and no loans shall be contracted in foreign countries without the approval of the President of the United States.

(7) The debts, liabilities, and obligations of the present Philippine Government, its Provinces, municipalities, and instrumentalities, valid and subsisting at the time of the adoption of the constitution, shall be assumed and paid by the new government.

(8) Provision shall be made for the establishment and maintenance of an adequate system of public schools, primarily conducted in the English language.

(9) Acts affecting currency, coinage, imports, exports, and immigration shall not become law until approved by the President of the United States.

(10) Foreign affairs shall be under the direct supervision and control of the United States.

(11) All acts passed by the Legislature of the Commonwealth of the Philippine Islands shall be reported to the Congress of the United States.

(12) The Philippine Islands recognizes the right of the United States to expropriate property for public uses, to maintain military and other reservations and armed forces in the Philippines, and, upon order of the President, to call into the service of such armed forces all military forces organized by the Philippine government.

(13) The decisions of the courts of the Commonwealth of the Philippine Islands shall be subject to review by the Supreme Court of the United States as provided in paragraph (6) of section 7.

(14) The United States may, by Presidential proclamation, exercise the right to intervene for the preservation of the government of

the Commonwealth of the Philippine Islands and for the maintenance of the government as provided in the constitution thereof, and for the protection of life, property, and individual liberty and for the discharge of government obligations under and in accordance with the provisions of the constitution.

(15) The authority of the United States High Commissioner to the government of the Commonwealth of the Philippine Islands, as provided in this Act, shall be recognized.

(16) Citizens and corporations of the United States shall enjoy in the Commonwealth of the Philippine Islands all the civil rights of the citizens and corporations, respectively, thereof.

(b) The constitution shall also contain the following provisions, effective as of the date of the proclamation of the President recognizing the independence of the Philippine Islands, as hereinafter provided:

(1) That the property rights of the United States and the Philippine Islands shall be promptly adjusted and settled, and that all existing property rights of citizens or corporations of the United States shall be acknowledged, respected, and safeguarded to the same extent as property rights of citizens of the Philippine Islands.

(2) That the officials elected and serving under the constitution adopted pursuant to the provisions of this Act shall be constitutional officers of the free and independent government of the Philippine Islands and qualified to function in all respects as if elected directly under such government, and shall serve their full terms of office as prescribed in the constitution.

(3) That the debts and liabilities of the Philippine Islands, its Provinces, cities, municipalities, and instrumentalities, which shall be valid and subsisting at the time of the final and complete withdrawal of the sovereignty of the United States, shall be assumed by the free and independent government of the Philippine Islands; and that where bonds have been issued under authority of an Act of Congress of the United States by the Philippine Islands, or any Province, city, or municipality therein, the Philippine government will make adequate provision for the necessary funds for the payment of interest and principal, and such obligations shall be a first lien on the taxes collected in the Philippine Islands.

(4) That the government of the Philippine Islands, on becoming independent of the United States, will assume all continuing obligations assumed by the United States under the treaty of peace with Spain ceding said Philippine Islands to the United States.

(5) That by way of further assurance the government of the Phil-

ippine Islands will embody the foregoing provisions (except paragraph (2)) in a treaty with the United States.

SUBMISSION OF CONSTITUTION TO THE PRESIDENT OF THE UNITED STATES

Sec. 3. Upon the drafting and approval of the constitution by the constitutional convention in the Philippine Islands, the constitution shall be submitted within two years after the enactment of this Act to the President of the United States, who shall determine whether or not it conforms with the provisions of this Act. If the President finds that the proposed constitution conforms substantially with the provisions of this Act he shall so certify to the Governor General of the Philippine Islands, who shall so advise the constitutional convention. If the President finds that the constitution does not conform with the provisions of this Act he shall so advise the Governor General of the Philippine Islands, stating wherein in his judgment the constitution does not so conform and submitting provisions which will in his judgment make the constitution so conform. The Governor General shall in turn submit such message to the constitutional convention for further action by them pursuant to the same procedure hereinbefore defined, until the President and the constitutional convention are in agreement.

SUBMISSION OF CONSTITUTION TO FILIPINO PEOPLE

Sec. 4. After the President of the United States has certified that the constitution conforms with the provisions of this Act, it shall be submitted to the people of the Philippine Islands for their ratification or rejection at an election to be held within four months after the date of such certification, on a date to be fixed by the Philippine Legislature, at which election the qualified voters of the Philippine Islands shall have an opportunity to vote directly for or against the proposed constitution and ordinances appended thereto. Such election shall be held in such manner as may be prescribed by the Philippine Legislature, to which the return of the election shall be made. The Philippine Legislature shall by law provide for the canvassing of the return and shall certify the result to the Governor General of the Philippine Islands, together with a statement of the votes cast, and a copy of said constitution and ordinances. If a majority of the votes cast shall be for the constitution, such vote shall be deemed an expression of the will of the people of the Philippine Islands in favor of Philippine independence, and the Governor General shall, within thirty days after receipt of the certification from the Philippine Legislature, issue a proclamation for the election of officers of the government of the Commonwealth of the Philippine Islands provided for in the constitution. The election shall take place not earlier than three months nor later than six months after the proclamation by the Governor General ordering such election. When the election of the officers provided for under the constitution has been held and the results determined, the Governor General of the Philippine Islands shall certify the results of the election to the President of the United States, who shall thereupon issue a proclamation announcing the results of the election, and upon the issuance of such proclamation by the President the existing Philippine government shall terminate and the new government shall enter upon its rights, privileges, powers, and duties, as provided under the constitution. The present government of the Philippine Islands shall provide for the orderly transfer of the functions of government.

If a majority of the votes cast are against the constitution, the existing government of the Philippine Islands shall continue without regard to the provisions of this Act.

TRANSFER OF PROPERTY AND RIGHTS TO PHILIPPINE COMMONWEALTH

Sec. 5. All the property and rights which may have been acquired in the Philippine Islands by the United States under the treaties mentioned in the first section of this Act, except such land or other property as has heretofore been designated by the President of the United States for military and other reservations of the Government of the United States, and except such land or other property or rights or interests therein as may have been sold or otherwise disposed of in accordance with law, are hereby granted to the government of the Commonwealth of the Philippine Islands when constituted.

RELATIONS WITH THE UNITED STATES PENDING COMPLETE INDEPENDENCE

Sec. 6. After the date of the inauguration of the government of the Commonwealth of the Philippine Islands trade relations between the United States and the Philippine Islands shall be as now provided by law, subject to the following exceptions:

(a) There shall be levied, collected, and paid on all refined sugars in excess of fifty thousand long tons, and on unrefined sugars, in excess of eight hundred thousand long tons, coming into the United States from the Philippine Islands in any calendar year, the same rates of duty which are required by the laws of the United States to be levied, collected, and paid upon like articles imported from foreign countries.

(b) There shall be levied, collected, and paid on all coconut oil coming into the United States from the Philippine Islands in any calendar year in excess of two hundred thousand long tons, the same rates of duty which are required by the laws of the United States to be levied, collected, and paid upon like articles imported from foreign countries.

(c) There shall be levied, collected, and paid on all yarn, twine, cord, cordage, rope and cable, tarred or untarred, wholly or in chief value of manila (abaca) or other hard fibers, coming into the United States from the Philippine Islands in any calendar year in excess of a collective total of three million pounds of all such articles hereinbefore enumerated, the same rates of duty which are required by the laws of the United States to be levied, collected, and paid upon like articles imported from foreign countries.

(d) In the event that in any year the limit in the case of any article which may be exported to the United States free of duty shall be reached by the Philippine Islands, the amount or quantity of such articles produced or manufactured in the Philippine Islands thereafter that may be so exported to the United States free of duty shall be allocated, under export permits issued by the government of the Commonwealth of the Philippine Islands, to the producers or manufacturers of such articles proportionately on the basis of their exportation to the United States in the preceding year; except that in the case of unrefined sugar the amount thereof to be exported annually to the United States free of duty shall be allocated to the sugar-producing mills of the islands proportionately on the basis of their average annual production for the calendar years 1931, 1932, and 1933, and the amount of sugar from each mill which may be so exported shall be allocated in each year between the mill and the planters on the basis of the proportion of sugar to which the mill and the planters are respectively entitled. The government of the Philippine Islands is authorized to adopt the necessary laws and regulations for putting into effect the allocation hereinbefore provided.

(e) The government of the Commonwealth of the Philippine Islands shall impose and collect an export tax on all articles that may be exported to the United States from the Philippine Islands free of duty under the provisions of existing law as modified by the foregoing provisions of this section, including the articles enumerated in subdivisions (a), (b), and (c), within the limitations therein specified, as follows:

(1) During the sixth year after the inauguration of the new government the export tax shall be 5 per centum of the rates of duty which are required by the laws of the United States to be levied, collected, and paid on like articles imported from foreign countries;

(2) During the seventh year after the inauguration of the new government the export tax shall be 10 per centum of the rates of duty which are required by the laws of the United States to be levied, collected, and paid on like articles imported from foreign countries;

(3) During the eighth year after the inauguration of the new government the export tax shall be 15 per centum of the rates of duty which are required by the laws of the United States to be levied, collected, and paid on like articles imported from foreign countries;

(4) During the ninth year after the inauguration of the new government the export tax shall be 20 per centum of the rates of duty which are required by the laws of the United States to be levied, collected, and paid on like articles imported from foreign countries;

(5) After the expiration of the ninth year after the inauguration of the new government the export tax shall be 25 per centum of the rates of duty which are required by the laws of the United States to be levied, collected, and paid on like articles imported from foreign countries.

The government of the Commonwealth of the Philippine Islands shall place all funds received from such export taxes in a sinking fund, and such funds shall, in addition to other moneys available for that purpose, be applied solely to the payment of the principal and interest on the bonded indebtedness of the Philippine Islands, its Provinces, municipalities, and instrumentalities, until such indebtedness has been fully discharged.

When used in this section in a geographical sense, the term "United States" includes all Territories and possessions of the United States, except the Philippine Islands, the Virgin Islands, American Samoa, and the island of Guam.

Sec. 7. Until the final and complete withdrawal of American sovereignty over the Philippine Islands—

(1) Every duly adopted amendment to the constitution of the government of the Commonwealth of the Philippine Islands shall be submitted to the President of the United States for approval. If the President approves the amendment or if the President fails to disapprove such amendment within six months from the time of its submission, the amendment shall take effect as a part of such constitution.

(2) The President of the United States shall have authority to suspend the taking effect of or the operation of any law, contract, or

executive order of the government of the Commonwealth of the Philippine Islands, which in his judgment will result in a failure of the government of the Commonwealth of the Philippine Islands to fulfill its contracts, or to meet its bonded indebtedness and interest thereon or to provide for its sinking funds, or which seems likely to impair the reserves for the protection of the currency of the Philippine Islands, or which in his judgment will violate international obligations of the United States.

(3) The Chief Executive of the Commonwealth of the Philippine Islands shall make an annual report to the President and Congress of the United States of the proceedings and operations of the government of the Commonwealth of the Philippine Islands and shall make such other reports as the President or Congress may request.

(4) The President shall appoint, by and with the advice and consent of the Senate, a United States High Commissioner to the government of the Commonwealth of the Philippine Islands who shall hold office at the pleasure of the President and until his successor is appointed and qualified. He shall be known as the United States High Commissioner to the Philippine Islands. He shall be the representative of the President of the United States in the Philippine Islands and shall be recognized as such by the government of the Commonwealth of the Philippine Islands, by the commanding officers of the military forces of the United States, and by all civil officials of the United States, in the Philippine Islands. He shall have access to all records of the government or any subdivision thereof, and shall be furnished by the Chief Executive of the Commonwealth of the Philippine Islands with such information as he shall request.

If the government of the Commonwealth of the Philippine Islands fails to pay any of its bonded or other indebtedness or the interest thereon when due or to fulfill any of its contracts, the United States High Commissioner shall immediately report the facts to the President, who may thereupon direct the High Commissioner to take over the customs offices and administration of the same, administer the same, and apply such part of the revenue received therefrom as may be necessary for the payment of such overdue indebtedness or for the fulfillment of such contracts. The United States High Commissioner shall annually, and at such other times as the President may require, render an official report to the President and Congress of the United States. He shall perform such additional duties and functions as may be delegated to him from time to time by the President under the provisions of this Act.

The United States High Commissioner shall receive the same compensation as is now received by the Governor General of the

Philippine Islands, and shall have such staff and assistants as the President may deem advisable and as may be appropriated for by Congress, including a financial expert, who shall receive for submission to the High Commissioner a duplicate copy of the reports of the insular auditor. Appeals from decisions of the insular auditor may be taken to the President of the United States. The salaries and expenses of the High Commissioner and his staff and assistants shall be paid by the United States.

The first United States High Commissioner appointed under this Act shall take office upon the inauguration of the new government of the Commonwealth of the Philippine Islands.

(5) The government of the Commonwealth of the Philippine Islands shall provide for the selection of a Resident Commissioner to the United States, and shall fix his term of office. He shall be the representative of the government of the Commonwealth of the Philippine Islands and shall be entitled to official recognition as such by all departments upon presentation to the President of credentials signed by the Chief Executive of said government. He shall have a seat in the House of Representatives of the United States, with the right of debate, but without the right of voting. His salary and expenses shall be fixed and paid by the government of the Philippine Islands. Until a Resident Commissioner is selected and qualified under this section, existing law governing the appointment of Resident Commissioners from the Philippine Islands shall continue in effect.

(6) Review by the Supreme Court of the United States of cases from the Philippine Islands shall be as now provided by law; and such review shall also extend to all cases involving the constitution of the Commonwealth of the Philippine Islands.

Sec. 8. (a) Effective upon the acceptance of this Act by concurrent resolution of the Philippine Legislature or by a convention called for that purpose, as provided in section 17—

(1) For the purposes of the Immigration Act of 1917, the Immigration Act of 1924 [except section 13 (c)], this section, and all other laws of the United States relating to the immigration, exclusion, or expulsion of aliens, citizens of the Philippine Islands, who are not citizens of the United States shall be considered as if they were aliens. For such purposes the Philippine Islands shall be considered as a separate country and shall have for each fiscal year a quota of fifty. This paragraph shall not apply to a person coming or seeking to come to the Territory of Hawaii who does not apply for and secure an immigration or passport visa, but such immigration shall be determined by the Department of the Interior on the basis of the needs of industries in the Territory of Hawaii.

(2) Citizens of the Philippine Islands who are not citizens of the United States shall not be admitted to the continental United States from the Territory of Hawaii (whether entering such Territory before or after the effective date of this section) unless they belong to a class declared to be nonimmigrants by section 3 of the Immigration Act of 1924 or to a class declared to be nonquota immigrants under the provisions of section 4 of such Act other than subdivision (c) thereof, or unless they were admitted to such Territory under an immigration visa. The Secretary of Labor shall by regulations provide a method for such exclusion and for the admission of such excepted classes.

(3) Any Foreign Service officer may be assigned to duty in the Philippine Islands, under a commission as a consular officer, for such period as may be necessary and under such regulations as the Secretary of State may prescribe, during which assignment such officer shall be considered as stationed in a foreign country; but his powers and duties shall be confined to the performance of such of the official acts and notarial and other services, which such officer might properly perform in respect of the administration of the immigration laws if assigned to a foreign country as a consular officer, as may be authorized by the Secretary of State.

(4) For the purposes of sections 18 and 20 of the Immigration Act of 1917, as amended, the Philippine Islands shall be considered to be a foreign country.

(b) The provisions of this section are in addition to the provisions of the immigration laws now in force, and shall be enforced as a part of such laws, and all the penal or other provisions of such laws not inapplicable, shall apply to and be enforced in connection with the provisions of this section. An alien, although admissible under the provisions of this section, shall not be admitted to the United States if he is excluded by any provision of the immigration laws other than this section, and an alien, although admissible under the provisions of the immigration laws other than this section, shall not be admitted to the United States if he is excluded by any provision of this section.

(c) Terms defined in the Immigration Act of 1924 shall, when used in this section, have the meaning assigned to such terms in that Act.

Sec. 9. There shall be no obligation on the part of the United States to meet the interest or principal of bonds and other obligations of the government of the Philippine Islands or of the Provincial and municipal governments thereof, hereafter issued during the continuance of United States sovereignty in the Philippine Islands: *Pro-*

vided, That such bonds and obligations hereafter issued shall not be exempt from taxation in the United States or by authority of the United States.

RECOGNITION OF PHILIPPINE INDEPENDENCE AND WITHDRAWAL OF AMERICAN SOVEREIGNTY

Sec. 10. (a) On the 4th day of July immediately following the expiration of a period of ten years from the date of the inauguration of the new government under the constitution provided for in this Act the President of the United States shall by proclamation withdraw and surrender all right of possession, supervision, jurisdiction, control, or sovereignty then existing and exercised by the United States in and over the territory and people of the Philippine Islands, including all military and other reservations of the Government of the United States in the Philippines (except such naval reservations and fueling stations as are reserved under section 5), and on behalf of the United States, shall recognize the independence of the Philippine Islands as a separate and self-governing nation and acknowledge the authority and control over the same of the government instituted by the people thereof, under the constitution then in force.

(b) The President of the United States is hereby authorized and empowered to enter into negotiations with the government of the Philippine Islands, not later than two years after his proclamation recognizing the independence of the Philippine Islands, for the adjustment and settlement of all questions relating to naval reservations and fueling stations of the United States in the Philippine Islands and pending such adjustment and settlement the matter of naval reservations and fueling stations shall remain in its present status.

NEUTRALIZATION OF PHILIPPINE ISLANDS

Sec. 11. The President is requested, at the earliest practicable date, to enter into negotiations with foreign powers with a view to the conclusion of a treaty for the perpetual neutralization of the Philippine Islands, if and when Philippine independence shall have been achieved.

NOTIFICATION TO FOREIGN GOVERNMENTS

Sec. 12. Upon the proclamation and recognition of the independence of the Philippine Islands, the President shall notify the governments with which the United States is in diplomatic correspondence thereof and invite said governments to recognize the independence of the Philippine Islands.

TARIFF DUTIES AFTER INDEPENDENCE

Sec. 13. After the Philippine Islands have become a free and independent nation there shall be levied, collected, and paid upon all articles coming into the United States from the Philippine Islands the rates of duty which are required to be levied, collected, and paid upon like articles imported from other foreign countries: *Provided,* That at least one year prior to the date fixed in this Act for the independence of the Philippine Islands, there shall be held a conference of representatives of the Government of the United States and the government of the Commonwealth of the Philippine Islands, such representatives to be appointed by the President of the United States and the Chief Executive of the Commonwealth of the Philippine Islands, respectively, for the purpose of formulating recommendations as to future trade relations between the Government of the United States and the independent government of the Philippine Islands, the time, place, and manner of holding such conference to be determined by the President of the United States; but nothing in this proviso shall be construed to modify or affect in any way any provision of this Act relating to the procedure leading up to Philippine independence or the date upon which the Philippine Islands shall become independent.

IMMIGRATION AFTER INDEPENDENCE

Sec. 14. Upon the final and complete withdrawal of American sovereignty over the Philippine Islands the immigration laws of the United States (including all the provisions thereof relating to persons ineligible to citizenship) shall apply to persons who were born in the Philippine Islands to the same extent as in the case of other foreign countries.

CERTAIN STATUTES CONTINUED IN FORCE

Sec. 15. Except as in this Act otherwise provided, the laws now or hereafter in force in the Philippine Islands shall continue in force in the Commonwealth of the Philippine Islands until altered, amended, or repealed by the Legislature of the Commonwealth of the Philippine Islands or by the Congress of the United States, and all references in such laws to the government or officials of the Philippines or Philippine Islands shall be construed, insofar as applicable, to refer to the government and corresponding officials respectively of the Commonwealth of the Philippine Islands. The government of the Commonwealth of the Philippine Islands shall be deemed successor to the present government of the Philippine Islands and of all the rights and obligations thereof. Except as otherwise provided in this Act, all laws or parts of laws relating to the present government of the Philippine Islands and its administration are hereby repealed as of the date of the inauguration of the government of the Commonwealth of the Philippine Islands.

Sec. 16. If any provision of this Act is declared unconstitutional or the applicability thereof to any person or circumstances is held invalid, the validity of the remainder of the Act and the applicability of such provisions to other persons and circumstances shall not be affected thereby.

EFFECTIVE DATE

Sec. 17. The foregoing provisions of this Act shall not take effect until accepted by concurrent resolution of the Philippine Legislature or by a convention called for the purpose of passing upon that question as may be provided by the Philippine Legislature.

Approved, March 24, 1934.

Appendix C

AMENDMENTS TO THE TYDINGS-McDUFFIE ACT

AN ACT To amend an Act entitled "An Act to provide for the complete independence of the Philippine Islands, to provide for the adoption of a constitution and a form of government for the Philippine Islands, and for other purposes."

Be it enacted by the Senate and House of Representatives of the United States of America in Congress assembled, That section 6 of the Act of March 24, 1934, entitled "An Act to provide for the complete independence of the Philippine Islands, to provide for the adoption of a constitution and a form of government for the Philippine Islands, and for other purposes" (48 Stat. 456), is hereby amended to read as follows:

"Section 6. During the period beginning January 1, 1940, and ending July 3, 1946, trade relations between the United States and the Philippines shall be as now provided by law, subject to the following exceptions:

"(a) On and after January 1, 1941, the Philippine Government shall impose and collect an export tax on every Philippine article shipped from the Philippines to the United States, except as otherwise specifically provided in this section. Said tax shall be computed in the manner hereinafter set forth in this subsection and in subsection (c) of this section. During the period January 1, 1941, through December 31, 1941, the export tax on every such article shall be 5 per centum of the United States duty; on each succeeding January 1 thereafter, the export tax shall be increased progressively by an additional 5 per centum of the United States duty, except that during the period January 1, 1946, through July 3, 1946, the export tax shall remain at 25 per centum of the United States duty.

"(b) (1) No export tax described in subsection (a) of this section shall be imposed or collected upon any Philippine article of a class or kind in respect of which a quota is established by subdivision

(3) of this subsection, nor upon copra or manila (abaca) fiber not dressed or manufactured in any manner.

"(2) The United States duty shall be levied, collected, and paid in the United States upon every article which is of a class or kind in respect of which a quota is established by subdivision (3) of this subsection and which is entered, or withdrawn from warehouse, for consumption after December 31, 1939, in excess of its respective quota: *Provided, however,* That nothing in this section or any subsection thereof shall be construed to exempt the quota of coconut oil therein provided for from the excise taxes provided for in section 2470 of the Internal Revenue Code (I.R.C., ch. 21, sec. 2470).

"(3) For the purposes indicated in subdivisions (1) and (2) of this subsection, there are hereby established the following quotas of the designated Philippine articles: For the calendar year 1940, the quotas, hereafter called original quotas, shall be as follows:

"a. cigars (exclusive of cigarettes, cheroots of all kinds, and paper cigars and cigarettes including wrappers), two hundred million cigars;

"b. scrap tobacco, and stemmed and unstemmed filler tobacco described in paragraph 602 of the Tariff Act of 1930, four million five hundred thousand pounds;

"c. coconut oil, two hundred thousand long tons;

"d. buttons of pearl or shell, eight hundred and fifty thousand gross.

For each calendar year thereafter through the calendar year 1945, each of the said quotas shall be the same as the corresponding quota for the immediately preceding calendar year, less 5 per centum of the corresponding original quota.

"For the period January 1, 1946, through July 3, 1946, each of said quotas shall be one-half of the corresponding quota specified for the calendar year 1945.

"(c) The Philippine Government, in imposing and collecting export taxes on Philippine embroideries, shall compute the tax in accordance with the formulas specified in subsection (a) of this section, except that in determining the taxable value of any such article, an allowance shall be made equal to the cost—cost, insurance, and freight to the Philippines—of any cloth of United States origin used in the production thereof.

"(d) The United States duty shall be levied, collected, and paid, in the United States, upon all Philippine sugars, which are entered, or withdrawn from warehouse, for consumption in any calendar year after 1939, in excess of eight hundred and fifty thousand long tons, of which not more than fifty thousand long tons may be refined sugars: *Provided, however,* That for the period January 1, 1946, through July 3, 1946, the quota of Philippine sugars, not subject to the United States duty, shall be four hundred and twenty-five thousand long tons, of which not more than twenty-five thousand long tons may be refined sugars. Any export tax imposed and collected on Philippine sugars entered or withdrawn from warehouse for consumption in excess of the quotas established by this subsection shall be refunded by the Philippine Government.

"(e) Upon the expiration of the Act of June 14, 1935 (49 Stat. 340), as extended to May 1, 1941, by proclamation of the President, dated January 26, 1938, the total amount of all Philippine cordage coming into the United States which may be entered or withdrawn from warehouse, for consumption during the remainder of the calendar year 1941, shall not exceed four million pounds and in any calendar year after 1941 shall not exceed six million pounds: *Provided, however,* That for the period January 1, 1946, through July 3, 1946, the total amount of Philippine cordage which may be entered, or withdrawn from warehouse, for consumption shall not exceed three million pounds.

"(f) (1) The quotas for sugars established by subsection (d) of this section shall be allocated annually as prescribed in section 6 (d) of the Act of March 24, 1934 (48 Stat. 456), which section in this respect is not repealed by this amendatory Act.

"(2) The quotas for cordage, established by subsection (e) of this section, and by the Act of June 14, 1935, shall be allocated by authorities of the Philippine Government among the manufacturers of such commodities proportionately upon the basis of the shipment of each such manufacturer to the United States during the twelve months immediately preceding the inauguration of the Commonwealth of the Philippines.

"(3) The quotas for all articles for which quotas are established by this section, except sugars and cordage, shall in each instance be allocated by authorities of the Philippine Government among the manufacturers whose products were shipped to the United States during the calendar year 1937, on the basis of the proportion which each manufacturer's maximum production shipped to the United States, directly or through other persons, in any calendar year during the five-year period, 1933 through 1937, bears to the total of such maximum shipments of all such manufacturers.

"(4) If, after the first nine months of any quota year, the holder of any allotment under any of the quotas established by this Act or by the Act of June 14, 1935, is or will be unable for any reason to ship to the United States by the end of the quota year the total amount of his allocation for that year, the Philippine Government shall apportion that amount of such allocation which it is established by sufficient evidence cannot be shipped to the United States during the remainder of the quota year in such manner and in accordance with such rules and regulations as it may prescribe.

"(g) (1) The Philippine Government shall pay to the Secretary of the Treasury of the United States, at the end of each calendar quarter, all of the moneys received during such quarter from export taxes (less refunds), imposed and collected in accordance with the provisions of this section, and said moneys shall be deposited in an account with the Treasurer of the United States and shall constitute a supplementary sinking fund for the payment of bonds of the Philippines, its Provinces, cities, and municipalities, issued prior to May 1, 1934, under authority of Acts of Congress: *Provided, however,* That moneys received from any export tax imposed on any article which is shipped from the Philippines to the United States prior to July 4, 1946, and which is entered, or withdrawn from warehouse for consumption, on or after July 4, 1946, shall be refunded by the independent Government of the Philippines.

"(2) The said Secretary of the Treasury is authorized to accept the deposits of the proceeds of the export taxes referred to in subdivision (1) of this subsection in accordance with the Act of June 11, 1934 (48 Stat. 929).

"(3) The Secretary of the Treasury of the United States, with the approval of the Philippine Government, is authorized to purchase with such supplementary sinking fund bonds of the Philippines, its Provinces, cities, and municipalities, issued prior to May 1, 1934, under authority of Acts of Congress and to invest such fund in interest-bearing obligations of the United States or in obligations guaranteed as to both principal and interest by the United States. Whenever the Secretary of the Treasury finds that such fund is in excess of an amount adequate to meet future interest and principal payments on all such bonds, he may, with the approval of the Philippine Government, purchase with such excess any other bonds of the Philippines, its Provinces, cities, municipalities, and instrumentalities. For the purpose of this subsection obligations may be acquired on original issue at par, or by purchase of outstanding obligations at the market price. Any obligations acquired by the fund may, with the approval of the Philippine Government, be sold by the Secretary of the Treasury at the market price and the proceeds of such sale and the proceeds of the payment upon maturity or redemption of any obligations held in the supplementary sinking fund, as well as all moneys in any manner earned by such fund or on any obligations acquired by said fund, shall be paid into the said fund.

"(4) During the three months preceding July 4, 1946, the Philippine Government and the Secretary of the Treasury of the United States shall confer to ascertain that portion of the bonds of the Philippines, its Provinces, cities, and municipalities, issued prior to May 1, 1934, under authority of Acts of Congress, which will remain outstanding on July 4, 1946; and the Philippine Government shall turn over to the Secretary of the Treasury of the United States for destruction all such bonds that are then held, canceled, or uncanceled, in any of the sinking funds maintained for the payment of such bonds. After such outstanding portion of this indebtedness is thus determined, and before July 4, 1946, (i) there shall be set up with the Treasurer of the United States a special trust account in the name of the Secretary of the Treasury of the United States to pay future interest and principal payments on such bonds; (ii) the Philippine Government shall pay the Secretary of the Treasury of the United States for deposit in this special trust account all of the sinking funds maintained for the payment of such bonds; and (iii) the Secretary of the Treasury of the United States shall transfer into this special trust account all the proceeds of the supplementary sinking fund referred to in subdivision (1) of this subsection. Any portion of such special trust account found by the Secretary of the Treasury of the United States on July 4, 1946, to be in excess of an amount adequate to meet future interest and principal payments on all such outstanding bonds shall be turned over to the Treasury of the independent Government of the Philippines to be set up as an additional sinking fund to be used for the purpose of liquidating and paying all other obligations of the Philippines, its Provinces, cities, municipalities, and instrumentalities. To the extent that such special trust account is determined by the Secretary of the Treasury of the United States to be insufficient to pay interest and principal on the outstanding bonds of the Philippines, its Provinces, cities, and municipalities, issued prior to May 1, 1934, under authority of Acts of Congress, the Philippine Government shall, on or before July 3, 1946, pay to the Secretary of the Treasury of the United States for deposit in such special trust account an amount which said Secretary of the Treasury determines is required to assure payment of principal and interest on such bonds: *Provided, however,* That if the Secretary of the Treasury of the United States finds that this requirement would impose an undue hardship upon the Philippines, then the Philippine Government shall continue to provide annually the necessary funds for the payment of interest and principal on such bonds until such time as the Secretary of the Treasury of the United States determines that the amount in the special trust account is adequate to meet interest and principal payments on such bonds.

"(5) On and after July 4, 1946, the Secretary of the Treasury of the United States is authorized, with the approval of the independent Government of the Philippines, to purchase at the market price for the special trust account bonds of the Philippines, its Provinces, cities, and municipalities, issued prior to May 1, 1934, under authority of Acts of Congress. The Secretary of the Treasury of the United States is also authorized, with the approval of the independent Government of the Philippines, to invest all or any part of such special trust account in any interest-bearing obligations of the United States or in any obligations guaranteed as to both principal and interest by the United States. Such obligations may be acquired on original issue at par or by purchase of outstanding obligations at the market price, and any obligations acquired by the special trust account may, with the approval of the independent Government of the Philippines, be sold by the Secretary of the Treasury at the market price, and the proceeds of the payment upon maturity or redemption of such obligations shall be held as a part of such special trust account. Whenever the special trust account is determined by the Secretary of the Treasury of the United States to be adequate to meet interest and principal payments on all outstanding bonds of the Philippines, its Provinces, cities, and municipalities, issued prior to May 1, 1934, under authority of Acts of Congress, the Secretary of the Treasury is authorized to pay from such trust account the principal of such outstanding bonds and to pay all interest due and owing on such bonds. All such bonds and interest coupons paid or purchased by the special trust account shall be canceled and destroyed by the Secretary of the Treasury of the United States. From time to time after July 4, 1946, any moneys in such special trust account found by the Secretary of the Treasury of the United States to be in excess of an amount adequate to meet interest and principal payments on all such bonds shall be turned over to the treasurer of the independent Government of the Philippines.

"(h) No article shipped from the Philippines to the United States on or after January 1, 1941, subject to an export tax provided for in this section, shall be admitted to entry in the United States until the importer of such article shall present to the United States collector of customs a certificate, signed by a competent authority of the Philippine Government, setting forth the value and quantity of the article and the rate and amount of the export tax paid, or shall give a bond for the production of such certificate within six months from the date of entry."

Sec. 2. Section 8 of the said Act of March 24, 1934, is hereby amended by adding thereto a new subsection as follows:

"(d) Pending the final and complete withdrawal of the sovereignty of the United States over the Philippine Islands, except as otherwise provided by this Act, citizens and corporation of the Philippine Islands shall enjoy in the United States and all places subject to its jurisdiction all of the rights and privileges which they respectively shall have enjoyed therein under the laws of the United States in force at the time of the inauguration of the Government of the Commonwealth of the Philippine Islands."

Sec. 3. Section 10 of the said Act of March 24, 1934, is hereby amended by adding the following subsection thereto:

"(c) (1) Whenever the President of the United States shall find that any properties in the Philippines, owned by the Philippine Government or by private persons, would be suitable for diplomatic or consular establishments of the United States after the inauguration of the independent Government, he may, with the approval of the Philippine Government, and in exchange for the conveyance of title to the United States, transfer to the said Government or private persons any properties of the United States in the Philippines. Title to any properties so transferred to private persons, and title to any properties so acquired by the United States, shall be vested in fee simple in such persons and the United States, respectively, notwithstanding the provisions contained in subsection (a) of this section.

"(2) Whenever, prior to July 4, 1946, the President of the United States shall find that any properties of the United States in the Philippines would be suitable for diplomatic and consular establishments of the United States after the inauguration of the independent Government, he shall designate the same by the issuance of a proclamation or proclamations, and title to any properties so designated shall continue to be vested in fee simple in the United States notwithstanding the provisions contained in subsection (a) of this section.

"(3) Title to the lands and buildings pertaining to the official residences of the United States High Commissioner to the Philippine Islands in the cities of Manila and Baguio, together with all fixtures and movable objects, shall continue to be vested in the United States after July 4, 1946, notwithstanding the provisions contained in subsection (a) of this section.

"(4) Administrative supervision and control over any properties acquired or designated by the President of the United States pursuant to this subsection, and over the official residences in the Philippines of the High Commissioner, shall, on and after July 4, 1946, be exercised by the Secretary of State, in accordance with Acts of Congress relating to property held by the United States in foreign countries for official establishments."

Sec. 4. Section 13 of the said Act of March 24, 1934, is hereby amended by striking out the proviso and inserting in lieu thereof the following: *"Provided,* That at least two years prior to the date fixed in this Act for the independence of the Philippine Islands, there shall be held a conference of representatives of the Government of the United States and the Government of the Commonwealth of the Philippine Islands, such representatives, on the part of the United States, to consist of three United States Senators appointed by the President of the Senate, three Members of the House of Representatives appointed by the Speaker of the House, and three persons appointed by the President of the United States, and, on the part of the Philippines, to consist of nine representatives to be appointed by the President of the Commonwealth of the Philippines, with the consent of the Commission on Appointments of the National Assembly, for the purpose of formulating recommendations as to future trade relations between the United States and the independent Philippine Republic, the time, place, and manner of holding such conference to be determined by the President of the United States; but nothing in this proviso shall be construed to modify or affect in any way any provision of this Act relating to the procedure leading up to Philippine Independence or the date upon which the Philippine Islands shall become independent.

"In the event any vacancy occurs in the Commission by reason of the death, resignation, or retirement, of any member thereof, such vacancy may be filled by the authority appointing the member whose death, resignation, or retirement caused the vacancy."

Sec. 5. The said Act of March 24, 1934, is further amended by the addition of the following new section:

' "Sec. 18. (a) As used in sections 6 and 10 of this Act—

"(1) The term 'United States,' when used in a geographical sense, but not the term 'continental United States,' includes all Territories and possessions of the United States, other than the Philippines.

"(2) The term 'cordage' includes yarns, twines (including binding twine described in paragraph 1622 of the Tariff Act of 1930 (46 Stat. 675)), cords, cordage, rope and cable, tarred or untarred, wholly or in chief value of manila (abaca) or other hard fiber.

"(3) The term 'Philippine Government' means the Government of the Commonwealth of the Philippines.

"(4) The term 'United States duty,' when used in connection with the computation of export taxes, means the lowest rate of ordinary customs duty in effect at the time of the shipment of the article concerned from the Philippines and applicable to like articles imported into the continental United States from any foreign country, except Cuba, or when more than one rate of ordinary customs duty is applicable to such like articles, the aggregate of such rates.

"(5) The term 'refined sugars' possesses the same meaning as the term 'direct-consumption sugar' as defined in section 101 of the Sugar Act of 1937.

"(6) The term 'Philippine article' means an article the growth, produce, or manufacture of the Philippines, in the production of which no materials of other than Philippine or United States origin valued in excess of 20 per centum of the total value of such article was used and which is brought into the United States from the Philippines.

"(7) The term 'American article' means an article the growth, produce, or manufacture of the United States, in the production of which no materials of other than Philippine or United States origin valued in excess of 20 per centum of the total value of such article was used and which is brought into the Philippines from the United States.

"(8) The term 'Philippine import duty' means the lowest rate of ordinary customs duty applicable at the port of arrival, at the time of entry, or withdrawal from warehouse, for consumption of the article concerned, to like articles imported into the Philippines from any other foreign country, or when more than one rate of ordinary customs duty is applicable to such like articles, the aggregate of such rates.

"(b) As used in subsection (a) of this section:

"(1) The terms 'includes' and 'including' shall not be deemed to exclude other things otherwise within the meaning of the term defined.

"(2) The term 'ordinary customs duty' shall not include any import duty or charge which is imposed to compensate for an internal tax imposed in respect of a like domestic product or in respect of a commodity from which the imported product has been manufactured or produced in whole or in part."

Sec. 6. The said Act of March 24, 1934, is further amended by the addition of the following new section:

"Sec. 19. (a) The proceeds of the excise taxes imposed by section

2470 of the Internal Revenue Code (I.R.C., ch. 21, sec. 2470), and of the import taxes imposed by sections 2490 and 2491 of the Internal Revenue Code (I.R.C., ch. 22, secs. 2490, 2491), collected on or after January 1, 1939, and accrued prior to July 4, 1946, and required to be held in separate or special funds and paid into the Treasury of the Philippines, together with any moneys hereafter appropriated in accordance with the authorization contained in section 503 of the Sugar Act of 1937 (50 Stat. 915) by virtue of accruals of excise and import taxes prior to July 4, 1946, shall be held as separate funds and paid into the treasury of the Philippines to be used for the purpose of meeting new or additional expenditures which will be necessary in adjusting Philippine economy to a position independent of trade preferences in the United States and in preparing the Philippines for the assumption of the responsibilities of an independent state: *Provided, however,* That the portion of such funds expended by the Government of the Commonwealth of the Philippines shall be budgeted, appropriated, and accounted for separately from other moneys of that Government.

"(b) If the President of the United States finds that the Government of the Commonwealth of the Philippines has failed or is about to fail to comply with any requirement of subsections (a) and (c) of this section, he shall direct the Secretary of the Treasury of the United States to withhold or discontinue, during any period or periods of time specified by the President of the United States further payments in whole or in part.

"(c) The provisions contained in section 2476 of the Internal Revenue Code (I.R.C., ch. 21, sec. 2476), prohibiting further payments in the event that the Government of the Commonwealth of the Philippines should provide by law for the subsidization of producers of copra, coconut oil, or allied products, and the provisions contained in the Sugar Act of 1937, specifying the purpose for which such appropriations could be used by the said government and the manner and condition of transfer, shall not apply to any moneys collected or appropriated pursuant to said Acts on or after January 1, 1939, and to this extent are hereby repealed: *Provided, however,* That the restriction contained in the proviso to section 503 of the Sugar Act of 1937 shall continue in full force and effect: *And provided further,* That no part of the proceeds of the excise taxes herein referred to shall be paid directly or indirectly as a subsidy to the producers or processors of copra, coconut oil or allied products, except that this provision shall not be construed as prohibiting the use of a portion of said funds for facilities for better curing of copra, or for bona fide production loans to Philippine copra producers.

"(d) Nothing contained herein shall be construed as obligating the United States to continue for any period of time any or all of the excise and import taxes imposed by sections 2470, 2490, 2491 of the Internal Revenue Code or by sections 3490, 3500, 3501 of the Internal Revenue Code (I.R.C., ch. 32, secs. 3490, 3500, 3501).

"(e) Notwithstanding the provisions of section 4 of the Act of March 8, 1902 (32 Stat. 54), or of any other provision of law, on or after the first day of the second month following the passage of this amendatory Act, except as otherwise provided in this section, all customs duties collected in accordance with sections 6 and 13 of this Act, on any article the growth, produce, or manufacture of the Philippines, in the production of which no materials of other than Philippine or United States origin valued in excess of 20 per centum of the total value of such article, was used and which is brought into the United States from the Philippines, and all customs duties collected on any other article brought into the United States from the Philippines, shall be covered into the general fund of the Treasury of the United States and shall not be paid into the Treasury of the Philippines."

Sec. 7. (a) Sections 1 to 5, inclusive, of this amendatory Act shall become effective on January 1, 1940, if before that date—

(1) Subsection 5 of section 1 of the Ordinance Appended to the Constitution of the Philippines shall have been amended in the manner now provided by law, by changing the final period of said subsection to a comma, and by adding thereto the words: "as amended by the Act of Congress of the United States approved (followed by the date of the approval of this amendatory Act)," and section 3 of the said ordinance shall have been amended by inserting immediately after the words "approved March 24, 1934" the same amendatory language mentioned above.

(2) The President of the United States shall have found and proclaimed that the Philippine Government has enacted, subsequent to the adoption of the amendments to the Constitution of the Philippines (as provided in subdivision (1) of this subsection), a law relating to export taxes (as provided in section 1), and has retained those Philippine laws relating to sinking-fund and currency matters which were in effect on May 20, 1938.

(b) Section 1 of this amendatory Act shall remain in full force and effect from the effective date thereof until July 4, 1946, unless the President of the United States shall, prior to July 4, 1946, have found and proclaimed that the Philippine Government has, in any substantial respect, repealed or amended, or failed or refused to enforce or administer any Philippine law referred to in subdivision (2) of subsection (a) of this section. In the event of such a finding and proclamation, section 1 shall immediately become ineffective and trade relations between the United States and the Philippines shall be as provided by section 6 of the Act of March 24, 1934, prior to the enactment of this amendatory Act and by section 13 of the said Act.

(c) Sections 6 and 7 of this amendatory Act shall become effective upon its enactment.

Sec. 8. Notwithstanding the provisions contained in section 8 (a) (3) of the Act of March 24, 1934 (48 Stat. 456), entitled "An Act to provide for the complete independence of the Philippine Islands, to provide for the adoption of a constitution and a form of government for the Philippine Islands, and for other purposes," Foreign Service officers may, under commissions as diplomatic and consular officers, be assigned to the Philippine Islands, during which assignments such officers shall be considered as stationed in a foreign country, for such periods of time and under such regulations as the Secretary of State may prescribe for the performance of any of the duties customarily performed by Foreign Service officers stationed in foreign countries and of additional duties in connection with advising and assisting the United States High Commissioner to the Philippine Islands in the supervision and control of the foreign affairs of the Commonwealth of the Philippines in accordance with section 2 (a) (10) of the Act approved March 24, 1934, and section 1 (10) of the ordinance appended to the constitution of the Philippines adopted February 8, 1935.

This section shall become effective upon its enactment.

Approved, August 7, 1939.

Appendix D

CONSTITUTION OF THE

PHILIPPINES *

The Filipino people, imploring the aid of Divine Providence, in order to establish a government that shall embody their ideals, conserve and develop the patrimony of the nation, promote the general welfare, and secure to themselves and their posterity the blessings of independence under a regime of justice, liberty, and democracy, do ordain and promulgate this Constitution.

ARTICLE I. THE NATIONAL TERRITORY

Section 1. The Philippines comprises all the territory ceded to the United States by the Treaty of Paris concluded between the United States and Spain on the tenth day of December, eighteen hundred and ninety-eight, the limits of which are set forth in Article III of said treaty, together with all the islands embraced in the treaty concluded at Washington, between the United States and Spain on the seventh day of November, nineteen hundred, and in the treaty concluded between the United States and Great Britain on the second day of January, nineteen hundred and thirty, and all territory over which the present Government of the Philippine Islands exercises jurisdiction.

ARTICLE II. DECLARATION OF PRINCIPLES

Section 1. The Philippines is a republican state. Sovereignty resides in the people and all government authority emanates from them.

---

* As amended by Resolution Numbered Seventy-three adopted by the Second National Assembly on the eleventh day of April, nineteen hundred and forty, and approved by the President of the United States on the second day of December, nineteen hundred and forty, and by a Resolution of Both Houses adopted by the First Congress of the Republic of the Philippines on the eighteenth day of September, nineteen hundred and forty-six, and approved by a majority of the votes cast at the election held on the eleventh day of March, nineteen hundred and forty-seven.

Sec. 2. The defense of the State is a prime duty of government, and in the fulfillment of this duty all citizens may be required by law to render personal military or civil service.

Sec. 3. The Philippines renounces war as an instrument of national policy, and adopts the generally accepted principles of international law as part of the law of the Nation.

Sec. 4. The natural right and duty of parents in the rearing of the youth for civic efficiency should receive the aid and support of the Government.

Sec. 5. The promotion of social justice to insure the well-being and economic security of all the people should be the concern of the State.

ARTICLE III. BILL OF RIGHTS

Section 1. (1) No person shall be deprived of life, liberty, or property without due process of law, nor shall any person be denied the equal protection of the laws.

(2) Private property shall not be taken for public use without just compensation.

(3) The right of the people to be secure in their persons, houses, papers, and effects against unreasonable searches and seizures shall not be violated, and no warrants shall issue but upon probable cause, to be determined by the judge after examination under oath or affirmation of the complainant and the witnesses he may produce, and particularly describing the place to be searched, and the persons or things to be seized.

(4) The liberty of abode and of changing the same within the limits prescribed by law shall not be impaired.

(5) The privacy of communication and correspondence shall be inviolable except upon lawful order of the court or when public safety and order require otherwise.

(6) The right to form associations or societies for purposes not contrary to law shall not be abridged.

(7) No law shall be made respecting an establishment of religion, or prohibiting the free exercise thereof, and the free exercise and enjoyment of religious profession and worship, without discrimination or preference, shall forever be allowed. No religious test shall be required for the exercise of civil or political rights.

(8) No law shall be passed abridging the freedom of speech, or of the press, or the right of the people peaceably to assemble and petition the Government for redress of grievances.

(9) No law granting a title of nobility shall be enacted, and no person holding any office of profit or trust shall, without the consent

of the Congress of the Philippines, accept any present, emolument, office, or title of any kind whatever from any foreign state.

(10) No law impairing the obligation of contracts shall be passed.

(11) No *ex post facto* law or bill of attainder shall be enacted.

(12) No person shall be imprisoned for debt or nonpayment of a poll tax.

(13) No involuntary servitude in any form shall exist except as a punishment for crime whereof the party shall have been duly convicted.

(14) The privilege of the writ of *habeas corpus* shall not be suspended except in cases of invasion, insurrection, or rebellion, when the public safety requires it, in any of which events the same may be suspended wherever during such period the necessity for such suspension shall exist.

(15) No person shall be held to answer for a criminal offense without due process of law.

(16) All persons shall before conviction be bailable by sufficient sureties, except those charged with capital offenses when evidence of guilt is strong. Excessive bail shall not be required.

(17) In all criminal prosecutions the accused shall be presumed to be innocent until the contrary is proved, and shall enjoy the right to be heard by himself and counsel, to be informed of the nature and cause of the accusation against him, to have a speedy and public trial, to meet the witnesses face to face, and to have compulsory process to secure the attendance of witnesses in his behalf.

(18) No person shall be compelled to be a witness against himself.

(19) Excessive fines shall not be imposed, nor cruel and unusual punishments inflicted.

(20) No person shall be twice put in jeopardy of punishment for the same offense. If an act is punished by a law and an ordinance, conviction or acquittal under either shall constitute a bar to another prosecution for the same act.

(21) Free access to the courts shall not be denied to any person by reason of poverty.

ARTICLE IV. CITIZENSHIP

Section 1. The following are citizens of the Philippines:

(1) Those who are citizens of the Philippine Islands at the time of the adoption of this Constitution.

(2) Those born in the Philippine Islands of foreign parents who, before the adoption of this Constitution, had been elected to public office in the Philippine Islands.

(3) Those whose fathers are citizens of the Philippines.

(4) Those whose mothers are citizens of the Philippines and, upon reaching the age of majority, elect Philippine citizenship.

(5) Those who are naturalized in accordance with law.

Sec. 2. Philippine citizenship may be lost or reacquired in the manner provided by law.

ARTICLE V. SUFFRAGE

Section 1. Suffrage may be exercised by male citizens of the Philippines not otherwise disqualified by law, who are twenty-one years of age or over and are able to read and write, and who shall have resided in the Philippines for one year and in the municipality wherein they propose to vote for at least six months preceding the election. The National Assembly shall extend the right of suffrage to women, if in a plebiscite which shall be held for that purpose within two years after the adoption of this Constitution, not less than three hundred thousand women possessing the necessary qualifications shall vote affirmatively on the question.

ARTICLE VI. LEGISLATIVE DEPARTMENT

Section 1. The Legislative power shall be vested in a Congress of the Philippines, which shall consist of a Senate and a House of Representatives.

Sec. 2. The Senate shall be composed of twenty-four Senators who shall be chosen at large by the qualified electors of the Philippines, as may be provided by law.

Sec. 3. The term of office of Senators shall be six years and shall begin on the thirtieth day of December next following their election. The first Senators elected under this Constitution shall, in the manner provided by the law, be divided equally into three groups, the Senators of the first group to serve for a term of six years; those of the second group, for four years; and those of the third group, for two years.

Sec. 4. No person shall be a Senator unless he be a natural-born citizen of the Philippines and, at the time of his election, is at least thirty-five years of age, a qualified elector, and a resident of the Philippines for not less than two years immediately prior to his election.

Sec. 5. The House of Representatives shall be composed of not more than one hundred and twenty Members who shall be apportioned among the several provinces as nearly as may be according to the number of their respective inhabitants, but each province shall have at least one Member. The Congress shall by law make an apportionment within three years after the return of every enumeration, and not otherwise. Until such apportionment shall have been made, the House of Representatives shall have the same number of Members as that fixed by law for the National Assembly, who shall be elected by the qualified electors from the present Assembly districts. Each representative district shall comprise, as far as practicable, contiguous and compact territory.

Sec. 6. The term of office of the Members of the House of Representatives shall be four years and shall begin on the thirtieth day of December next following their election.

Sec. 7. No person shall be a Member of the House of Representatives unless he be a natural-born citizen of the Philippines and, at the time of his election, is at least twenty-five years of age, a qualified elector, and a resident of the province in which he is chosen for not less than one year immediately prior to his election.

Sec. 8. (1) Elections for Senators and Members of the House of Representatives shall be held in the manner and on the dates fixed by law.

(2) In case of vacancy in the Senate or in the House of Representatives, a special election may be called to fill such vacancy in the manner prescribed by law, but the Senator or Member of the House of Representatives thus elected shall serve only for the unexpired term.

Sec. 9. The Congress shall convene in regular session once every year on the fourth Monday of January, unless a different date is fixed by law. It may be called in special session at any time by the President to consider general legislation or only such subjects as he may designate. No special session shall continue longer than thirty days and no regular session longer than one hundred days, exclusive of Sundays.

Sec. 10. (1) The Senate shall elect its President and the House of Representatives its Speaker.

Each House shall choose such other officers as may be required.

(2) A majority of each House shall constitute a quorum to do business, but a smaller number may adjourn from day to day and may compel the attendance of absent Members in such manner and under such penalties as such House may provide.

(3) Each House may determine the rules of its proceedings, punish its Members for disorderly behavior, and, with the concurrence of two-thirds of all its Members, expel a Member.

(4) Each House shall keep a Journal of its proceedings, and from time to time publish the same, excepting such parts as may in its judgment require secrecy; and the *yeas* and *nays* on any question shall, at the request of one-fifth of the Members present, be entered in the Journal.

(5) Neither House during the sessions of the Congress shall, without the consent of the other, adjourn for more than three days, nor to any other place than that in which the two Houses shall be sitting.

Sec. 11. The Senate and the House of Representatives shall each have an Electoral Tribunal which shall be the sole judge of all contests relating to the election, returns, and qualifications of their respective Members. Each Electoral Tribunal shall be composed of nine Members, three of whom shall be Justices of the Supreme Court to be designated by the Chief Justice, and the remaining six shall be Members of the Senate or of the House of Representatives, as the case may be, who shall be chosen by each House, three upon nomination of the party having the largest number of votes and three of the party having the second largest number of votes therein. The senior Justice in each Electoral Tribunal shall be its Chairman.

Sec. 12. There shall be a Commission on Appointments consisting of twelve Senators and twelve Members of the House of Representatives, elected by each House, respectively, on the basis of proportional representation of the political parties therein. The President of the Senate shall be the Chairman ex officio of the Commission, but shall not vote, except in cases of tie.

Sec. 13. The Electoral Tribunals and the Commission on Appointments shall be constituted within thirty days after the Senate and the House of Representatives shall have been organized with the election of their President and Speaker, respectively. The Commission on Appointments shall meet only while the Congress is in session, at the call of its Chairman or a majority of its Members, to discharge such powers and functions as are herein conferred upon it.

Sec. 14. The Senators and the Members of the House of Representatives shall, unless otherwise provided by law, receive an annual compensation of seven thousand two hundred pesos each, including per diems and other emoluments or allowances, and exclusive only of traveling expenses to and from their respective districts in the case of Members of the House of Representatives, and to and from their places of residence in the case of Senators, when attending sessions of the Congress. No increase in said compensation shall take effect until after the expiration of the full term of all the Members of the Senate and of the House of Representatives approving such increase. Until otherwise provided by law, the President of the Senate and the Speaker of the House of Representatives shall each receive an annual compensation of sixteen thousand pesos.

Sec. 15. The Senators and Members of the House of Representatives shall in all cases except treason, felony, and breach of the peace, be privileged from arrest during their attendance at the sessions of the Congress, and in going to and returning from the same; and for any speech or debate therein, they shall not be questioned in any other place.

Sec. 16. No Senator or Member of the House of Representatives may hold any other office or employment in the Government without forfeiting his seat, nor shall any Senator or Member of the House of Representatives, during the time for which he was elected, be appointed to any civil office which may have been created or the emoluments whereof shall have been increased while he was a Member of the Congress.

Sec. 17. No Senator or Member of the House of Representatives shall directly or indirectly be financially interested in any contract with the Government or any subdivision or instrumentality thereof, or in any franchise or special privilege granted by the Congress during his term of office. He shall not appear as counsel before the Electoral Tribunals or before any court in any civil case wherein the Government or any subdivision or instrumentality thereof is the adverse party, or in any criminal case wherein an officer or employee of the Government is accused of an offense committed in relation to his office, or collect any fee for his appearance in any administrative proceedings, or accept employment to intervene in any cause or matter where he may be called upon to act on account of his office. No Member of the Commission on Appointments shall appear as counsel before any court inferior to a collegiate court of appellate jurisdiction.

Sec. 18. All appropriation, revenue or tariff bills, bills authorizing increase of the public debt, bills of local application, and private bills, shall originate exclusively in the House of Representatives, but the Senate may propose or concur with amendments.

Sec. 19. (1) The President shall submit within fifteen days of the opening of each regular session of the Congress a budget of receipts and expenditures, which shall be the basis of the general appropriation bill. The Congress may not increase the appropriations recommended by the President for the operation of the Government as specified in the Budget, except the appropriations for the Congress and the Judicial Department. The form of the Budget and the information that it should contain shall be prescribed by law.

(2) No provision or enactment shall be embraced in the general appropriation bill unless it relates specifically to some particular appropriation therein; and any such provision or enactment shall be limited in its operation to such approriation.

Sec. 20. (1) Every bill passed by the Congress shall, before it becomes a law, be presented to the President. If he approves the same, he shall sign it; but if not, he shall return it with his objections to the House where it originated, which shall enter the objections at large on its Journal and proceed to reconsider it. If, after such reconsideration, two-thirds of all the Members of such House shall agree to pass the bill, it shall be sent, together with the objections, to the other House by which it shall likewise be reconsidered, and if approved by two-thirds of all the Members of that House, it shall become a law. In all such cases, the votes of each House shall be determined by *yeas* and *nays,* and the names of the Members voting for and against shall be entered on its Journal. If any bill shall not be returned by the President as herein provided within twenty days (Sundays excepted) after it shall have been presented to him, the same shall become a law in like manner as if he had signed it, unless the Congress by adjournment prevent its return, in which case it shall become a law unless vetoed by the President within thirty days after adjournment.

(2) The President shall have the power to veto any particular item or items of an appropriation bill, but the veto shall not affect the item or items to which he does not object. When a provision of an appropriation bill affects one or more items of the same, the President cannot veto the provision without at the same time vetoing the particular item or items to which it relates. The item or items objected to shall not take effect except in the manner heretofore provided as to bills returned to the Congress without the approval of the President. If the veto refers to a bill or any item of an appropriation bill which appropriates a sum in excess of ten *per centum* of the total amount voted in the appropriation bill for the general expenses of the Government for the preceding year, or if it should refer to a bill authorizing an increase of the public debt, the same shall not become a law unless approved by three-fourths of all the Members of each House.

(3) The President shall have the power to veto any separate item or items in a revenue or tariff bill, and the item or items vetoed shall not take effect except in the manner provided as to bills vetoed by the President.

Sec. 21. (1) No bill which may be enacted into law shall embrace more than one subject which shall be expressed in the title of the bill.

(2) No bill shall be passed by either House unless it shall have been printed and copies thereof in its final form furnished its Members at least three calendar days prior to its passage, except when the President shall have certified to the necessity of its immediate enactment. Upon the last reading of a bill no amendment thereof shall be allowed, and the question upon its passage shall be taken immediately thereafter, and the *yeas* and *nays* entered on the Journal.

Sec. 22. (1) The rule of taxation shall be uniform.

(2) The Congress may by law authorize the President, subject to such limitations and restrictions as it may impose, to fix, within specified limits, tariff rates, import or export quotas, and tonnage and wharfage dues.

(3) Cemeteries, churches, and parsonages or convents appurtenant thereto, and all lands, buildings, and improvements used exclusively for religious, charitable, or educational purposes shall be exempt from taxation.

Sec. 23. (1) All money collected on any tax levied for a special purpose shall be treated as a special fund and paid out for such purpose only. If the purpose for which a special fund was created has been fulfilled or abandoned, the balance, if any, shall be transferred to the general funds of the Government.

(2) No money shall be paid out of the Treasury except in pursuance of an appropriation made by law.

(3) No public money or property shall ever be appropriated, applied, or used, directly or indirectly, for the use, benefit, or support of any sect, church, denomination, sectarian institution, or system of religion, or for the use, benefit, or support of any priest, preacher, minister, or other religious teacher or dignitary as such, except when such priest, preacher, minister, or dignitary is assigned to the armed forces or to any penal institution, orphanage, or leprosarium.

Sec. 24. The heads of departments upon their own initiative or upon the request of either House may appear before and be heard by such House on any matter pertaining to their departments, unless the public interest shall require otherwise and the President shall so state in writing.

Sec. 25. The Congress shall, with the concurrence of two-thirds of all the Members of each House, have the sole power to declare war.

Sec. 26. In times of war or other national emergency, the Congress may by law authorize the President, for a limited period and subject to such restrictions as it may prescribe, to promulgate rules and regulations to carry out a declared national policy.

ARTICLE VII. EXECUTIVE DEPARTMENT

Section 1. The Executive power shall be vested in a President of the Philippines.

Sec. 2. The President shall hold his office during a term of four years and, together with the Vice-President chosen for the same term, shall be elected by a direct vote of the people. The returns of every election for President and Vice-President, duly certified by the board of canvassers of each province or city, shall be transmitted to the seat of the National Government, directed to the President of the Senate, who shall, in the presence of the Senate and the House of Representatives, open all the certificates, and the votes shall then be counted. The persons respectively having the highest number of votes for President and Vice-President shall be declared elected; but in case two or more shall have an equal and the highest number of votes for either office, one of them shall be chosen President or Vice-President, as the case may be, by a majority vote of the Members of the Congress in joint session assembled.

Sec. 3. No person may be elected to the office of President or Vice-President unless he be a natural-born citizen of the Philippines, a qualified voter, forty years of age or over, and has been a resident of the Philippines for at least ten years immediately preceding the election.

Sec. 4. Elections for President and Vice-President shall be held once every four years on a date to be fixed by law.

The terms of the President and Vice-President shall end at noon on the thirtieth day of December following the expiration of four years after their election, and the terms of their successors shall begin from such time.

Sec. 5. No person shall serve as President for more than eight consecutive years. The period of such service shall be counted from the date he shall have commenced to act as President. Voluntary renunciation of the office for any length of time shall not be considered as an interruption in the continuity of the service of the incumbent for the full term for which he was elected.

Sec. 6. If, at the time fixed for the beginning of the term of the President, the President-elect shall have died, the Vice-President-elect shall become President. If a President shall not have been chosen before the time fixed for the beginning of his term, or if the Vice-President shall have failed to qualify, then the Vice-President shall act as President until a President shall have qualified, and the Congress may by law provide for the case wherein neither a President-elect nor a Vice-President-elect shall have qualified, declaring who shall then act as President, or the manner in which one who is to act shall be selected, and such person shall act accordingly until a President or Vice-President shall have qualified.

Sec. 7. Before he enter on the execution of his office, the President shall take the following oath or affirmation.

"I do solemnly swear (or affirm) that I will faithfully and conscientiously fulfill my duties as President of the Philippines, preserve and defend its Constitution, execute its laws, do justice to every man, and consecrate myself to the service of the Nation. So help me God." (In case of affirmation, last sentence will be omitted.)

Sec. 8. In the event of the removal of the President from office, or of his death, resignation, or inability to discharge the powers and duties of the said office, the same shall devolve on the Vice-President, and the Congress shall by law provide for the case of removal, death, resignation, or inability, both of the President and Vice-President, declaring what officer shall then act as President, and such officer shall act accordingly, until the disability be removed, or a President shall be elected.

Sec. 9. The President shall have an official residence and receive a compensation to be ascertained by law which shall be neither increased nor diminished during the period for which he shall have been elected, and he shall not receive within that period any other emolument from the Government or any of its subdivisions or instrumentalities. Until the Congress shall provide otherwise, the President shall receive an annual salary of thirty thousand pesos. The Vice-President, when not acting as President, shall receive an annual compensation of fifteen thousand pesos until otherwise provided by law.

Sec. 10. (1) The President shall have control of all the executive departments, bureaus, or offices, exercise general supervision over all local governments as may be provided by law, and take care that the laws be faithfully executed.

(2) The President shall be commander-in-chief of all armed forces of the Philippines and, whenever it becomes necessary, he may call out such armed forces to prevent or suppress lawless violence, invasion, insurrection, or rebellion. In case of invasion, when the public safety requires it, he may suspend the privileges of the writ of *habeas corpus,* or place the Philippines or any part thereof under martial law

(3) The President shall nominate and with the consent of the Commission on Appointments, shall appoint the heads of the executive departments and bureaus, officers of the Army from the rank of colonel, of the Navy and air forces from the rank of captain or commander, and all other officers of the Government whose appointments are not herein otherwise provided for, and those whom he may be authorized by law to appoint; but the Congress may by law vest the appointment of inferior officers, in the President alone, in the courts, or in the heads of departments.

(4) The President shall have the power to make appointments dur-

ing the recess of the Congress, but such appointments shall be effective only until disapproval by the Commission on Appointments or until the next adjournment of the Congress.

(5) The President shall from time to time give to the Congress information of the state of the Nation, and recommend to its consideration such measures as he shall judge necessary and expedient.

(6) The President shall have the power to grant reprieves, commutations, and pardons, and remit fines and forfeitures, after conviction, for all offenses, except in cases of impeachment, upon such conditions and with such restrictions and limitations as he may deem proper to impose. He shall have the power to grant amnesty with the concurrence of the Congress.

(7) The President shall have the power, with the concurrence of two-thirds of all the Members of the Senate, to make treaties, and with the consent of the Commission on Appointments, he shall appoint ambassadors, other public ministers, and consuls. He shall receive ambassadors and other public ministers duly accredited to the Government of the Philippines.

Sec. 11. (1) The executive departments of the present Government of the Philippine Islands shall continue as now authorized by law until the Congress shall provide otherwise.

(2) The heads of departments and chiefs of bureaus or offices and their assistants shall not, during their continuance in office, engage in the practice of any profession, or intervene, directly or indirectly, in the management or control of any private enterprise which in any way may be affected by the functions of their office; nor shall they, directly or indirectly, be financially interested in any contract with the Government, or any subdivision or instrumentality thereof.

(3) The President may appoint the Vice-President as a member of his cabinet and also as head of an executive department.

ARTICLE VIII. JUDICIAL DEPARTMENT

Section 1. The Judicial power shall be vested in one Supreme Court and in such inferior courts as may be established by law.

Sec. 2. The Congress shall have the power to define, prescribe, and apportion the jurisdiction of the various courts, but may not deprive the Supreme Court of its original jurisdiction over cases affecting ambassadors, other public ministers, and consuls, nor of its jurisdiction to review, revise, reverse, modify, or affirm on appeal, certiorari, or writ of error, as the law or the rules of court may provide, final judgments and decrees of inferior courts in—

(1) All cases in which the constitutionality or validity of any treaty, law, ordinance, or executive order or regulations is in question.

(2) All cases involving the legality of any tax, impost, assessment, or toll, or any penalty imposed in relation thereto.

(3) All cases in which the jurisdiction of any trial court is in issue.

(4) All criminal cases in which the penalty imposed is death or life imprisonment.

(5) All cases in which an error or question of law is involved.

Sec. 3. Until the Congress shall provide otherwise, the Supreme Court shall have such original and appellate jurisdiction as may be possessed and exercised by the Supreme Court of the Philippine Islands at the time of the adoption of this Constitution. The original jurisdiction of the Supreme Court shall include all cases affecting ambassadors, other public ministers, and consuls.

Sec. 4. The Supreme Court shall be composed of a Chief Justice and ten Associate Justices and may sit either *in banc* or in two divisions unless otherwise provided by law.

Sec. 5. The members of the Supreme Court and all judges of inferior courts shall be appointed by the President with the consent of the Commission on Appointments.

Sec. 6. No person may be appointed member of the Supreme Court unless he has been five years a citizen of the Philippines, is at least forty years of age, and has for ten years or more been a judge of a court of record or engaged in the practice of law in the Philippines.

Sec. 7. No judge appointed for a particular district shall be designated or transferred to another district without the approval of the Supreme Court. The Congress shall by law determine the residence of judges of inferior courts.

Sec. 8. The Congress shall prescribe the qualifications of judges of inferior courts, but no person may be appointed judge of any such courts unless he is a citizen of the Philippines and has been admitted to the practice of law in the Philippines.

Sec. 9. The members of the Supreme Court and all judges of inferior courts shall hold office during good behavior, until they reach the age of seventy years, or become incapacitated to discharge the duties of their office. They shall receive such compensation as may be fixed by law, which shall not be diminished during their continuance in office. Until the Congress shall provide otherwise, the Chief Justice of the Supreme Court shall receive an annual compensation of sixteen thousand pesos.

Sec. 10. All cases involving the constitutionality of a treaty or law shall be heard and decided by the Supreme Court *in banc,* and no treaty or law may be declared unconstitutional without the concurrence of two-thirds of all the members of the Court.

Sec. 11. The conclusions of the Supreme Court in any case submitted to it for decision shall be reached in consultation before the case is assigned to a Justice for the writing of the opinion of the Court. Any Justice dissenting from a decision shall state the reasons for his dissent.

Sec. 12. No decision shall be rendered by any court of record without expressing therein clearly and distinctly the facts and the law on which it is based.

Sec. 13. The Supreme Court shall have the power to promulgate rules concerning pleading, practice, and procedure in all courts, and the admission to the practice of law. Said rules shall be uniform for all courts of the same grade and shall not diminish, increase, or modify substantive rights. The existing laws on pleading, practice, and procedure are hereby repealed as statutes, and are declared Rules of Courts, subject to the power of the Supreme Court to alter and modify the same. The Congress shall have the power to repeal, alter, or supplement the rules concerning pleading, practice, and procedure, and the admission to the practice of law in the Philippines.

ARTICLE IX. IMPEACHMENT

Section 1. The President, the Vice-President, the Justices of the Supreme Court, and the Auditor General, shall be removed from office on impeachment for, and conviction of, culpable violation of the Constitution, treason, bribery, or other high crimes.

Sec. 2. The House of Representatives, by a vote of two-thirds of all its members, shall have the sole power of impeachment.

Sec. 3. The Senate shall have the sole power to try all impeachments. When sitting for that purpose, the Senators shall be on oath or affirmation. When the President of the Philippines is on trial, the Chief Justice of the Supreme Court shall preside. No person shall be convicted without the concurrence of three-fourths of all the Members of the Senate.

Sec. 4. Judgment in cases of impeachment shall not extend further than to removal from office and disqualification to hold and enjoy any office of honor, trust, or profit under the Government of the Philippines, but the party convicted shall nevertheless be liable and subject to prosecution, trial, and punishment, according to law.

ARTICLE X. COMMISSION ON ELECTIONS

Section 1. There shall be an independent Commission on Elections composed of a Chairman and two other Members to be appointed by the President with the consent of the Commission on Appointments, who shall hold office for a term of nine years and may not be reappointed. Of the Members of the Commission first appointed, one shall hold office for nine years, another for six years, and the third for three years. The Chairman and the other Members of the Commission on Elections may be removed from office only by impeachment in the manner provided in this Constitution.

Until the Congress shall provide otherwise, the Chairman of the Commission shall receive an annual salary of twelve thousand pesos, and the other Members, ten thousand pesos each. Their salaries shall be neither increased nor diminished during their term of office.

Sec. 2. The Commission on Elections shall have exclusive charge of the enforcement and administration of all laws relative to the conduct of elections and shall exercise all other functions which may be conferred upon it by law. It shall decide, save those involving the right to vote, all administrative questions, affecting elections, including the determination of the number and location of polling places, and the appointment of election inspectors and of other election officials. All law enforcement agencies and instrumentalities of the Government, when so required by the Commission, shall act as its deputies for the purpose of insuring free, orderly, and honest elections. The decisions, orders, and rulings of the Commission shall be subject to review by the Supreme Court.

No pardon, parole, or suspension of sentence for the violation of any election law may be granted without the favorable recommendation of the Commission.

Sec. 3. The Chairman and Members of the Commission on Elections shall not, during their continuance in office, engage in the practice of any profession, or intervene, directly or indirectly, in the management or control of private enterprise which in any way may be affected by the functions of their office; nor shall they, directly or indirectly, be financially interested in any contract with the Government or any subdivision or instrumentality thereof.

Sec. 4. The Commission on Elections shall submit to the President and the Congress, following each election, a report on the manner in which such election was conducted.

ARTICLE XI. GENERAL AUDITING OFFICE

Section 1. There shall be a General Auditing Office under the direction and control of an Auditor General, who shall hold office for a term of ten years and may not be reappointed. The Auditor General shall be appointed by the President with the consent of the Commission on Appointments, and shall receive an annual compensation to be fixed by law which shall not be diminished during his continuance in office. Until the Congress shall provide otherwise, the Auditor General shall receive an annual compensation of twelve thousand pesos.

Sec. 2. The Auditor General shall examine, audit, and settle all accounts pertaining to the revenues and receipts from whatever source, including trust funds derived from bond issues; and audit, in accordance with law and administrative regulations, all expenditures of funds or property pertaining to or held in trust by the Government or the provinces or municipalities thereof. He shall keep the general accounts of the Government and preserve the vouchers pertaining thereto. It shall be the duty of the Auditor General to bring to the attention of the proper administrative officer expenditures of funds or property which, in his opinion, are irregular, unnecessary, excessive, or extravagant. He shall also perform such other functions as may be prescribed by law.

Sec 3. The decisions of the Auditor General shall be rendered within the time fixed by law, and the same may be appealed to the President whose action shall be final. When the aggrieved party is a private person or entity, an appeal from the decision of the Auditor General may be taken directly to a court of record in the manner provided by law.

Sec. 4. The Auditor General shall submit to the President and the Congress an annual report covering the financial condition and operations of the Government, and such other reports as may be required.

ARTICLE XII. CIVIL SERVICE

Section 1. A Civil Service embracing all branches and subdivisions of the Government shall be provided by law. Appointments in the Civil Service, except as to those which are policy-determining, primarily confidential or highly technical in nature, shall be made only according to merit and fitness, to be determined as far as practicable by competitive examination.

Sec. 2. Officers and employees in the Civil Service, including members of the armed forces, shall not engage directly or indirectly in partisan political activities or take part in any election except to vote.

Sec. 3. No officer or employee of the Government shall receive additional or double compensation unless specifically authorized by law.

Sec. 4. No officer or employee in the Civil Service shall be removed or suspended except for cause as provided by law.

ARTICLE XIII. CONSERVATION AND UTILIZATION
OF NATURAL RESOURCES

Section 1. All agricultural, timber, and mineral lands of the public domain, waters, minerals, coal, petroleum, and other mineral oils, all forces of potenital energy, and other natural resources of the Philippines belong to the State, and their disposition, exploitation, development, or utilization shall be limited to citizens of the Philippines, or to corporations or associations at least sixty per centum of the capital of which is owned by such citizens, subject to any existing right, grant, lease, or concession at the time of the inauguration of the Government established under this Constitution. Natural resources, with the exception of public agricultural land, shall not be alienated, and no license, concession, or lease for the exploitation, development, or utilization of any of the natural resources shall be granted for a period exceeding twenty-five years, renewable for another twenty-five years, except as to water right for irrigation, water supply, fisheries, or industrial uses other than the development of water power, in which cases beneficial use may be the measure and the limit of the grant.

Sec. 2. No private corporation or association may acquire, lease, or hold public agricultural lands in excess of one thousand and twenty-four hectares, nor may any individual acquire such lands by purchase in excess of one hundred and forty-four hectares, or by lease in excess of one thousand and twenty-four hectares, or by homestead in excess of twenty-four hectares. Lands adapted to grazing, not exceeding two thousand hectares, may be leased to an individual, private corporation, or association.

Sec. 3. The Congress may determine by law the size of private agricultural land which individuals, corporations, or associations may acquire and hold, subject to rights existing prior to the enactment of such law.

Sec. 4. The Congress may authorize, upon payment of just compensation, the expropriation of lands to be subdivided into small lots and conveyed at cost to individuals.

Sec. 5. Save in cases of hereditary succession, no private agricultural land shall be transferred or assigned except to individuals, corporations, or associations qualified to acquire or hold lands of the public domain in the Philippines.

Sec. 6. The State may, in the interest of national welfare and defense, establish and operate industries and means of transportation and communication, and, upon payment of just compensation, transfer to public ownership utilities and other private enterprises to be operated by the Government.

ARTICLE XIV. GENERAL PROVISIONS

Section 1. The flag of the Philippines shall be red, white, and blue, with a sun and three stars, as consecrated and honored by the people and recognized by law.

Sec. 2. All public officers and members of the armed forces shall take an oath to support and defend the Constitution.

Sec. 3. The Congress shall take steps toward the development and adoption of a common national language based on one of the existing native languages. Until otherwise provided by law, English and Spanish shall continue as official languages.

Sec. 4. The State shall promote scientific research and invention. Arts and letters shall be under its patronage. The exclusive right to writings and inventions shall be secured to authors and inventors for a limited period.

Sec. 5. All educational institutions shall be under the supervision of and subject to regulation by the State. The Government shall establish and maintain a complete and adequate system of public education, and shall provide at least free public primary instruction, and citizenship training to adult citizens. All schools shall aim to develop moral character, personal discipline, civic conscience, and vocational efficiency, and to teach the duties of citizenship. Optional religious instruction shall be maintained in the public schools as now authorized by law. Universities established by the State shall create scholarships in arts, science, and letters for specially gifted citizens.

Sec. 6. The State shall afford protection to labor, especially to working women and minors, and shall regulate the relations between landowner and tenant, and between labor and capital in industry and in agriculture. The State may provide for compulsory arbitration.

Sec. 7. The Congress shall not, except by general law, provide for the formation, organization, or regulation of private corporations, unless such corporations are owned or controlled by the Government or any subdivision or instrumentality thereof.

Sec. 8. No franchise, certificate, or any other form of authorization for the operation of a public utility shall be granted except to citizens of the Philippines or to corporations or other entities organized under the laws of the Philippines, sixty per centum of the capital of which is owned by citizens of the Philippines, nor shall such franchise, certificate, or authorization be exclusive in character or for a longer period than fifty years. No franchise or right shall be granted to any individual, firm, or corporation, except under the condition that it shall be subject to amendment, alteration, or repeal by the Congress when the public interest so requires.

Sec. 9. The Government shall organize and maintain a national police force to preserve public order and enforce the law.

Sec. 10. This Constitution shall be officially promulgated in English and Spanish, but in case of conflict the English text shall prevail.

ARTICLE XV. AMENDMENTS

Section 1. The Congress in joint session assembled, by a vote of three-fourths of all the Members of the Senate and of the House of Representatives voting separately, may propose amendments to this Constitution or call a convention for that purpose. Such amendments shall be valid as part of this Constitution when approved by a majority of the votes cast at an election at which the amendments are submitted to the people for their ratification.

ARTICLE XVI. TRANSITORY PROVISIONS

Section 1. The first election of the officers provided in this Constitution and the inauguration of the Government of the Commonwealth of the Philippines shall take place as provided in Public Act Numbered One hundred and twenty-seven of the Congress of the United States, approved March twenty-four, nineteen hundred and thirty-four.

Sec. 2. All laws of the Philippine Islands shall continue in force until the inauguration of the Commonwealth of the Philippines; thereafter, such laws shall remain operative, unless inconsistent with this Constitution, until amended, altered, modified, or repealed by the Congress of the Philippines, and all references in such laws to the Government or officials of the Philippine Islands shall be construed, in so far as applicable, to refer to the Government and corresponding officials under this Constitution.

Sec. 3. All courts existing at the time of the adoption of this Constitution shall continue and exercise their jurisdiction, until otherwise provided by law in accordance with this Constitution, and all cases, civil and criminal, pending under the laws then in force.

Sec. 4. All officers and employees in the existing Government of the Philippine Islands shall continue in office until the Congress shall provide otherwise, but all officers whose appointments are by this Constitution vested in the President shall vacate their respective offices upon the appointment and qualification of their successors, if such appointment is made within a period of one year from the date of the inauguration of the Commonwealth of the Philippines.

Sec. 5. The members of the House of Representatives for the Mountain Province shall be elected as may be provided by law. The voters of municipalities and municipal districts formerly belonging to

344 *Philippine Constitution*

a special province and now forming part of regular provinces shall vote in the election for Members of the House of Representatives in such districts as may be provided by law.

Sec. 6. The provisions of this Constitution, except those contained in this article and in Article V, and those which refer to the election and qualifications of officers to be elected under this Constitution, shall not take effect until the inauguration of the Commonwealth of the Philippines.

ARTICLE XVII. SPECIAL PROVISIONS EFFECTIVE UPON
THE PROCLAMATION OF THE INDEPENDENCE
OF THE PHILIPPINES

Section 1. Upon the proclamation of the President of the United State recognizing the independence of the Philippines

(1) The property rights of the United States and the Philippines shall be promptly adjusted and settled, and all existing property rights of citizens or corporations of the United States shall be acknowledged, respected, and safeguarded to the same extent as property rights of citizens of the Philippines.

(2) The officials elected and serving under this Constitution shall be constitutional officers of the free and independent Government of the Philippines and qualified to function in all respects as if elected directly under such Government, and shall serve their full terms of office as prescribed in this Constitution.

(3) The debts and liabilities of the Philippines, its provinces, cities, municipalities, and instrumentalities, which shall be valid and subsisting at the time of the final and complete withdrawal of the sovereignty of the United States, shall be assumed by the free and independent Government of the Philippines; and where bonds have been issued under authority of an Act of Congress of the United States by the Philippine Islands, or any province, city, or municipality therein, the Government of the Philippines will make adequate provision for the necessary funds for the payment of interest and principal, and such obligations shall be a first lien on all taxes collected.

(4) The Government of the Philippines will assume all continuing obligations of the United States under the Treaty of Peace with Spain ceding the Philippine Islands to the United States.

(5) The Government of the Philippines will embody the foregoing provisions of this article [except subsection (2)] in a treaty with the United States.

ARTICLE XVIII. THE COMMONWEALTH AND THE REPUBLIC

Section 1. The government established by this Constitution shall be known as the Commonwealth of the Philippines. Upon the final and complete withdrawal of the sovereignty of the United States and the proclamation of Philippine independence, the Commonwealth of the Philippines shall thenceforth be known as the Republic of the Philippines.

ORDINANCE APPENDED TO THE CONSTITUTION

Notwithstanding the provisions of section one, Article Thirteen, and section eight, Article Fourteen, of the foregoing Constitution, during the effectivity of the Executive Agreement entered into by the President of the Philippines with the President of the United States on the fourth of July, nineteen hundred and forty-six, pursuant to the provisions of Commonwealth Act Numbered Seven hundred and thirty-three, but in no case to extend beyond the third of July, nineteen hundred and seventy-four, the disposition, exploitation, development, and utilization of all agricultural, timber, and mineral lands of the public domain, waters, minerals, coal, petroleum, and other mineral oils, all forces and sources of potential energy, and other natural resources of the Philippines, and the operation of public utilities, shall, if open to any person, be open to citizens of the United States and to all forms of business enterprise owned or controlled, directly or indirectly, by citizens of the United States in the same manner as to, and under the same conditions imposed upon, citizens of the Philippines or corporations or associations owned or controlled by citizens of the Philippines.

Note.—The first amendment embodied in Resolution No. 39 adopted by the Second National Assembly on September 15, 1939, and approved by the President of the United States on November 10, 1939, was automatically superseded upon the establishment of the Republic of the Philippines.

Appendix E

PHILIPPINE TRADE AGREEMENT
REVISION ACT OF 1955 *

AN ACT Relating to revisions of the executive agreement concerning trade and related matters entered into by the President of the United States and the President of the Philippines on July 4, 1946. *Be it enacted by the Senate and House of Representatives of the United States of America in Congress assembled,*

201. AUTHORITY TO REVISE THE 1946 AGREEMENT

In order to make revisions proposed by the delegations of the Governments of the United States of America and of the Republic of the Philippines in the "Final Act of Negotiations Relative to Revision of the 1946 Trade Agreement Between the United States of America and the Republic of the Philippines" signed at Washington, December 15, 1954, as corrected, the President of the United States is hereby authorized to enter into an agreement with the President of the Philippines revising the executive agreement concerning trade and related matters entered into by the President of the United States and the President of the Philippines on July 4, 1946, so that such executive agreement, as so revised, will read as follows:

"AGREEMENT BETWEEN THE UNITED STATES OF AMERICA AND THE REPUBLIC OF THE PHILIPPINES CONCERNING TRADE AND RELATED MATTERS DURING A TRANSITIONAL PERIOD FOLLOWING THE INSTITUTION OF PHILIPPINE INDEPENDENCE, SIGNED AT MANILA ON JULY 4, 1946, AS REVISED

"The President of the United States of America and the President of the Republic of the Philippines, mindful of the close economic ties between the people of the United States and the people of the Philippines during many years of intimate political relations, and desiring to enter into an agreement in keeping with their long friend-

---

* Passed the House of Representatives July 7; passed the Senate July 20, 1955; signed by the President Aug. 1, 1955.

ship, which will be mutually beneficial to the two peoples and will strengthen the economy of the Philippines so as to enable that Republic to contribute more effectively to the peace and prosperity of the free world, have agreed to the following Articles:

"ARTICLE I

"1. The ordinary customs duty to be collected on United States articles as defined in Subparagraph (e) of Paragraph 1 of the Protocol, which during the following portions of the period from January 1, 1956, to July 3, 1974, both dates inclusive, are entered, or withdrawn from warehouse, in the Philippines for consumption, shall be determined by applying the following percentages of the Philippine duty as defined in Subparagraph (h) of Paragraph 1 of the Protocol:

"(a) During the period from January 1, 1956, to December 31, 1958, both dates inclusive, twenty-five per centum.

"(b) During the period from January 1, 1959, to December 31, 1961, both dates inclusive, fifty per centum.

"(c) During the period from January 1, 1962, to December 31, 1964, both dates inclusive, seventy-five per centum.

"(d) During the period from January 1, 1965, to December 31, 1973, both dates inclusive, ninety per centum.

"(e) During the period from January 1, 1974, to July 3, 1974, both dates inclusive, one hundred per centum.

"2. The ordinary customs duty to be collected on Philippine articles as defined in Subparagraph (f) of Paragraph 1 of the Protocol, other than those specified in the Schedule to Paragraph 2 of Article II, which during such portions of such period are entered, or withdrawn from warehouse, in the United States for consumption, shall be determined by applying the following percentages of the United States duty as defined in Subparagraph (g) of Paragraph 1 of the Protocol:

"(a) During the period from January 1, 1956, to December 31, 1958, both dates inclusive, five per centum.

"(b) During the period from January 1, 1959, to December 31, 1961, both dates inclusive, ten per centum.

"(c) During the period from January 1, 1962, to December 31, 1964, both dates inclusive, twenty per centum.

"(d) During the period from January 1, 1965, to December 31, 1967, both dates inclusive, forty per centum.

"(e) During the period from January 1, 1967, to December 31, 1970, both dates inclusive, sixty per centum.

"(f) During the period from January 1, 1971, to December 31, 1973, both dates inclusive, eighty per centum.

"(g) During the period from January 1, 1974, to July 3, 1974, both dates inclusive, one hundred per centum.

"3. Customs duties on United States articles, and on Philippine articles, other than ordinary customs duties, shall be determined without regard to the provisions of Paragraphs 1 and 2 of this Article, but shall be subject to the provisions of Paragraph 4 of this Article.

"4. With respect to United States articles imported into the Philippines, and with respect to Philippine articles imported into the United States, no duty on or in connection with importation shall be collected or paid in an amount in excess of the duty imposed with respect to like articles which are the product of any other foreign country, or collected or paid in any amount if the duty is not imposed with respect to such like articles. As used in this Paragraph, the term 'duty' includes taxes, fees, charges, or exactions, imposed on or in connection with importation, but does not include internal taxes or ordinary customs duties.

"5. With respect to products of the United States which do not come within the definition of United States articles, imported into the Philippines, no duty on or in connection with importation shall be collected or paid in an amount in excess of the duty imposed with respect to like articles which are the product of any foreign country, or collected or paid in any amount if the duty is not imposed with respect to such like articles which are the product of any other foreign country. As used in this Paragraph the term 'duty' includes taxes, fees, charges, or exactions, imposed on or in connection with importation, but does not include internal taxes.

"6. With respect to products of the Philippines, which do not come within the definition of Philippine articles, imported into the United States, no duty on or in connection with importation shall be collected or paid in an amount in excess of the duty imposed with respect to like articles which are the product of any other foreign country (except Cuba), or collected or paid in any amount if the duty is not imposed with respect to such like articles which are the product of any other foreign country (except Cuba). As used in this Paragraph the term 'duty' includes taxes, fees, charges, or exactions, imposed on or in connection with importation, but does not include internal taxes.

"7. Notwithstanding the provisions of Paragraph 1 of this Article, the Philippines shall impose a temporary special import tax, in lieu of the present tax on the sale of foreign exchange, on any article or product imported or brought into the Philippines, irrespective of source; provided that such special levy is applied in a non-discriminatory manner pursuant to Paragraphs 4 and 5 of this Article, that the initial tax is at a rate no higher than the present rate of the foreign exchange tax, and that the tax be progressively reduced at a rate no less rapid than that specified in the following Schedule. If, as a result of applying this Schedule, the total revenue from Philippine customs duties and from the special import tax on goods coming from the United States is less in any calendar year than the proceeds from the exchange tax on such goods during the calendar year 1955, no reduction need be made in the special import tax for the next succeeding calendar year, and, if necessary to restore revenues collected on the importation of United States goods to the level of the exchange tax on such goods in calendar year 1955, the Philippines may increase the rate for such succeeding calendar year to any previous level provided for in this Schedule which is considered to be necessary to restore such revenues to the amount collected from the exchange tax on United States goods in calendar year 1955. Rates for the special import levy in subsequent years shall be fixed in accordance with the schedules specified in this Article, except as the Philippine Government may determine that higher rates are necessary to maintain the above-mentioned level of revenues from the importation of United States goods. In this event, such rate shall be determined by the Philippine Government, after consultation with the United States Government, at a level of the Schedule calculated to cover any anticipated deficiency arising from the operation of this provision.

"Schedule for Reducing Special Import Tax

"(a) After December 31, 1956, ninety per centum.
"(b) After December 31, 1957, eighty per centum.
"(c) After December 31, 1958, seventy per centum.
"(d) After December 31, 1959, sixty per centum.
"(e) After December 31, 1960, fifty per centum.
"(f) After December 31, 1961, forty per centum.
"(g) After December 31, 1962, thirty per centum.
"(h) After December 31, 1963, twenty per centum.
"(i) After December 31, 1964, ten per centum.
"(j) On and after January 1, 1966, nil.

"ARTICLE II

"1. During the period from January 1, 1956, to December 31, 1973, both dates inclusive, the total amount of the articles falling within one of the classes specified in Items A and A-1 of the Schedule to this Paragraph, which are Philippine articles as defined in Subparagraph (f) of Paragraph 1 of the Protocol, and which, in any calendar year, may be entered, or withdrawn from warehouse, in the United States for consumption, shall not exceed the amounts specified in such Schedule as to each class of articles. During the period from January 1, 1956, to December 31, 1973, both date's inclusive, the total amount of the articles falling within the class specified in Item B of the Schedule to this Paragraph which are the product of the Philippines, and which, in any calendar year, may be entered, or withdrawn from warehouse, in the United States for consumption, shall not exceed the amount specified in such Schedule as to such class of articles. During the period from January 1, 1974, to July 3, 1974, both dates inclusive, the total amounts referred to in the preceding sentences of this Paragraph shall not exceed one-half of the amount specified in such Schedule with respect to each class of articles, respectively. The establishment herein of the limitations on the amounts of Philippine raw and refined sugar that may be entered, or withdrawn from warehouse, in the United States for consumption, shall be without prejudice to any increases which the Congress of the United States might allocate to the Philippines in the future. The following Schedule to Paragraph 1 shall constitute an integral part thereof:

"Schedule of Absolute Quotas

"Item	Classes of Articles	Amounts
A	Sugars	952,000 short tons
	A-1 of which not to exceed	56,000 short tons
	may be refined sugars, meaning 'direct-consumption sugar' as defined in Section 101 of the Sugar Act of 1948, as amended, of the United States which is set forth in part as Annex I to this Agreement.	
B	Cordage, including yarns, twines (including binding twine described in Paragraph 1622 of the Tariff Act of 1930 of the United States, as amended, which is set forth as Annex II to this Agreement), cords, cordage, rope, and cable, tarred or untarred, wholly or in chief value of manila (abaca) or other hard fiber.	6,000,000 lbs.

"2. Philippine articles as defined in Subparagraph (f) of Paragraph 1 of the Protocol falling within one of the Classes specified in the items included in the Schedule to this Paragraph, which, during the following portions of the period from January 1, 1956, to December 31, 1973, both dates inclusive, are entered, or withdrawn from warehouse, in the United States for consumption, shall be free of ordinary customs duty, in quantities determined by applying the following percentages to the amounts specified in such Schedule as to each such class of articles:

"(a) During each of the calendar years 1956 to 1958, inclusive, ninety-five per centum.

"(b) During each of the calendar years 1959 to 1961, inclusive, ninety per centum.

"(c) During each of the calendar years 1962 to 1964, inclusive, eighty per centum.

"(d) During each of the calendar years 1965 to 1967, inclusive, sixty per centum.

"(e) During each of the calendar years 1968 to 1970, inclusive, forty per centum.

"(f) During each of the calendar years 1971 to 1973, inclusive, twenty per centum.

"(g) On and after January 1, 1974, nil.

The following Schedule to Paragraph 2 shall constitute an integral part thereof:

"Schedule of Tariff Quotas

"Item	Classes of Articles	Amounts
A	Cigars (exclusive of cigarettes, cheroots of all kinds, and paper cigars and cigarettes, including wrapper).	200,000,000 cigars
B	Scrap tobacco, and stemmed and unstemmed filler tobacco described in Paragraph 602 of the Tariff Act of 1930 of the United States, as amended, which is set forth as Annex III to this Agreement.	6,500,000 lbs.
C	Coconut oil	200,000 long tons
D	Buttons of pearl or shell	850,000 gross

The quantities shown in the Schedule to this Paragraph represent base quantities for the purposes of computing the tariff-free quota and are not absolute quotas. Any such Philippine article so entered, or withdrawn from warehouse, in excess of the duty-free quota provided in this Paragraph shall be subject to one hundred per centum of the United States duty as defined in Subparagraph (g) of Paragraph 1 of the Protocol.

"ARTICLE III

"1. Except as otherwise provided in Article II or in Paragraph 2 of this Article, neither country shall impose restrictions or prohibitions on the importation of any article of the other country, or on the exportation of any article to the territories of the other country, unless the importation of the like article of, or the exportation of the like article to, all third countries is similarly restricted or prohibited. If either country imposes quantitative restrictions on the importation or exportation of any article in which the other country has an important interest and if it makes allotments to any third country, it shall afford such other country a share proportionate to the amount of the article, by quantity or value, supplied by or to it during a previous representative period, due consideration being given to any special factors affecting the trade in such article.

"2. (a) Notwithstanding the provisions of Paragraph 1 of this Article, with respect to quotas on United States articles as defined in Subparagraph (e) of Paragraph 1 of the Protocol or with respect to quotas on Philippine articles as defined in Subparagraph (f) of Paragraph 1 of the Protocol (other than the articles for which quotas are provided in Paragraph 1 of Article II) a quota may be established only if—

"(1) The President of the country desiring to impose the quota, after investigation, finds and proclaims that, as the result of preferential treatment accorded pursuant to this Agreement, any article of the other country is being imported in such increased quantities and under such conditions as to cause or threaten serious injury to domestic producers of like or directly competitive articles; or

"(2) The President of the country desiring to impose the quota finds that such action is necessary to forestall the imminent threat of, or to stop a serious decline in its monetary reserves, or, in the event its monetary reserves are very low, to achieve a reasonable rate of increase in its reserves.

"(b) Any quota imposed for any twelve-month period under (a) (1) above for the purpose of protecting domestic industry shall not be less than the amount determined by the President of the importing country as the total amount of the articles of such class which, during the twelve months preceding entry into effect of the quota, was entered, or withdrawn from warehouse, for consumption, after deduction of the amount by which he finds domestic production can be increased during the twelve-month period of the quota; or if the quota is established for any period other than a twelve-month period, it shall not be less than a proportionate amount.

"(c) Each Party agrees not to apply restrictions so as to prevent unreasonably the importation of any description of goods in minimum commercial quantities, the exclusion of which would seriously impair regular channels of trade, or restrictions which would prevent the importation of commercial samples, or prevent compliance with patent, trade-mark, copyright, or similar procedures.

"(d) Any quota established pursuant to this Paragraph shall not continue in effect longer than necessary to achieve the purposes for its imposition, at which time the President of the country imposing the quota, following investigation, shall find and proclaim that the conditions which gave rise to the establishment of such quota no longer exist.

"3. Either country taking action pursuant to the provisions of this Article shall give notice to the other country as far in advance as may be practicable, and shall afford it an opportunity to consult in respect of the proposed action. It is understood that this right of consultation does not imply that the consent of the other country to the establishment of the quota is needed in order for the quota to be put into effect.

"ARTICLE IV

"1. With respect to articles which are products of the United States coming into the Philippines, or with respect to articles manufactured in the Philippines wholly or in part from such articles, no internal tax shall be—

"(a) Collected or paid in an amount in excess of the internal tax imposed with respect to like articles which are the product of the Philippines, or collected or paid in any amount if the internal tax is not imposed with respect to such like articles;

"(b) Collected or paid in an amount in excess of the internal tax imposed with respect to like articles which are the product of any other foreign country, or collected or paid in any amount if the internal tax is not imposed with respect to such like articles. Where an internal tax is imposed with respect to an article which is the product of a foreign country to compensate for an internal tax imposed (1) with respect to a like article which is the product of the Philippines, or (2) with respect to materials used in the production of a like article which is the product of the Philippines, if the amount of the internal tax which is collected and paid with respect to the article which is the product of the United States is not in excess of that permitted by Paragraph 1 (b) of Article IV such collection and payment shall not be regarded as in violation of the first sentence of this Paragraph.

"2. With respect to articles which are products of the Philippines coming into the United States, or with respect to articles manufactured in the United States wholly or in part from such articles, no internal tax shall be

"(a) Collected or paid in an amount in excess of the internal tax imposed with respect to like articles which are the product of the United States, or collected or paid in any amount if the internal tax is not imposed with respect to such like articles;

"(b) Collected or paid in an amount in excess of the internal tax imposed with respect to like articles which are the product of any other foreign country, or collected or paid in any amount if the internal tax is not imposed with respect to such like articles. Where an internal tax is imposed with respect to an article which is the product of a foreign country to compensate for an internal tax imposed (1) with respect to a like article which is the product of the United States, or (2) with respect to materials used in the production of a like article which is the product of the United States, if the amount of the internal tax which is collected and paid with respect to the article which is the product of the Philippines is not in excess of that permitted by Paragraph 2 (b) of Article IV such collection and payment shall not be regarded as in violation of the first sentence of this Paragraph. This Paragraph shall not apply to the taxes imposed under Sections 4591, 4812, or 4831 of the Internal Revenue Code of the United States which are set forth in part as Annexes IV, V, and VI of this Agreement.

"3. No processing tax or other internal tax shall be imposed or collected in the United States with respect to articles coming into such country for the official use of the Government of the Philippines or of the United States, respectively, or any department or agency thereof.

"4. No processing tax or other internal tax shall be imposed or collected in the United States with respect to manila (abaca) fiber not dressed or manufactured in any manner.

"5: The United States will not reduce the preference of two cents per pound provided in Section 4513 of the Internal Revenue Code of the United States (relating to processing taxes on coconut oil, etc.), which is set forth as Annex VII to this Agreement, with respect to articles 'wholly the production of the Philippine Islands' or articles 'produced wholly from materials the growth or production of the Philippine Islands'; except that it may suspend the provisions of Section 4511 (b) of the Internal Revenue Code of the United States during any period as to which the President of the United States, after consultation with the President of the Philippines, finds that adequate supplies of neither copra nor coconut oil, the product of the Philippines, are readily available for processing in the United States.

"ARTICLE V

"The Republic of the Philippines will take the necessary legislative and executive actions, prior to or at the time of the entry into force of the revisions of this Agreement authorized by the Congress of the United States and the Congress of the Philippines in 1955, to enact and implement legislation similar to that already enacted by the Congress of the United States as Public Law 419, 83rd Congress, Chapter 323, 2d Session, to facilitate the entry of Philippine traders.

"ARTICLE VI

"1. The disposition, exploitation, development, and utilization of all agricultural, timber, and mineral lands of the public domain, waters, minerals, coal, petroleum and other mineral oils, all forces and sources of potential energy, and other natural resources of either Party, and the operation of public utilities, shall, if open to any person, be open to citizens of the other Party and to all forms of business enterprise owned or controlled, directly or indirectly, by citizens of the other Party in the same manner as to and under the same conditions imposed upon citizens or corporations or associations owned or controlled by citizens of the Party granting the right.

"2. The rights provided for in Paragraph 1 may be exercised, in the case of citizens of the Philippines with respect to natural resources in the United States which are subject to Federal control or regulations, only through the medium of a corporation organized under the laws of the United States or one of the States thereof and likewise, in the case of citizens of the United States with respect to natural resources in the public domain in the Philippines, only through the medium of a corporation organized under the laws of the Philippines and at least 60% of the capital stock of which is owned or controlled by citizens of the United States. This provision, however, does not affect the right of citizens of the United States to acquire or own private agricultural lands in the Philippines or citizens of the Philippines to acquire or own land in the United States which is subject to the jurisdiction of the United States and not within the jurisdiction of any State and which is not within the public domain. The Philippines reserves the right to dispose of its public lands in small quantitites on especially favorable terms exclusively to actual settlers or other users who are its own citizens. The United States reserves the right to dispose of its public lands in small quantities on especially favorable terms exclusively to actual settlers or other users who are its own citizens or aliens who have declared their intention to become citizens. Each Party reserves the right to limit the extent to which aliens may engage in fishing or engage in enterprises which furnish communications services and air or water transport. The United States also reserves the right to limit the extent to which aliens may own land in its outlying territories and possessions, but the Philippines will extend to American nationals who are residents of any of those outlying territories and possessions only the same rights, with respect to ownership of lands, which are granted therein to citizens of the Philippines. The rights provided for in this Paragraph shall not, however, be exercised by either Party so as to derogate from the rights previously acquired by citizens or corporations or associations owned or controlled by citizens of the other Party.

"ARTICLE VII

"1. The Republic of the Philippines and the United States of America each agrees not to discriminate in any manner, with respect to their engaging in business activities, against the citizens or any form of business enterprise owned or controlled by citizens of the other and that new limitations imposed by either Party upon the extent to which aliens are accorded national treatment with respect to carrying on business activities within its territories, shall not be applied as against enterprises owned or controlled by citizens of the other Party which are engaged in such activities therein at the time such new limitations are adopted, nor shall such new limitations be applied to American citizens or corporations or associations owned or controlled by American citizens whose States do not impose like limitations on citizens or corporations or associations owned or controlled by citizens of the Republic of the Philippines.

"2. The United States of America reserves the rights of the several States of the United States to limit the extent to which citizens or corporations or associations owned or controlled by citizens of the Philippines may engage in any business activities. The Republic of the Philippines reserves the power to deny any rights to engage in business activities to citizens of the United States who are citizens of States, or to corporations or associations at least 60% of the capital stock or capital of which is owned or controlled by citizens of States, which deny like rights to citizens of the Philippines or to corporations or associations owned or controlled by citizens of the Philippines. The exercise of this reservation on the part of the Philippines shall not affect previously acquired rights, provided that in the event that any State of the United States of America should in the future impose restrictions which would deny to citizens or corporations or associations owned or controlled by citizens of the Philippines the right to continue to engage in business activities in which they were engaged therein at the time of the imposition of such restrictions, the Republic of the Philippines shall be free to apply like limitations to the citizens or corporations or associations owned or controlled by citizens of such States.

"ARTICLE VIII

"Nothing in this Agreement shall be construed:

"(1) to require either Party to furnish any information the disclosure of which it considers contrary to its essential security interests; or

"(2) to prevent either Party from taking any action which it considers necessary for the protection of its essential security interests—

"(a) relating to fissionable materials or the materials from which they are derived;

"(b) relating to the traffic in arms, ammunition and implements of war and to such traffic in other goods and materials as is carried on directly or indirectly for the purpose of supplying a military establishment;

"(c) taken in time of war or other emergency in international relations; or

"(3) to prevent either Party from taking any action in pursuance of its obligations under the United Nations Charter for the maintenance of international peace and security.

"ARTICLE IX

"1. Upon the taking effect of this Agreement, and upon the taking effect of the revisions thereof authorized by the Congress of the United States and the Congress of the Philippines in 1955, the provisions placing obligations on the United States: (a) if in effect as laws of the United States at the time of such taking effect, shall continue in effect as laws of the United States during the effectiveness of the Agreement; or (b) if not so in effect, shall take effect and continue in effect as laws of the United States during the effectiveness of the Agreement; in the Philippines will continue in effect as laws of the Philippines, during the effectiveness of this Agreement, the provisions thereof placing obligations on the Philippines.

"2. The United States and the Philippines will promptly enact, and shall keep in effect during the effectiveness of this Agreement, such legislation as may be necessary to supplement the laws of the

United States and the Philippines, respectively, referred to in Paragraph 1 of this Article, and to implement the provisions of such laws and the provisions of this Agreement placing obligations on the United States and the Philippines, respectively.

"ARTICLE X

"The United States and the Philippines agree to consult with each other with respect to any questions as to the interpretation or the application of this Agreement, concerning which either Government may make representations to the other. Not later than July 1, 1971, the United States and the Philippines agree to consult with each other as to joint problems which may arise as a result or in anticipation of the termination of this Agreement.

"ARTICLE XI

"1. This Agreement shall have no effect after July 3, 1974. It may be terminated by either the United States or the Philippines at any time, upon not less than five years' written notice. If the President of the United States or the President of the Philippines determines and proclaims that the other country has adopted or applied measures or practices which would operate to nullify or impair any right or obligation provided for in this Agreement, then the Agreement may be terminated upon not less than six months' written notice.

"2. The revisions of this Agreement authorized by the Congress of the United States and the Congress of the Philippines in 1955 shall enter into force on January 1, 1956.

"PROTOCOL TO ACCOMPANY THE AGREEMENT BETWEEN THE UNITED STATES OF AMERICA AND THE REPUBLIC OF THE PHILIPPINES CONCERNING TRADE AND RELATED MATTERS DURING A TRANSITIONAL PERIOD FOLLOWING THE INSTITUTION OF PHILIPPINE INDEPENDENCE, SIGNED AT MANILA ON JULY 4, 1946, AS REVISED

"The undersigned duly empowered Plenipotentiaries have agreed to the following Protocol to the Agreement between the United States of America and the Republic of the Philippines concerning trade and related matters during a transitional period following the institution of Philippine Independence, signed at Manila on July 4, 1946, as revised, which shall constitute an integral part of the Agreement:

"1. For the purpose of the Agreement—

"(a) The term 'person' includes partnerships, corporations, and associations.

"(b) The term 'United States' means the United States of America and, when used in a geographical sense, means the States, the District of Columbia, the Territories of Alaska and Hawaii, and Puerto Rico.

"(c) The term 'Philippines' means the Republic of the Philippines and, when used in a geographical sense, means the territories of the Republic of the Philippines, whether a particular act in question took place, or a particular situation in question existed, within such territories before or after the institution of the Republic of the Philippines. As used herein the territories of the Republic of the Philippines comprise all the territories specified in Section 1 of Article I of the Constitution of the Philippines which is set forth as Annex X to this Agreement.

"(d) The term 'ordinary customs duty' means a customs duty based on the article as such (whether or not such duty is also based in any manner on the use, value, or method of production of the article, on the amount of like article imported, or on any other factor); but does not include—

"(1) A customs duty based on an act or omission of any person with respect to the importation of the article, or of the country from which it comes; or

"(2) A countervailing duty imposed to offset a subsidy, bounty, or grant; or

"(3) An anti-dumping duty imposed to offset the selling of merchandise for exportation at a price less than the prevailing price in the country of export; or

"(4) Any tax, fee, charge, or exaction, imposed on or in connection with importation unless the law of the country imposing it designates or imposes it as a customs duty or contains a provision to the effect that it shall be treated as a duty imposed under the customs laws; or

"(5) The tax imposed by Section 4581 of the Internal Revenue Code of the United States, which is set forth as Annex VIII to this Agreement, with respect to an article, merchandise, or combination, ten per centum or more of the quantity by weight of which consists of, or is derived directly or indirectly from, one or more of the oils, fatty acids, or salts specified in Section 4511 of such Code which is set forth as Annex VII to this Agreement; or the tax imposed by Section 4501 (b) of such Code which is set forth as Annex IX to this Agreement.

"(e) The term 'United States article' means an article which is the product of the United States, unless, in the case of an article produced with the use of materials imported into the United States from any foreign country (except the Philippines) the aggregate value of such imported materials at the time of importation into the United States was more than twenty per centum of the value of the article imported into the Philippines, the value of such article to be determined in accordance with, and as of the time provided by, the customs laws of the Philippines in effect at the time of importation of such article. As used in this Subparagraph the terms 'value,' when used in reference to a material imported into the United States, includes the value of the material ascertained under the customs laws of the United States in effect at the time of importation into the United States, and, if not included in such value, the cost of bringing the material to the United States, but does not include the cost of landing it at the port of importation, or customs duties collected in the United States. For the purposes of this Subparagraph any imported material, used in the production of an article in the United States, shall be considered as having been used in the production of an article subsequently produced in the United States, which is the product of a chain of production in the United States in the course of which an article, which is the product of one stage of the chain, is used by its producer or another person, in a subsequent stage of the chain, as a material in the production of another article. It is understood that 'United States articles' do not lose their status as such, for the purpose of Philippine tariff preferences, by reason of being imported into the Philippines from a country other than the United States or from an insular possession of the United States or by way of or via such a country or insular possession.

"(f) The term 'Philippine article' means an article which is the product of the Philippines, unless, in the case of an article produced with the use of materials imported into the Philippines from any foreign country (except the United States) the aggregate value of such imported materials at the time of importation into the Philippines was more than twenty per centum of the value of the article imported into the United States, the value of such article to be determined in accordance with, and as of the time provided by, the customs laws of the United States in effect at the time of importation of such article. As used in this Subparagraph the term 'value,' when used in reference to a material imported into the Philippines, includes the value of the material ascertained under the customs laws of the Philippines in effect at the time of importation into the Philippines, and, if not included in such value, the cost of bringing the material to the Philippines, but does not include the cost of landing it at the port of importation, or customs duties collected in the Philippines. For the purposes of this Subparagraph any imported material, used in the production of an article in the Philippines, shall be considered as having been used in the production of an article subsequently produced in the Philippines, which is the product of a chain of production in the Philippines in the course of which an article, which is the product of one stage of the chain, is used by its producer or another person, in a subsequent stage of the chain, as a material in the production of another article. It is understood that 'Philippine articles' do not lose their status as such, for the purpose of United States tariff preferences, by reason of being imported into the United States from a country other than the Philippines or from an insular possession of the United States or by way of or via such a country or insular possession.

"(g) The term 'United States duty' means the rate or rates of ordinary customs duty which (at the time and place of entry, or withdrawal from warehouse, in the United States for consumption, of the Philippine article) would be applicable to a like article if imported from that foreign country which is entitled to the lowest rate, or the lowest aggregate of rates, of ordinary customs duty with respect to such like article.

"(h) The term 'Philippine duty' means the rate or rates of ordinary customs duty which (at the time and place of entry, or withdrawal from warehouse, in the Philippines for consumption, of the United States article) would be applicable to a like article if imported from that foreign country which is entitled to the lowest rate, or the lowest aggregate of rates, of ordinary customs duty with respect to such like article.

"(i) The term 'internal tax' includes an internal fee charge, or exaction, and includes—

"(1) The tax imposed by Section 4581 of the Internal Revenue Code of the United States which is set forth as Annex VIII to this Agreement, with respect to an article, merchandise, or combination, ten per centum or more of the quantity by weight of which consists of, or is derived directly or indirectly from, one or more of the oils, fatty acids, or salts specified in Section 4511 of such Code which is set forth as Annex VII to this Agreement; and the tax imposed by Section 4501 (b) of such Code which is set forth as Annex IX to this Agreement; and

"(2) Any other tax, fee, charge, or exaction, imposed on or in connection with importation unless the law of the country imposing it designates or imposes it as a customs duty or contains a provision to the effect that it shall be treated as a duty imposed under the customs laws.

"2. For the purposes of Subparagraphs (g) and (h) of Paragraph 1 of this Protocol—

"(a) If an article is entitled to be imported from a foreign country free of ordinary customs duty, that country shall be considered as the country entitled to the lowest rate of ordinary customs duty with respect to such article; and

"(b) A reduction in ordinary customs duty granted any country, by law, treaty, trade agreement, or otherwise, with respect to any article, shall be converted into the equivalent reduction in the rate of ordinary customs duty otherwise applicable to such article.

"3. For the purposes of Paragraphs 1 and 2 of Article IV, any material, used in the production of an article, shall be considered as having been used in the production of an article subsequently produced, which is the product of a chain of production in the course of which an article, which is the product of one stage of the chain, is used by its producer or another person, in a subsequent stage of the chain, as a material in the production of another article.

"4. The terms 'includes' and 'including' when used in a definition contained in this Agreement shall not be deemed to exclude other things otherwise within the meaning of the term defined."

SEC. 202. MODIFICATION OF TEXT OF REVISED AGREEMENT

The text of the revised agreement which is set forth in section 201 may be modified before the agreement authorized by such section is signed, but only—

(1) to the extent necessary (A) to correct errors, (B) to correct references to laws, or (C) to reflect action taken by the Republic of the Philippines with respect to article V of such agreement; or

(2) if such modifications are merely changes of style.

SEC. 301. PROCLAMATION; EFFECTIVE DATE OF TITLE

(a) *Proclamation.* If the agreement authorized by section 201 has been entered into before January 1, 1956, the President of the United States shall so proclaim, and the revised agreement shall be effective in the United States in accordance with its terms.

(b) *Effective Date of Title.* The provisions of this title (other than this section) shall take effect on January 1, 1956, but only if the President of the United States has made the proclamation referred to in subsection (a).

SEC. 302. PHILIPPINE TRADE ACT OF 1946

The Philippine Trade Act of 1946 (except section 506 (a) relating to termination of payments into Philippine Treasury, and except amendments and repeals made by such Act) shall not apply during such time as the revised agreement is in effect.

SEC. 303. QUOTAS ON PHILIPPINE ARTICLES

The rights reserved to the United States by paragraph 2 of article III of the revised agreement shall be exercised by the President, subject to the terms and conditions contained in such article. The President is authorized to prescribe such procedures and regulations for carrying out his functions as he may deem appropriate. Quotas shall be established pursuant to such article III by proclamation of the President, shall be effective for such period or periods as the President shall specify in his proclamation, and shall terminate upon finding and proclamation of the President in accordance with paragraph (2) (d) of such article III.

SEC. 304. SUSPENSION OF 2 CENTS PER POUND ADDITIONAL PROCESSING TAX ON COCONUT OIL

The authority contained in paragraph 5 of article IV of the revised agreement to suspend the provisions of section 4511 (b) of the Internal Revenue Code of 1954 may be exercised by the President by proclamation.

SEC. 305. TRADE AGREEMENTS WITH THE REPUBLIC OF THE PHILIPPINES

Until July 4, 1974, no trade agreement shall be entered into with the Republic of the Philippines under section 350, as amended, of the Tariff Act of 1930, which is inconsistent with this Act or with the revised agreement, unless, prior to such time, the revised agreement has been terminated.

SEC. 306. RIGHTS OF THIRD COUNTRIES

The benefits granted by this Act, and by the revised agreement, to the Republic of the Philippines, Philippine article or products, and Philippine citizens, shall not, by reason of any provision of any treaty or agreement existing on the date of the enactment of this Act with any third country, be extended to such country or its products, citizens, or subjects.

SEC. 307. ADMINISTRATION OF REVISED AGREEMENT

The provisions of articles I, II, III, and IV of the revised agreement which are in effect in the United States which relate to customs or internal revenue matters shall be administered as parts of the customs and internal revenue laws of the United States.

SEC. 308. TECHNICAL AMENDMENT

Section 9 of the Act of March 2, 1917, as amended (48 U. S. C., sec. 734), is hereby amended by inserting after "the Philippine Trade Act of 1946" the following: "or the Philippine Trade Agreement Revision Act of 1955."

Approved August 1, 1955.

INDEX

Abacá and cordage: production, 63, 67, 118, 226, 227, 274; export, 64, 66, 225, 270; quotas, 98, 128
Abode and movement, freedom of, 14, 89-90
Absentee landlordism, 65, 66, 140, 173-74
Administrative Code for the Philippines, 78
Africa, 3, 213, 214, 219
Aglipay, Bishop Gregorio, 23, 95-96
Agno River, 178, 271
Agricultural Credit and Cooperative Financing Administration, 176
Agricultural Credit Law, 254
Agricultural Tenancy Act, 173
Agriculture: United States legislation for Philippine, 98-99; World War II and, 116; Magsaysay administration programs for, 172-83; credit, 175-76; markets, cooperative, 176-77; Japanese holdings in the Philippines, 226; production outlook, 271, 272, 273; see also under specific subject, e.g., Animal husbandry
Aguinaldo, Emilio, Malolos Constitution and, 18-19, 20; election of 1935 and, 94, 95-96
Agusan Province, 180
Air force, 100, 102-3, 105
Ambuklao project, 178-79
Ang Bagong Katipunan, 30
Animal husbandry, 59, 116, 176

Anti-colonialism, 2, 10, 12, 202, 213-14
Arab states, 214, 219
Army, 102, 103-4, 105; Hukbalahap revolt and, 145-46, 155-57
Army surplus scandals, 119-21
Asia, 195-234; nationalism in, 2-3; Communism in, 10, 213-14, 215; land reform in, 175; United States interest in, 204, 205, 208; see also specific countries, e.g., Japan
Asian-Arab bloc, 12
Assembly, freedom of, 14, 30, 90

Baghdad Pact, 207
Baguio, 112; Conference, 201-3
Bandung Conference, 213, 214-20
Bangkok, 210
Bases Agreement of 1947, 133
Bataan: significance of, 17, 39, 107; defense of, 105-6, 144, 197
Bell Bill, see Philippine Trade Act of 1946
Bell, C. Jasper, 127
Dell, Daniel W., 127, 131
Bell Report, 127, 131, 132
Beyer, Otley H., cited, 48
Birth rate, 55, 61
Black market, 120, 142, 241
Bohol, province of, 239
Bondoc Peninsula, 276
Bonifacio, Andres, 46
Buryats, 2
Busuanga, 275
Buttons, 63, 128, 188

Philippines (*Continued*)
—— *American occupation:* established, 19-20, 22, 39; civil government established, 21-22; American and Spanish occupations compared, 22-24
—— *Commonwealth:* transition to Republic, 94-114; problems of, 97-105; Japanese occupation, 105-11
—— *Republic:* constitutional convention and, 82, 84; inauguration of, 114; problems of, 115-35, 137-47, 160-61, 165, 166, 170-71; rebuilding after World War II, 169-94; in international affairs, 195-234; "austerity" program of, 266-69, 273; political outlook for, 277-81
—— *See also* specific subjects, e.g., Agriculture; *and* leaders, e.g., Magsaysay
Philippine Scouts, 40, 101, 105
Philippine Trade Act of 1946, 127-30; revision, 184-91, 194, 241, 254, 271, 346-64 (text)
Philippine Weather Bureau, 24
Political parties, *see* specific party, e.g., Liberal party, *and* Opposition parties
Polygamy, 27
Population, 55, 61, 130; agricultural production and, 273
Presidency, Philippine Constitution on the, 88, 92, 333-36 (text)
Presidential Complaints and Action Committee, 171, 256
Press, freedom of, 28-30, 90, 112
Progressive party, 257
Prosser, Charles E., 53
Public Education Law (1901), 45
Public health, 42, 54-62, 112; appropriations, 63; World War II and, 116; health service and water supply, 181-83

Public works, 99, 177-78, 274
Puyat, Gil J., 185

Quezon-MacArthur defense plan, 102
Quezon, Manuel, quoted, 16, 280; Wood and, 32; character of, 73; Murphy and, 76; as president of the Senate, 77; Tydings-McDuffie Act and, 79; constitutional convention and, 82, 87; election and inauguration as president of the Commonwealth, 94-96; MacArthur and, 101-2; death of, 111, 238; Laurel and, 122-23; Garcia and, 239
Quezon, Mrs. Aurora, 146
Quirino, Antonio, 257, 258, 264
Quirino, Elpidio, presidential administration of, 132, 137-39, 238; character of, 136, 164; Hukbalahap revolt and, 144-45, 146, 154-55, 165; election of 1951 and, 160-64; Magsaysay and, 154-55, 160, 161-65, 166; Baguio Conference and, 201; death of, 252
Quirino-Foster Agreement, 132
Quotas, *see* Trade, quotas

Racial discrimination, 23, 214, 215, 217
Reconstruction Finance Corporation, 118
Recto, Claro M., constitutional convention and, 83; puppet regime and, 122, 123; Magsaysay and, 193-94; political record of, 257-58; election of 1957 and, 262-63, 264
Rehabilitation Act of 1946, 117, 119; Philippine Trade Act of 1946 and, 129-30
Religion, freedom of, 13, 27, 28
Reparations, 223-25
Rhee, Syngman, 200, 229